This book asks why some countries have responded to the external constraints and opportunities arising from their global and regional economic context by opening up their economies. In particular, the authors examine the role domestic political and economic factors play in shaping the decision to become more open, or more inward-looking. The countries of Southeast Asia have generally enjoyed economic success in the postwar period. The authors argue that one of the explanations for this success has been their integration into the global division of labor, and analyze decision-makers' reasons for following this course. They place particular emphasis on external events, notably the two oil shocks of the 1970s, and the more recent outflow of investment capital and manufacturing capacity from Japan and East Asia.

THE POLITICS OF OPEN ECONOMIES

CAMBRIDGE ASIA-PACIFIC STUDIES

Cambridge Asia-Pacific Studies aims to provide a focus and forum for scholarly work on the Asia-Pacific region as a whole, and its component sub-regions, namely Northeast Asia, Southeast Asia and the Pacific Islands. The series is produced in association with the Research School of Pacific and Asian Studies at the Australian National University and the Institute of International Affairs.

Editor: John Ravenhill

Editorial Board: James Cotton, Donald Denoon, Mark Elvin, David Goodman, Stephen Henningham, Hal Hill, David Lim, Ron May, Anthony Milner, Tessa Morris-Suzuki.

R. Gerard Ward and Elizabeth Kingdon (eds.) *Land, Custom and Practice in the South Pacific*

Stephanie Lawson *Tradition Versus Democracy in the South Pacific*

Walther Hatch and Kozo Yamamura *Asia in Japan's Embrace*

THE POLITICS OF OPEN ECONOMIES

Indonesia, Malaysia, the Philippines, and Thailand

ALASDAIR BOWIE

George Washington University

and

DANNY UNGER

Georgetown University

CAMBRIDGE
UNIVERSITY PRESS

PUBLISHED BY THE PRESS SYNDICATE OF THE UNIVERSITY OF CAMBRIDGE
The Pitt Building, Trumpington Street, Cambridge CB2 1RP, United Kingdom

CAMBRIDGE UNIVERSITY PRESS
The Edinburgh Building, Cambridge, CB2 2RU, United Kingdom
40 West 20th Street, New York, NY 10011-4211, USA
10 Stamford Road, Oakleigh, Melbourne 3166, Australia

First published 1997

Printed in the United Kingdom at the University Press, Cambridge

Typeset in 10/12 Monotype Baskerville [SE]

A catalogue record for this book is available from the British Library

Library of Congress Cataloguing in Publication data

Bowie, Alasdair.
The politics of open economies: Indonesia, Malaysia, the
Philippines, and Thailand / Alasdair Bowie and Danny Unger.
p.   cm. – (Cambridge Asia-Pacific Studies)
Includes bibliographical references.
ISBN 0 521 58343 8 (hc) – ISBN 0 521 58683 6 (pb)
1. Asia, Southeastern – Economic policy.   2. Asia, Southeastern –
Economic conditions.   I. Unger, Danny, 1955–   II. Title.   III. Series.
HC441.B69   1997
330.959 – dc21   96-49358   CIP

ISBN 0 521 58343 8 hardback
ISBN 0 521 58683 6 paperback

To Karl D. Jackson
in thanks for his ceaseless enthusiasm.

Contents

Figures and tables

Figures

Tables

Acknowledgments

We would first like to acknowledge Rick Doner's enthusiastic participation in the early stages of thinking about this book. The Southeast Asia Committee of the Social Science Research Council in 1990 provided a small seed grant from its Program of Grants to Isolated Scholars, funded by the Henry Luce Foundation, which supported our early meetings. The Catholic University of America provided partial travel support for Alasdair Bowie to visit Southeast Asia, and to conduct research at the University of Washington library in Seattle, with the able guidance of Southeast Asia librarian, Judith Henchy. Kohar Rony, Southeast Asia Area Specialist in the Asian Division of the Library of Congress, provided cheerful assistance during many Library of Congress visits. The Department of Political Science at the George Washington University funded research assistance in the summer of 1994. The very competent research help of Koichi Kawamura in 1994 and Traci Swanson during the last leg in 1996 was invaluable. Our thanks to Shojiro Tokunaga for his work in organizing conferences at which Danny Unger presented parts of this book. The comments we received from conference participants in Fukuoka and Honolulu were very helpful.

Colleague and friend Susan Sell read parts of the manuscript, as did Rick Doner, Robert Goldfarb, Hal Hill, Susan Lusi, Robert Scalapino, and David Wurfel. Our thanks to all for their generosity with their time and for the helpful comments we received. Likewise to the anonymous reviewers who gave the manuscript careful attention and provided us with valuable comments. Columbia and Cornell University Presses kindly granted permission for us to draw on previously published material by Alasdair Bowie.

Lastly, thanks to Susan Lusi for research assistance, forbearance, and support in ways both large and small that have made this work possible.

CHAPTER ONE

Introduction

This book attempts to explain why some developing countries adopt economic policies that are relatively open to cross-border movements of goods, services, and capital. In particular, it focuses on national economic policy responses to changing external economic conditions and asks what factors account for the propensity of some countries to maintain or increase their economic openness while others opt to reduce it.[1] The analysis is limited to the economic policies of four Southeast Asian states – Indonesia, Malaysia, the Philippines, and Thailand (the ASEAN[2] four) – during the half-century following the end of the Pacific War.

Indonesia, Malaysia, the Philippines, and Thailand are, along with Vietnam, the most populous members of ASEAN. Unlike Vietnam, they have chosen market-oriented development strategies since they gained independence (Thailand never was colonized). As a group, their economic performance has been very strong over the last thirty years (see table 1.1). While the Philippines stands out within this group as a laggard, its record, when measured against the entire population of developing economies, has been at least average (see table 1.2). For these and other reasons (explained below), we have chosen to use these four countries to understand better those factors that lead officials in developing countries to maintain or adopt open economic policies.

Our interest in developing countries' open economic policies stems in considerable part from the relative rareness of such policies before the 1980s. Government officials in many developing countries eschewed open economic policies due to fears of the economic dependence on larger, wealthier economies that would ensue. How can we account for the fact that in terms of economic openness, the ASEAN Four in the 1960s and 1970s were, to greater or lesser degrees, practicing the orthodoxy of the 1980s and 1990s?[3] More importantly, as we shall show, there is considerable evidence suggesting that open economic policies, while inadequate by themselves, are likely to feature

Table 1.1. *Economic performance of ASEAN Four, 1960–94*

	Average annual growth in GDP (percent)		Recent expansion in exports (US $ billion)	
	1960–90	1985–94[a]	1980–90	1990–94
Indonesia	3.2	6.0	5.3	21.3
Malaysia	3.9	5.6	11.5	17.8
Philippines	1.4	1.7	2.9	10.2
Thailand	4.8	8.6	14.3	21.6

Note:
[a] GNP.
Sources: Vinod Thomas and Yan Wang, *The Lessons of East Asia, Government Policy and Productivity Growth, Is East Asia an Exception?*, Washington, D.C.: World Bank, 1993, p. 14; ASEAN Centre, *ASEAN–Japan Statistical Pocketbook*, Tokyo: ASEAN Centre, 1993, p. 19; World Bank, *World Tables, 1994*, Baltimore: Johns Hopkins University Press, 1994; World Bank, *World Development Report, 1994*, New York: Oxford University Press, 1994, table 1, pp. 162–3; *World Development Report 1996*, New York: Oxford University Press, 1996, pp. 188–9, 216–17.

Table 1.2. *GNP per capita: selected countries, 1972–92 (US$ million)*

	1972	1977	1982	1987	1992
Bolivia	270	410	530	530	680
Côte d'Ivoire	290	710	970	770	670
Ecuador	310	800	1490	1070	1070
India	110	190	280	310	310
Indonesia	**90**	**320**	**610**	**490**	**670**
Kenya	180	270	400	340	310
Malaysia	**450**	**1010**	**1900**	**1830**	**2790**
Pakistan	160	190	350	360	420
Philippines	**200**	**430**	**760**	**580**	**770**
South Korea	330	910	1930	2960	6790
Thailand	**220**	**460**	**770**	**860**	**1840**

Source: World Tables, 1994, Baltimore: Johns Hopkins University Press, table 1.

prominently in the economic policy portfolios of poor countries that succeed in achieving sustained economic growth.

The United Nations Development Program's human development index ranks Thailand and Malaysia among the top developing countries (at numbers 16 and 17) with the Philippines and Indonesia ranking above the median (at numbers 38 and 41). All but Indonesia move up the ladder when one looks only

Table 1.3. *Structure of production: ASEAN Four, 1970 and 1993 (percentages)*

	Agriculture		Industry		Services	
	1970	1993	1970	1993	1970	1993
Indonesia	45	19	19	39	36	40
Malaysia	29	n.a.	25	n.a.	46	n.a.
Philippines	30	22	32	33	39	45
Thailand	26	10	25	39	49	51

Source: World Bank, *World Development Report, 1994,* New York: Oxford University Press, 1994, table 3, pp. 166–7; World Bank, *World Development Report, 1995,* New York: Oxford University Press, 1995, pp. 166–7.

at rates of infant mortality and all but Malaysia rise when one considers only rates of adult literacy. And all four countries, with the Philippine record somewhat less impressive, have registered dramatic improvements in terms of these indices since 1960.[4] In terms of per capita gross national product (GNP), Indonesia rose from $90 in 1972 to $670 in 1992; Malaysia's increase was from $450 to $2790; the Philippines' from $200 to $770; and Thailand's from $220 to $1840.[5] Over those same twenty years, per capita gross domestic investment increased between 30 percent (the Philippines) and 567 percent (Indonesia) and gross domestic product (GDP) rose between 3.3 (Indonesia) and 4.4 (Thailand) times (with the Philippines' gross domestic product not quite doubling).[6] The Philippines had a much slower rate of growth in gross domestic investment as a share of GDP (the share reaching 22.6 percent in 1992, with 34.6, 33.9, and 40.2 percent for Indonesia, Malaysia, and Thailand respectively during that same year).[7] Finally, over the period from 1972 to 1992, merchandise exports expanded 9.5 times for the Philippines, 19 times for Indonesia, and 24 and 31 times for Malaysia and Thailand respectively.[8]

Over the last forty years, fairly steady economic growth, except in the Philippines, has produced marked structural economic changes in these economies. Within manufacturing, food and tobacco's share of value added in Indonesia dropped from 65 to 24 percent between 1970 and 1991, in Malaysia from 26 to 11 percent, and in Thailand from 43 to 28 percent over those same years.[9] Average annual growth in Indonesian merchandise exports fell from 7.2 percent during the 1970s, to 5.6 percent from 1980 to 1992. The comparable figures for Malaysia were 4.8 and 11.3 percent; for the Philippines 6 and 3.7 percent; and for Thailand 10.3 and 14.7 percent.[10] The composition of these exports also changed dramatically over these years (see table 1.4).

In short, as tables 1.1–1.4 make clear, the ASEAN Four have demonstrated considerable success at rapidly increasing their production and changing the structure of their economies. The importance of agriculture in all these

Table 1.4. *Composition of merchandise exports: ASEAN Four, 1970 and 1992 (percentages)*

	Indonesia	Malaysia	Philippines	Thailand
Fuels, minerals, metals				
1970	44	30	23	15
1992	38	17	8	2
Other primary commodities				
1970	54	63	70	77
1992	15	22	19	32
Machinery and transport equipment				
1970	0	2	0	0
1992	4	38	17	22
Textiles, clothing				
1970	0	1	1	1
1992	18	6	10	17
Other manufactures				
1970	1	6	8	8
1992	44	23	56	45

Source: World Bank, *World Development Report, 1994*, New York: Oxford University Press, 1994, table 15, pp. 190–1.

countries has declined and manufactured exports have become increasingly important. While, in almost every respect, the Philippines has trailed as the "sick man of Asia," its record is more creditable when compared with countries such as Bolivia, Côte d'Ivoire, India, Kenya, or Pakistan.

The focus of this study

Trying to understand why some nation-states are more successful than others at securing advantageous positions within the global division of labor strikes us as an important task. After all, as a result of the central emphasis that most societies place on raising material living standards, policymakers and scholars long have been concerned to understand those factors that produce economic growth. Anthropologists, economists, historians, political scientists, sociologists, and others contribute to this effort, often embracing divergent explanations that underline differing factors in explaining economic growth. Economists, in particular, stress the efficiency gains that can accrue from participation in a wider international division of labor and exposure to broader economic competition.

This study focuses on those concepts and variables that have the greatest influence on the decisions of developing-country elites to opt for economic openness. We place less emphasis on the wide range of other factors often employed to explain economic growth. We do not try to explain, for example, savings and investment rates, although these often do figure in the explanation for policy choices on which we concentrate.

Our concern is with the links between individual developing economies, the regional economies in which they are situated, and the global economy.[11] We conceive of the regional and global economies as providing the broader context – a changing structure of exogenous constraints and opportunities – within which policymakers in developing countries fashion and implement economic policies.

Our central question is: "What factors make some developing-economy policymakers prefer policies favoring economic openness?"[12] Opting for economic openness is likely, all else being equal, to enhance the likelihood of developing countries being able to respond successfully to the economic constraints and opportunities presented by the regional and global systems.[13] Given the growing importance of external factors in the national–international economic balance, we feel it is worthwhile to pursue the question of why elites opt for economic openness.

In approaching the study of policymakers' preferences for openness, we are concerned with how and why policymakers adapt to particular externally generated structural changes. When oil prices rise, why do some policymakers respond by sheltering their economies while others increase the exposure of their economies to international influences? Understanding these issues also sheds light on why some economies bounce back from adverse shocks while others take much longer to recover.

We have chosen as our cases specific instances of national response.[14] By an instance of national response, we mean the policy adjustments made by a country's elite policymakers in response to a particular change in the constellation of externally shaped incentive structures. We have sixteen cases: the response of each of the four developing economies to four (more or less) discrete challenges stemming from changes in the regional and world economies. This approach has the advantage that it enables us to compare policymaking across countries at the same time, and in each country across various points in time.[15]

Treating episodes of national response as cases is admittedly artificial, for the values of our dependent variable, economic openness, are not entirely independent from one case to the next. Path-dependence – the effects that past choices have on future options and choices – ensures that levels of economic growth, coalitions forged, sectors that expand,[16] and the policies pursued in one period will all influence to some extent the choices made in subsequent periods.[17] As a result, our sixteen cases are not fully independent of one another. Despite these problems, however, we believe the advantages of structuring our analysis in this fashion justify the choices we make.

Having introduced briefly our analytical framework, we now explain why we have chosen degree of economic openness as the dependent variable for this study. We conceive of our sixteen cases as discrete instances of national policy response to exogenous challenges. Each response is shaped by an array of specified domestic economic and political variables. Responses may differ along a number of dimensions. We here are concerned with just one – the degree to which a response moves toward or away from economic openness.[18] We rely on both quantitative measures and qualitative assessments to distinguish degrees of economic openness, referring primarily to movements of goods, but also to capital. We believe we are justified in concentrating on this one aspect of policy response because of the potential significance of economic openness as a loose predictor of long-term economic growth.[19]

Indeed, we narrow our focus further still by emphasizing openness to flows of goods rather than of services, labor, or capital. However, we do not ignore such flows entirely. In fact, we give considerable attention to external changes and domestic policies that influence capital flows. We emphasize merchandise trade, however, because of its greater prominence in the comparative political economy literature from which we derive some of our hypotheses and, more critically, for ease of analysis and comparison. We recognize the increasing importance of capital flows in the contemporary world political economy and remain sensitive to their influences in our analysis. In particular, we try to remain alert to instances where degrees of openness in the two areas do not move in tandem, that is, where policy opening in trade is accompanied by closure to capital flows, or the reverse. Officials in developing countries at times opened their trade regimes while retaining controls on international capital flows. In some cases, officials hoped thereby to nurture strong firms locally before exposing them to competition from foreign enterprises. We argue, however, that the ASEAN Four were relatively open to flows of capital as well as of goods and services.

Economic openness as a dependent variable

For some readers, the choice of economic openness as our dependent variable may seem peculiar. Most studies of this sort use as their dependent variables rates of economic growth or economic adjustment or reform (meaning, broadly, increasing reliance on market mechanisms to allocate resources).[20] Why do we care about economic openness?

David Ricardo showed more than 150 years ago that all countries benefit from specialization in production and trade. Surely, then, the advantages of openness are no more subject to challenge than the joys of fatherhood? Developing countries, by definition, face shortages of capital and can boost economic performance by drawing on externally generated savings. Surely, then, policymakers in all developing countries should opt for openness.

In fact, it ain't necessarily so. There is a wide gap between what the theory of comparative advantage says is good for us and actual trade policy.[21] An open trade strategy, David Lake suggests, represents a country's willingness to accept the trade outcomes of international market forces.[22] But, as Robert Gilpin argues, societies have tended to value social stability or self-sufficiency more highly than the putative gains of openness to the international market.[23] Officials also may protect firms from inflows of either goods or capital in order to foster domestic firms that eventually will be able to compete in international markets. This suggests that states' decisions not to protect their markets are worthy of more careful study.[24]

Indeed, champions of free trade almost everywhere and at all times face considerable opposition. Many of the sources of this contention are familiar and can be found anywhere. For example, while the consumers who gain from free trade are many, the gains typically are modest, relatively intangible, and become apparent only later. Further, the many consumers are often geographically dispersed, and face problems in mobilizing their collective interests for effective political action. In contrast, those producers who lose from free trade are few, and often geographically concentrated; their potential losses are significant and they feel immediately threatened. Such losers are more intensely motivated to lobby for their interests than are the gainers and the former often face fewer collective action obstacles in doing so. Politicians, the targets of these lobbying efforts, will often be persuaded to restrict trade even if the public interest suggests the wisdom of an open trade strategy.

In some respects, the hurdles that open trade proponents must overcome are greater in developing countries than in advanced economies. Protectionists can more easily make a case for infant industry protection in developing countries than can their counterparts in advanced economies. Some scholars suggest that countries with low labor productivity gain less from trade than do those with high labor productivity.[25] Others find an open trade strategy appropriate for developing economies only during certain periods when trade grows rapidly along with large flows of capital.[26]

In most developing countries, labor is the only relatively abundant factor of production and, hence, labor is likely to be the only group in favor of open trade. (Imports of goods will not tend to increase the relative supply of labor. More precisely, those goods likely to be imported will comprise relatively more capital than labor. Hence, imports will not tend to bid down the cost of labor by increasing its supply.)[27] Given the political weakness of workers or peasant producers (both groups face significact obstacles to collective action), this would lead us to expect forces opposed to an open trade strategy to prevail.[28] Further, developing countries generally do not have the kinds of social welfare policies that in many small European states compensate losers for the adjustment costs they incur as their economies move toward more open trade.[29] Hence, we would expect opposition to open trade policies to be more intense in developing countries.

Another reason to expect the ASEAN Four, in particular, to prefer protectionist policies is that their relative resource wealth makes such policies at least minimally possible, unlike resource-poor economies such as Singapore, South Korea or Taiwan. Gustav Ranis sees the availability of commodity exports as reducing political leaderships' willingness or ability to impose market discipline on vested interests.[30] Joan Nelson suggests that politicians who rely for their support on their abilities to dispense patronage – a fair characterization of the clientelistic politics evident among the ASEAN Four – are unlikely to adopt policies that shift the allocation of resources to impersonal market mechanisms and deny themselves their discretionary authority.[31]

Massed against this array of considerations, the apparently invincible logic of neoclassical economic arguments on behalf of open trade policies appears less compelling. It is also true, however, that producers operating in small markets cannot hope to achieve scale economies without access to external markets. In addition, for small economies, accommodating external shocks requires domestic responses – either adjustment, at least in part through open trade strategies, or insulation through trade protection. Small, weak states do not have the option available to a large economy such as the United States of attempting to avoid adjustment costs by foisting them onto other economies.[32] Further, a complex of shared factors, ethnic (the roles of the immigrant Chinese), geographical (archipelagic and littoral states), and historical (ties to imperialist powers that differed in nature from South Korean and Taiwanese colonial ties to Japan), has long oriented the ASEAN Four toward external markets. The arguments presented above, however, serve to support our assertion that trade policy openness is in general problematic and in need of explanation, rather than a default policy we can simply assume states will pursue unless particular intervening factors come into play.

We do assume that economic openness implies a broad commitment to the market mechanism and a minimalist conception of states' appropriate goals. As noted above, in many European economies, economic openness is combined with active state policies that compensate economic losers. Several scholars working on developing countries have noted the "orthodox paradox," that only states with considerable capacities appear to be able to implement market-oriented reforms successfully.[33]

Nonetheless, consistent with Anne Krueger's observation that liberal approaches in one policy area tend to be associated with similar approaches in others,[34] the ASEAN Four, comparatively speaking, are relatively liberal in their broad economic policy approach. In this respect, their policies differ considerably, in our interpretation, from those of Singapore, South Korea, or Taiwan in the 1960s and 1970s. As a group, the strong performances of the ASEAN Four throw some doubt on the assumption that "late development" necessarily requires that state officials play central roles in fitting their national economies into the international division of labor.[35] Indeed, we concur with the view of the authors of the World Bank's study *East Asian Miracle* that the Southeast Asian economies are much more relevant as exemplars to countries outside the region than are those of Northeast Asia.[36]

We suggested above that economic openness is likely to be associated with economic growth, all else equal. Every relatively successful national economy over the last thirty years has opened itself to foreign flows of capital, goods, and services (as have many unsuccessful ones, of course). Unlike the 1930s, in no country has the response to economic difficulties in the 1980s and 1990s been a major move toward diminishing its links to the international economy.[37] Despite recent periods of relatively successful economic expansion in comparatively autarkic continental economies (China in the 1950s, India in the 1960s, the Soviet Union through the 1950s, and the United States through the 1960s), the broad correlation between economic openness and growth appears sufficiently strong and our understanding of the causes at work adequately clear so as nearly to constitute a rule of contemporary political economy. In any case, the autarkic option has never been as attractive to less developed economies, particularly those of less than continental scale. Further, the increasing opportunity costs of such a strategy make it increasingly unattractive. These costs include diminished access to foreign capital and technology, whether through private or public flows, and possible sanctions diminishing access to markets in rich countries. We therefore feel comfortable viewing openness to international flows of capital, goods, and services as a loose proxy variable for successful national response, that is, for economic growth.[38] It is no doubt also true that the rich opt for openness while the poor are more apt to avoid it. That is, causality may run in the opposite direction, from success to trade openness, or in both directions. We believe, however, that the weight of evidence suggests that openness itself tends to stimulate growth. (For those who read this statement as a leap of faith, we urge recognition of relative openness as an intrinsically important variable, even if not correlated with prosperity.)

We recognize that there have been many significant exceptions to the correlation between economic openness and growth, and that most industrialized countries passed through periods in which they protected their markets. Indeed, as Henry Nau notes, during the postwar period in which trade and production grew most rapidly, the principal economies labored under fixed exchange rates and restrictions on capital flows.[39] Furthermore, in one of our countries, Thailand, there is considerable evidence that economic openness between the mid nineteenth and mid twentieth centuries on both the capital and trade accounts produced almost no real per capita economic growth.[40] Nonetheless, we feel that the preponderance of evidence suggests an impressive causal relationship between economic openness and growth.[41]

Were the economies of the ASEAN Four in fact more open than those of comparable developing countries in other regions, and have they become more so over time? Table 1.5 shows variation in our dependent variable, economic

Table 1.5. *Relative openness to trade in goods: selected countries, 1973 and 1993*
Merchandise trade as a percentage of GDP[a]

Rank[b]	Country	Wealth GNP/capita	Size GDP	Openness to trade Merch.trade/GDP	
		1993 ($)	1993 ($ billion)	1973	1993
43	*Egypt*	*660*	*35.8*	*21.2*	*26.5*
47	**Indonesia**	**740**	**144.7**	**34.6**	**42.6**
48	Senegal	750	5.8	44.4	31.9[c]
49	Bolivia	760	5.4	38.3	35.9
50	Cameroon	820	11.1	39.1	27.0[c]
53	**Philippines**	**850**	**54.1**	**36.0**	**55.2**
54	Congo	950	2.4	39.3	63.2
56	*Morocco*	*1040*	*26.6*	*32.9*	*40.0*
73	*Algeria*	*1780*	*39.8*	*47.7*	*36.2*
77	**Thailand**	**2110**	**124.9**	**33.5**	**66.4**
78	Costa Rica	2150	7.6	52.3	64.7
80	*Poland*	*2260*	*85.9*	*..*	*38.2*
82	Panama	2600	6.6	44.1	41.8
89	Brazil	2930	444.2	16.7	14.4
90	*S. Africa*	*2980*	*105.6*	*29.5*	*35.3*
93	**Malaysia**	**3140**	**64.5**	**69.4**	**144.0**
94	*Chile*	*3170*	*43.7*	*22.0*	*45.6*
95	*Hungary*	*3350*	*38.1*	*95.3*	*56.4*
96	Mexico	3610	343.5	9.9	23.4
72[d]	**ASEAN Four**	**1710[e]**	**97.1[f]**	**43.4**	**77.1**
				40.7w	**68.9w**
76	**M15[g]**	**1987**	**80.1**	**38.1**	**38.7**
				22.7w	**25.5w**
79	**R7[h]**	**2177**	**53.6**	**41.4**	**39.7**
				37.9w	**38.9w**

Notes:
[a]All figures unless otherwise stated are in US$ current.
[b]World Bank ranking of 132 countries by GNP/capita in 1993 (lowest=1).
[c]Figures for 1992.
[d]Putative ranking of the average country within this grouping.
[e]Average of the GNP/capita figures for the countries within this grouping.
[f]Average of the GDP figures for the countries within this grouping.
[g]M15 (Middle-Income-15) includes all countries in the table except the ASEAN Four.
That is, in order of GNP per capita: Egypt, Senegal, Bolivia, Cameroon, Congo,
Morocco, Algeria, Costa Rica, Poland, Panama, Brazil, South Africa, Chile, Hungary,
and Mexico. These countries are selected for this reference group because their GNP
per capita is comparable to that of one or more of the ASEAN Four. All but Egypt are
classified as middle-income by the World Bank – Egypt is among the three wealthiest
of the low-income countries – and five are assigned to the subcategory upper-middle
income: Brazil, South Africa, Chile, Hungary and Mexico.

openness in trade, both between the ASEAN Four and comparable countries at the same time, and in terms of changes over time. We do not intend the tables to prove, or even suggest, that the ASEAN Four's open economic policies engendered growth. The tables simply demonstrate that these economies were relatively open to trade flows.

Trade openness, measured with reference to merchandise trade (exports f.o.b. and imports c.i.f.) as a percentage of GDP, comes closest to what we mean by "openness." Table 1.5 shows that the ASEAN Four were already marginally more open to trade in 1973, before the first of our four international events unfolded, than were comparable economies, as represented by the Middle-Income-15 (M15) or the Reference-Group-7 (R7). Merchandise trade in the average ASEAN Four economy represented 43.4 percent of GDP. The same figure for the average M15 country was 38.1 percent, and for the average R7 country, 41.4 percent.

Twenty years later, the ASEAN Four were roughly twice as open to international trade as the M15 or R7. Merchandise trade soared to the equivalent of 77.1 percent of GDP in the ASEAN Four (144 percent in the case of Malaysia), whereas the proportion of merchandise trade to GDP remained virtually unchanged at 38.7 percent in the M15 and declined slightly, to 39.7 percent, in the R7.[42] In short, while most comparable countries were neither more nor less open than they had been in 1973, the ASEAN Four were dramatically more open.[43]

Table 1.6 illuminates trends in the intervening years.

Notes (cont.)
[h]R7 (Reference-Group-7, shown in italics) represents a subset of the Middle-Income-15 countries. It consists of Egypt, Morocco, Algeria, Poland, South Africa, Chile, and Hungary. It excludes from the latter grouping those economies that are much smaller (defined as less than half the size measured in terms of GDP) than the smallest ASEAN Four economy, that of the Philippines. Such countries are: Senegal, Bolivia, Cameroon, Congo, Costa Rica, and Panama. It also excludes those countries whose economies are much larger (defined as more than twice the size) than the largest ASEAN Four economy, that of Indonesia. Thus Mexico and Brazil are excluded.
..   Data not yet available
w   Weighted average. Weights are calculated by taking the size of an economy in terms of GDP ($ billion) and expressing it as a proportion of the aggregate GDP ($ billion) of all countries in the category (i.e., ASEAN Four, Middle-Income-15, or Reference-Group-7).
Sources: Calculated from World Bank, *World Development Report, 1995*, New York: Oxford University Press, for the World Bank, 1995, pp. 156, 162–3; World Bank, *World Tables, 1995*, Baltimore: Johns Hopkins University Press, for the World Bank, 1995, pp. 2–5, 26–9, 74–81.

Table 1.6. *Relative openness to trade in goods: selected countries, 1950–93*
Merchandise trade as a percentage of GDP[a]

Rank[b]	Country	1950	1960	1970	1973	1975	1983	1986	1993
43	*Egypt*	*18.9*	*30.8*	*28.8*	*21.2*	*46.7*	*47.9*	*30.4*	*26.5*
47	**Indonesia**	**9.3**	**16.2**	**23.7**	**34.6**	**36.9**	**43.9**	**31.9**	**42.6**
48	Senegal	..	46.7	41.9	44.4	55.0	63.8	42.0	31.9[c]
49	Bolivia	..	29.1	31.9	38.3	58.2	48.1	31.9	35.9
50	Cameroon	28.2	32.7	35.3	39.1	38.0	27.5	24.0	27.0[c]
53	**Philippines**	**20.4**	**16.7**	**32.2**	**36.0**	**40.8**	**39.1**	**33.4**	**55.2**
54	Congo	..	..	47.4	39.3	45.5	83.6	73.3	63.2
56	*Morocco*	..	*36.1*	*28.1*	*32.9*	*46.6*	*40.6*	*36.6*	*40.0*
73	*Algeria*	*58.3*	*60.5*	*46.0*	*47.7*	*68.6*	*44.2*	*27.1*	*36.2*
77	**Thailand**	..	**33.8**	**25.9**	**33.5**	**38.0**	**42.1**	**43.2**	**66.4**
78	Costa Rica	45.1	39.0	52.6	52.3	60.5	58.9	49.0	64.7
80	*Poland*	..	..	..	..	..	*29.3*	*31.5*	*38.2*
82	Panama	33.1	32.4	45.4	44.1	64.0	38.8	31.0	41.8
89	Brazil	..	..	14.8	16.7	18.1	18.4	13.6	14.4
90	*S. Africa*	*39.7*	*39.9*	*41.9*	*29.5*	*33.8*	*29.5*	*36.4*	*35.3*
93	**Malaysia**	..	**72.5**	**69.8**	**69.4**	**76.0**	**90.7**	**88.6**	**144.0**
94	*Chile*	..	*25.3*	*23.5*	*22.0*	*40.0*	*34.4*	*41.7*	*45.6*
95	*Hungary*	..	..	*67.5*	*95.3*	*120.9*	*81.2*	*76.5*	*56.4*
96	Mexico	19.2	16.2	9.4	9.9	10.1	21.0	21.6	23.4
72[d]	**ASEAN Four**	..	**34.8**	**37.9**	**43.4**	**47.9**	**54.0**	**49.3**	**77.1**
		..	**24.8w**	**33.3w**	**40.7w**	**43.2w**	**50.1w**	**43.5w**	**68.9w**
76	**M15**[e]	..	**35.3**	**36.8**	**38.1**	**50.4**	**44.5**	**37.8**	**38.7**
		..	**30.0w**	**23.1w**	**22.7w**	**24.3w**	**28.6w**	**25.1w**	**25.5w**
79	**R7**[f]	..	**38.5**	**39.3**	**41.4**	**59.4**	**43.9**	**40.0**	**39.7**
		..	**37.7w**	**38.9w**	**37.9w**	**53.8w**	**46.1w**	**36.0w**	**38.9w**

Notes:
[a-f] see notes *a–f* in table 1.5.
Sources: Calculated from World Bank, *World Development Report, 1995* and *1984*, New York: Oxford University Press, for the World Bank, 1995 and 1984; World Bank, *World Tables, 1995, 1992,* and *1976,* Baltimore: Johns Hopkins University Press, for the World Bank, 1995, 1992, and 1976; International Monetary Fund, *International Financial Statistics Yearbook, 1981* and *1979,* Washington, D.C.: IMF, 1981 and 1979; International Monetary Fund, *International Financial Statistics: Supplement on Trade Statistics No. 4,* 1982, Washington, D.C.: IMF, 1982; United Nations, *Yearbook of International Trade Statistics, 1960,* New York: United Nations, 1960.

Specifying the exogenously produced parameters

We have selected four sets of international developments to enable us to examine separate instances of challenges arising from the external environment that precipitate specific policy responses. Each event places specific demands on the national economies and those demands condition the particular national responses. The four events are: the first round of oil price increases and the ensuing stagflation in most of the advanced economies, 1974–75; the second round of oil price increases followed by high interest rates, a strong dollar (that increased the burdens assumed by developing debtor nations), sharp global recession, and stagnation in world trade, 1979–83; the collapse of commodity prices, 1984–86; and, finally, the net capital outflows (private and public) from the developing world beginning in 1986; in the cases of the ASEAN Four, the event corresponds to the significant net inflows beginning in 1987. During this period, Japanese official development assistance increased sharply and Japanese and other East Asian direct foreign investment flows into the ASEAN Four also rose rapidly.

We have selected these four events because we believe they have presented the most critical external challenges and opportunities to developing countries in general, and those in East Asia in particular. Each of these international developments has in important ways influenced relative factor scarcities (i.e., relative prices of capital, labor, and land) within developing countries, conditioned their access to externally mobilized savings and, as a result, has significantly affected domestic policy and political debates within them.

There are differences in these events. They vary considerably in length. The first lasted but a couple of years while the fourth is still ongoing. They also differed in the structures of externally shaped constraints and opportunities they presented to developing countries. During each, at least some developing countries proved able to sustain or intensify their commitment to development strategies rooted in economic openness. Some events, however, produced incentive structures that led to widespread defection from openness. Others, in contrast, may have facilitated moves toward openness. And, of course, in all instances there was variation in the particular national responses among individual developing countries. The first and second events introduced major international economic instabilities that open economies then imported into their own economies. Large pools of savings in unregulated offshore Eurodollar accounts offered the option in the 1970s of more *dirigiste* and closed development strategies (e.g., indebted industrialization) and less economic adjustment.[44] However, those countries that attempted to limit their exposure to externally induced instability by extending regulation of international flows of capital, goods, and services, experienced much more acute problems later on. By the third event, policymakers in most developing (as well as advanced) economies saw few options other than attempting to attract foreign capital and expand their exports by deregulating flows of capital, goods, and services.

Our four events represent instances when new external conditions presented policymakers in developing countries with altered structures of incentives. One way in which external events shaped those structures was by shifting relative factor costs. This not only changed comparative advantages, but also favored some local groups at the expense of others, a point we develop further below.

The impacts of these four events were neither uniform nor randomly distributed across the population of developing countries. In the fourth event – falling and negative net capital flows to the developing world – the developing economies of East Asia gained, not only because they had not incurred as much debt but also because private capital flows going to developing nations, particularly from Japan and later the East Asian NICs, and growing Japanese official development flows concentrated in Asia, compensated for reduced access to offshore financial markets. Hence, the impacts that capitalists, workers, landowners, and policymakers felt in different developing countries during the same episode often differed and helped to yield divergent national responses.

Selecting the ASEAN Four

We have chosen to study four countries from a single region for a variety of reasons. First, proximity can serve as a proxy for several interactive variables (we develop this idea further in chapter 2).[45] One of the reasons we have selected four geographically proximate countries for this analysis, however, concerns the tendency for geographical closeness to serve as a marker for other variables reflecting shared experience of external pressures and opportunities (as well as, in some cases, common attitudes and ideologies). Hence, we reduce the variance in the external contexts facing these countries in order better to isolate those domestic factors that account for differences in national policy responses.[46]

A second reason for selecting our countries from a single region relates to our particular analytic focus on the relationships linking domestic, regional, and global economies, and our conviction that the regional economy is of real independent significance.[47] In addition, despite the trend in the field of comparative politics to move away from "area" studies, we suspect that many of our readers will be interested not only in our theoretical claims but also in our analyses of four developing countries within a region in which they have particular interest. Relative to developing countries in other regions, the theoretical interest of the ASEAN Four is yet to be reflected, in our view, in the extent or quality of research on their political economies.

The third reason for selecting these four countries is that, in important ways, these economies are similar beyond what proximity alone would lead us to expect. Unlike the East Asian NICs, all are rich in resources and capable of producing and exporting agricultural surpluses, hence casting doubt on the alleged inverse relationship between natural bounty and economic growth.[48] The ASEAN Four are readily distinguished from, for example, city-state Singapore, which we exclude from this analysis, or semi-socialist economies such as Cambodia, China, Laos, Myanmar, and Vietnam. Indeed, these four political economies appear to be particularly similar to one another when compared with the East Asian NIEs. The ASEAN Four long were able to earn foreign exchange and raise government revenue by exporting agricultural and mineral commodities. In short, unlike the East Asian NIEs, the four had choices and might have opted to limit their exposure to international competition and open development strategies. They are important precisely because their policymakers had the luxury of entertaining choices.

To a very substantial degree, economic expansion in the ASEAN Four has been tied to regional and global economic trends. This is, of course, true of almost all states, and becoming more true. In important respects, however, it marks a broad distinction between the ASEAN Four and Japan, South Korea, and Taiwan.

While the ASEAN Four are of course somewhat diverse in their experiences and performances (we have already pointed out that the Philippines is something of an outlier among them), in important respects they are alike. None of the ASEAN Four are primarily Confucian (although their business elites largely are ethnic Chinese). Key policymakers in the ASEAN Four provide less strategic direction to the economy and are less aloof from societal and bureaucratic interests than are their Northeast Asian counterparts. The latter, as well as Japan, enjoy benefits deriving from effective state administrative structures that are comparatively small in size and relatively free of problems of goal displacement. The latter also are relatively homogeneous ethnically and unusually rich in human skills for their respective levels of development.

By contrast, in none of the ASEAN Four is state administration particularly efficient. Almost no-one views the Southeast Asian states as capitalist developmental states.[49] While there are many exceptions to this generalization, as a group these states have concentrated more on macroeconomic concerns – realistic exchange rates, control over state finances, steady monetary policies – than on sector-specific industrial policies. All of them enjoyed relatively great leeway as a result of their agricultural and resource wealth which long enabled them to earn foreign exchange without concentrating on industrial development. Ease of access to revenue and foreign exchange limited the extent to which state and business elites felt themselves bound to common destinies. Their distinct ethnic identities reinforced the limited interdependence between private and public elites. In addition, direct foreign investment played a more important role in the Southeast Asian states than in the NIEs. In short, the ASEAN Four, with their strong records of economic growth, offer means of expanding our understanding of the ways in which poor states can become richer.[50]

Having established the rationale for selecting our four countries, we turn in the next section to laying out a model of state, societal, and cognitive factors likely to induce responses of economic openness. This model reflects our concern to achieve a compromise between, on the one hand, excessive parsimony that does violence to the complexity of reality and, on the other, inordinate complexity that would frustrate efforts to provide analytical and comparative clarity. Our model attempts to operationalize our analytical framework linking domestic policy responses to changes in external contexts. We lay out five hypotheses (and variations on these) that we expect to explain decision-makers' preferences for either closed or open economic policies.

Hypotheses

What factors do we expect to affect the extent of economic openness in response to external challenges and opportunities? Identifying these variables requires us to propose a simplified model of political economy. Admittedly, our task would be easier if we limited ourselves to either domestic state-related factors (e.g., how do officials enhance state revenue, sustain political support, or devise effective industrial policies?) or domestic societal factors (e.g., what groups form, with what goals, and how do they exert influence on state policy?). Instead, while we seek to isolate these different kinds of variables for analytic purposes, we encompass both. We derive our model both deductively and inductively, drawing on both logically compelling hypotheses and the existing literature.[51] The model is by no means exhaustive or universally applicable. It includes variables that ultimately turn out not to be powerful explanatory factors and excludes others that clearly were not relevant to our cases.[52]

We begin by formulating a set of hypotheses that attempt to capture the causal paths from state, societal, and external variables to economic openness. Looking first at variables specific to states,[53] we observe that state authorities require revenue in order to maintain state operations and system stability, and that the economies they promote and regulate require foreign exchange. If state officials are able to extract adequate revenue from society without inordinate recourse to import tariffs, the economy is more likely to be open. If import taxes comprise a significant share of revenue, officials are prone to worry that opening their markets will result in (larger) fiscal deficits. Whether any given level of revenue is adequate, of course, depends on expenditure levels that are results of, among other factors: first, the extent to which state officials perceive significant security threats, internal or external, to their rule; and, second, the degree to which nonstate actors (as well as competing actors within the state) successfully can press expenditure demands on the state.

In short, the lower the level of external or internal threat of violence against the state, the less the need to extract revenue from society and the greater the potential to encourage economic growth by fostering property rights, breaking up distributional coalitions,[54] and opening up the economy.[55] And the greater the state's relative capacity, that is, the more easily the state is able to extract a given level of revenue from society, the more likely it is to pursue economic openness.[56] While it is possible that a surfeit of revenue would allow policy-makers to avoid politically difficult adjustment policies and, perhaps, to launch *dirigiste* policies (those involving government control or intervention in trade), it is at least as plausible that policymakers would elect to use fiscal surpluses to compensate losers while retaining or increasing economic openness.

As with revenue, the need for foreign exchange will vary with the local demand for foreign goods and services. To the extent that such demand is strong and exceeds existing supplies of foreign exchange, state actors will tend to favor policies that either minimize that demand (import substitution) or increase the supply of foreign exchange (export promotion). Foreign exchange shortages, of course, can be addressed either on the capital or the current account, through merchandise or services trade flows, official transfers, or short- or long-term capital inflows. A foreign exchange windfall may induce a turn away from open economic policies by reducing the pressures to enhance export earnings.

Our first hypothesis, then, is as follows:

Given that state officials require revenue, their ability to pursue open trade policies will vary with the extent of their dependence on import tariffs. Hence,

H1a: The greater state officials' capacity to generate revenues from domestic sources, rather than from import tariffs, the more likely state officials are to respond to an external development with policies that favor economic openness.

Foreign exchange shortages, expressed as periodic balance-of-payments crises, will nudge state officials to move toward either import-substituting or export-promoting strategies as means of either saving or earning foreign exchange. Officials may elect to reduce demand for foreign exchange, by means for example of tighter import restrictions. In the face of repeated failures to balance the current account through such policies, however, there is good reason to expect that the supply-side approach is more likely. Efforts to increase the supply of foreign exchange by encouraging openness are more far-sighted in that they envision long-run structural change in the economy. Their potential to alleviate the foreign exchange constraint in the long run is greater than is the case with the static, short-term expedient of saving foreign exchange by reducing the volume of existing imports.[57] If the advantages of a supply-increasing strategy over a demand-reducing one are not inherently compelling, the relative success of developing countries pursuing those divergent strategies is likely to encourage recourse to the former. This leads to a consideration of demonstration effects, which we discuss below. Policies to increase foreign exchange may include strategies that are not really intended to increase exports but (as in the Philippines case – see chapter 5) are largely window-dressing designed to hoodwink creditors and secure foreign public aid or private loans. Therefore,

H1b: The greater an economy's shortage of foreign exchange, and the more extensive the experience of failed efforts to save foreign exchange through resort to import-substituting policies, the more likely state officials are to respond to an external challenge by adopting policies designed to increase the supply of foreign exchange.

External events may of course bring windfall gains, from unexpected foreign exchange earnings. Such opportunities are likely to afford decision-makers the space to pursue policies that fly in the face of conventional economic rationality or that reduce the level of economic openness in the short term with a view to improving the technological sophistication of domestic industry (the Korean model of the 1970s). Thus,

> H1c: Where external events result in foreign exchange windfalls, state officials are more likely to respond by embracing closed policies.

This first group of hypotheses attempts to explain some of the potential sources of officials' policy preferences. Note that we do not assume a strictly short-term, utilitarian view of the state. The foreign policy executive, in particular, is often sensitive to the state's international setting and more prone to act on behalf of a perceived broader public good (to act consistently with the model of a guardian state). Regardless of the sources of preferences, however, translating preferences into policies and implementing these successfully require particular state capacities. Otherwise, policymakers may pull the policy levers to no avail.[58] State capacity, in turn, is linked to a wide variety of factors too complex to incorporate into our model.[59] Of particular importance, however, is the relative influence within the state of agencies responsible for macroeconomic policymaking and those line agencies that implement policies and regulate various actors. More generally, the extent to which the national executive delegates policymaking to economic technocrats influences the degree to which the selection of economic policies responds to economic rather than political logics. Political leaders sometimes delegate critical economic decision-making powers in order to depoliticize the decision process or to ensure that decisions reflect the interests of politicians' support coalitions. Examples include autonomous central banks and budget-making agencies, and policy commitments that sharply constrain policy options (as when Indonesia removed capital controls in 1971).[60] Our second hypothesis, then, is as follows:

> H2: Where technocrats and macroeconomic policymaking officials have dominant policymaking roles within the state, responses to shifts in external conditions are more likely to move in the direction of economic openness.

This hypothesis not only addresses the state capacity to implement policies successfully, but also assumes that structural characteristics of the state are linked to policy preferences (for an open or for a closed economy). Certain kinds of institutional arrangements, we assume, are more apt to be associated with particular sets of policy choices. Our assumption is rooted in the collective action hypothesis that, all else being equal (in the absence of state officials exercising their preferences), the majority whose interests are served by economic openness will fail to outweigh the organizational efforts aimed at achieving a more closed policy on the part of the minority who are hurt by openness. Institutional features that delegate decision authority to technocrats can help to redress this imbalance that works to favor closed economic policies.

State capacity to pursue long-term strategies promoting growth also may get a boost serendipitously. Sharp political disjunctures sometimes afford leaders particularly favorable circumstances for asserting their policy preferences.[61] Political leaders may enjoy honeymoons, respites from the most intense partisan conflict. Hence, when new governments assume office, breaks with vested interests may be more likely to occur, and officials more apt to be able to effect policy changes.[62] Similarly, such disjunctures may facilitate the forging of growth coalitions to take advantage of external opportunities. If business, labor, and other interests that gain from economic openness can be mobilized politically, then the collective action hypothesis no longer suggests a bias against open economic policies. Societal actors can, of course, identify their own interests and, viewed from a different perspective (discussed below), play a crucial role in shaping the state and its preferences. Within limits, however, those who control the state can manipulate information and policies to forge coalitions in support of their rule and their policy preferences. A given distribution of societal preferences may or may not be politically mobilized effectively in support of economic openness depending on the political leadership's commitments and political skills. Thus, our third hypothesis is:

> H3a: To the extent that the political coalitions that state leaders employ to sustain their rule favor openness, then state officials' policy responses to exogenous events are more apt to favor economic openness than closedness.

And, further:

> H3b: Governments coming to power after sharp political disjunctures, including coups and elections, are more prone to break from vested interests and more likely to redirect policy in the direction of economic openness.

Statist hypotheses tend to exhibit either mechanical (utilitarian) determinacy or a voluntarist view of policymaking.[63] That is, they tend to assume either that policymakers are tightly constrained and have little room for policy choices, that policymakers' preferences are given by particular features of the national economy and polity, or, in contrast, that policymakers are entirely free to select those policies they prefer. We can compensate for these common weaknesses in statist approaches by extending our view beyond the institutions of the state in order to look at the preferences and relative influence of societal actors (the demand side of policy)[64] and how these shape national economic responses to external challenges. First, drawing on Ronald Rogowski[65] (who draws, in turn, on the Stolper–Samuelson theorem), we note that in any economy owners of factors of production that are in relative abundance should tend to favor openness, while owners of relatively scarce factors should oppose it. The reason for this is that when factors are relatively scarce their value increases and so does the wealth of their owners. Trade will tend to diminish the relative scarcity and value of such factors. Hence, owners of relatively scarce factors should favor protection against imports of such factors. Conversely, those who own relatively abundant factors should favor openness. Trade will help to bring down the prices of those factors they do not own. In all of the four cases we consider in this study, capital is a relatively scarce factor and, following Rogowski, we therefore would expect those who control capital to oppose economic openness.[66]

Relative factor scarcity can change. This may occur as a result of either domestic upheaval or externally induced adjustments. Where the external changes reduce the relative abundance of a particular factor, they will increase the incentive of the owners of that factor to support a policy response that reduces openness. Alternatively, those changes that increase a factor's abundance should push owners of that factor to lean more in support of open economic policies.

Despite the intuitive appeal of this argument and its successful application in other contexts, there are a priori grounds for questioning its utility for our purposes here. First, the power of the hypothesis depends on an expectation that all actors have more or less equal ability to mobilize for political action. Generally, capital faces fewer collective action problems than either labor or landed interests where the latter are dominated by decentralized peasant production. Among the ASEAN Four, only the Philippines and, to a lesser degree, Malaysia have significant plantation production that we might expect to be more amenable to landed interests' efforts at overcoming collective action problems. In all of the ASEAN Four, the lack of effective labor organization is a major hindrance to labor's ability to overcome collective action obstacles and to develop the political strength promised by its abundance.

The second ground for concern about the usefulness of this hypothesis for our purposes is that relative factor scarcities vary little across our four countries or within them over time. As developing countries, all are relatively capital-poor and labor-rich. During the half-century that concerns us here, all also have been relatively land-poor. In short, relative factor scarcities have not varied significantly over the last half-century. The one significant exception is capital. As capital has moved more rapidly and readily around the globe, the relative scarcity of capital in at least some developing countries, including the ASEAN Four, has decreased. This may help to explain the declining force of protectionist pressures among firms in the ASEAN Four.

Further, knowing the relative scarcities of different factors of production is not sufficient to predict policy responses to external challenges. After all, individuals, firms, or groups may control more than one factor. At the time that parliament repealed the Corn Laws in Britain, for example, many of those landed interests that were hurt by the policy change also had significant investment in emerging industrial sectors. This tended to diminish their resistance to tariff changes.[67] Hence, to understand the political impact of relative factor scarcities, we need to know something about who controls them. This point is in fact crucial to our cases as the economically dominant Chinese business groups often have interests that spread across a variety of businesses characterized by different relative factor intensities. The same business group may be involved in agribusiness, finance, capital-intensive industry, and labor-intensive export manufacturing. Predicting their trade policy preferences based on factor scarcities becomes problematic.

It is also true that certain factors are inherently more flexible than others.[68] Independent of patterns of ownership of specific sectors, we might also expect that where investment capital is more readily redeployed, resistance to policy departures is likely to be less than in those cases where investments are more dedicated in nature.[69] Hence, ease of redeployment of capital – an admittedly difficult characteristic to measure – might be a further consideration here; as might high levels of intra-industry trade, which tend to diminish opposition to open trade. This relationship holds, allegedly, first, because the heterogeneity of trade interests within any given sector impedes the development of an effective coalition in favor of diminishing trade and, second, because assets are more easily shifted within a single industry rather than having to be moved to an unrelated area of production.[70]

Just as state capacity is relevant to understanding the extent to which officials' preferences can be converted into effective policies, so a variety of institutions can help us understand the relative prospects of different societal interests shaping national economic policies. These institutional factors range from the nature of party systems to the size of electoral districts. However, many are not relevant to the four countries that concern us here. Hence, we focus only on those institutions that link business interests and the state. We suggest that corporatist institutions are more likely to express the national interest in economic openness than are clientelistic policy channels operating through state officials or poorly institutionalized political parties lacking mass bases or effective organizational infrastructures. The latter policy channels put a premium on the intensity of actors' policy preferences. Since interests threatened with bankruptcy and joblessness by import competition have great motivation to use political influence to block imports, protectionist policies are more apt to result. In contrast, institutionalized corporatist channels may be more likely to give voice to a broader range of preferences, including those of actors favoring economic openness who might might not be disposed to invest resources to secure their less intensely felt policy interests. Hence,

> H4: Where business and the state are linked by corporatist institutions, state officials are more prone to respond to external challenges by adopting economic policies that shift the economy in the direction of economic openness.

We now turn briefly to the role of ideas and how they affect the extent of economic openness. Ideas can of course originate from abroad, can take root within societal actors, or can be propagated by the state. While the origins of ideas are difficult to pinpoint, their importance can be readily demonstrated. One of the great obstacles to change, as noted in a celebrated quotation from Machiavelli, is that while those who stand to lose from it can readily see how their interests stand to be damaged, those who may gain are less certain of the advantages they can reap.[71] This is one of the great challenges facing political leadership in creating coalitions in favor of change (see hypotheses H3).

We noted in H3a that state actors' ability to forge coalitions favoring economic openness is an important determinant of the adoption of open economic policies. Here we are concerned with factors that affect societal actors' propensity to respond to external challenges by creating coalitions that favor greater economic openness. We have already discussed several objective economic variables that influence the trade interests of different actors. Frequently, however, those interests are far from obvious. This is in part a reflection of the difficulty of predicting the future and of estimating utilities in complex environments.[72] Where widely perceived external models are available, however, they can demonstrate to individuals, firms, and state actors elsewhere how their interests likely will be affected by particular policy changes. For example, where a shift toward economic openness in country A has appeared to produce rapid economic growth and fast expansion in textile exports, this experience is more likely to be taken as a lesson in country B and to influence policy deliberations there if elites are aware of developments in country A and in significant ways identify with the experiences of country A. This is important because in a context of inevitable information inadequacy, actors are prone to draw imperfect (or even misleading) parallels from experiences elsewhere in estimating their expected gains and losses.[73] Hence, they are more likely to mobilize political pressure based on their interests as estimated through use of such analogies. Our fifth hypothesis then concerns the role of demonstration effects:

> H5: Where elites perceive and identify with successful examples of open economic strategies in other countries, they are more apt to believe that their own interests can be served by comparable strategies, and state officials are more likely to respond to an external development with policies that favor economic openness. The reverse also holds.

Our hypotheses and the independent variables they incorporate are not intended to be exhaustive (for example, we do not consider regime types, the role of ideologies, party systems, power balances between executive and legislative branches, leadership, or the impacts of particular state institutions or types of financial systems). We believe, however, that our five hypotheses (and their variations) capture important variables that influence the extent to which developing countries respond to external events with greater economic openness or closedness.

We should note that we do not expect the values of our independent variables to change frequently in the course of our four events. Indeed, in the cases of some variables when applied to particular countries, we anticipate finding no, or perhaps only a single, shift in value across the four events. In chapters 3 through 6, therefore, as we review the specific countries, we will for each external event concentrate only on those variables that appear to us to be critically

Figure 1.1. *Operationalization of the five hypotheses*

Hypothesis	Operationalization
H1a: Revenue	Fiscal balances; dependence on import taxes
H1b: Foreign exchange	Current-account balances; duration of ISI-linked chronic external imbalances
H1c: Sudden increases in foreign exchange	Foreign exchange surges
H2: Relative influence of (macroeconomic policy-making) technocrats	Subjective evaluation (process tracing)
H3a: Backing for the national executive on the part of actors favoring economic openness	Sources of electoral and other funding; advisors and cabinet members; voting blocs
H3b: Political disjunctures	Subjective evaluation
H4: Corporatist channels	Corporatist institutions; institutionalized parties; clientelist vs. Weberian state
H5: Demonstration effects	Subjective evaluation (process tracing)

important in explaining the national responses to the challenges posed by that specific event.

Finally, we show in figure 1.1 the ways in which we operationalize our independent variables, derived from the five hypotheses (and their modified forms) outlined above. The causal relationships suggested by the five hypotheses are summarized in figure 1.2.

Structure of the book

In chapter 2 we provide readers with a fuller discussion of the postwar development of the East Asian political economy, focusing on the US role in promoting an open international economy, creating the institutions to underpin that openness, and indirectly stimulating economic growth in East Asia through its regional containment policies. In chapter 2 we also highlight the important features of the subsequent four events.

Chapters 3 through 6 examine, respectively, Indonesia, Malaysia, the Philippines, and Thailand. In each chapter, we begin by providing an overview of key political and economic institutions (including sections on social organization, politics and the bases of state power, and linkages between business and

Figure 1.2. *Causal relationships suggested by the five hypotheses*

Independent variable	Increased economic openness?
H1a: Low import revenue dependence	Yes
H1b: Sustained foreign exchange shortages under ISI	Yes
H1c: Foreign exchange windfall	No
H2: Relatively great policy influence of (macroeconomic policymaking) technocrats	Yes
H3a: Political coalition favoring openness	Yes
H3b: Political disjuncture	Yes/indeterminate
H4: Corporatist channels link business and state	Yes
H5: Demonstration effects	Indeterminate

the state). We then turn, in each of the chapters, to a systematic examination of each of the four events. In every case, we begin by describing the impact that the exogenous shocks had on the particular country. Subsequently, we describe the economic policy record in each country. We conclude our discussion of each case with an analysis of the factors explaining that policy record. We do not examine every hypothesis for each event. Rather, we concentrate on those independent variables that have changed and look to see whether or not the result in terms of economic openness is consistent with the predictions made by our hypotheses. Finally, each of the country chapters concludes with an evaluation of the performance of each of the hypotheses introduced above. Chapter 7 presents our conclusions, drawn from a consideration of the four countries and the sixteen cases of policy response, and points to outstanding questions and areas for further research.

CHAPTER TWO

Southeast Asian economic growth: the international context

The international economic and strategic environments have presented both opportunities and constraints for growth and economic development in the Southeast Asian region. Exploiting these opportunities successfully has required some degree of openness, at least to foreign technology and foreign markets. As the cases of Japan in the 1950s and 1960s and South Korea into the 1980s make clear, however, success has not required full openness of capital and trade regimes.

This chapter presents a broad overview of the changing global and regional context for Southeast Asian development during the postwar years, and discusses how that context has shaped economic possibilities and affected economic openness among the ASEAN Four. We discuss the economic, political, strategic, and international institutional forces at work. We reserve for chapters 3 through 6 a more detailed and analytic consideration of the impact of the external environment on state policymaking and business planning in the individual countries. In those chapters, we also describe the nature of specific policy responses and seek to explain the reasons for individual countries responding to the external context in particular ways.

The initial section of this chapter concentrates on the Japanese and, in particular, US roles in shaping the context for early postwar Southeast Asian development. These include US commitment to the containment of communism, backed by high levels of US aid and military spending, and establishment of an open international economy featuring rapid growth and trade expansion. We then sketch briefly four developments ("events") over the past quarter-century that have represented specific international challenges to which developing countries in general, and the ASEAN Four in particular, have had to respond (we introduced these very briefly in chapter 1).

25

The United States and postwar Asia

In the period after World War II, the United States played the most important role of any country in shaping the context within which all economies operated. Economic and security interests led the United States to create global economic and strategic environments favorable to the success of open development policies. It also propagated economic ideas – economic liberalism – that influenced decision-makers in developing countries, particularly those of certain East Asian ones. And the United States directly influenced developing economies through the provision of capital, technology and managerial skills, and, not least, access to the US market.

In Asia, security interests led to US involvement in the Korean and Vietnam wars. American aid, military procurement, and spending expanded the range of economic possibilities for other Asian nations. The United States as the regionally dominant power, nurtured Japan's postwar take-off and linked it to Southeast Asia's markets and raw materials, thereby shaping many aspects of Southeast Asian development. And the United States played the leading role in fostering the international economic institutions that facilitated the expansion of an open international economy. Thus, the economic choices of Southeast Asian decision-makers ought to be seen, in the first instance, as responses to the security concerns and geopolitical considerations of the United States and their regional consequences.[1]

There are three ways in which a regionally dominant state can affect the development prospects of countries in a region. The first involves the creation of a wider international environment that spawns opportunities for growth, in particular by lowering transaction costs. Rapid global or regional economic growth enhances the prospects for any given national economy and such growth will both tend to stimulate, and be stimulated by, the expansion of capital flows from, and trade with, the dominant power. Similarly, a commitment to global diffusion of technological innovation has the potential to stimulate economic activity in a given economy. Further, given a particular level of economic activity and of technological innovation, institutional innovation by the dominant power may lower transaction costs and foster specialization and gains from trade. To encourage others to accept as appropriate the institution of a relatively open trade regime, the dominant power may employ both carrots and sticks, including provision of public goods, such as access to the power's markets (and bearing the adjustment costs of opening these markets to imports), sponsorship of global and regional institutions that facilitate cooperation in liberalizing trade and helping finance balance-of-payments shortfalls, and availability of a stable currency that can be used as the unit of account for international transactions. By acting in any or several of these ways, a dominant power may tend to shift transaction and relative factor costs within any given economy, with significant political and economic implications.[2]

The second way a regionally dominant state may influence the development prospects of countries in the region is by encouraging policies more likely to yield rapid growth.[3] Political pressure may be brought to bear on developing states to adopt public policies deemed appropriate by the dominant power (whether motivated by a desire to open developing-country markets and resources to the dominant state's firms, to stimulate economic development, or both). Procurement policies, concessional loans or outright grants, and a host of other tools may be used by the dominant power to give weight to such pressures. Alternatively, the dominant power may employ ideological appeal, or use the demonstration effect of its economy to encourage pro-growth policies.

The third means of influence is more direct, involving trade and the provision of capital, managerial skills, technology, and access to the consumer market of the dominant power.

The United States was the dominant regional power in Asia after World War II and shaped the constellation of opportunities and constraints confronting decision-makers in Asia. Despite the priority given to the rebuilding of Western Europe, the onset of the Cold War and its extension to East Asia – particularly with the start of the Korean War – forced American leaders to give the task of containing communism in East Asia greater attention. From these security concerns stemmed economic initiatives.

The United States at the global level set about creating an international environment favorable to the growth of capitalist economies. US leadership provided the impetus for global economic institutions governing balance-of-payments financing (the International Monetary Fund in 1944), development finance (the International Bank for Reconstruction and Development [World Bank] in 1945), and trade (the General Agreement on Tariffs and Trade [GATT] in 1947). By the time Asian economies had recovered sufficiently to take real advantage of these contributions, the United States was also providing global liquidity and encouraging use of the dollar as an international reserve currency and unit of account. As first Japan and then others adopted export-led growth strategies, these international institutions played crucial roles in fostering international capital mobility, balance-of-payments financing, and international economic stability. As foreseen immediately after the war in the report of a group of Japanese economists commissioned by the Japanese Ministry of Foreign Affairs, American domination of the world economy made autarky less viable and instead offered the potential for a system of international trade with a minimum of barriers which promised full employment and higher standards of living throughout the world.[4]

Japan-centric policies

In Asia, Japan was the centerpiece of US strategic policy. Initially (1945–47), the American Occupation authorities in Japan under General Douglas

MacArthur focused on the "twin evils," imperial militarism and military-industrial conglomerates, which Occupation authorities believed had fomented Japanese expansion into Northeast and, after 1940, Southeast Asia. By destroying the Japanese Imperial Army, breaking up the *zaibatsu*, and eliminating rural landlords, the Occupation "New Dealers" sought to bequeath to the world a reformed Japan that would never again mix aggression with economic prowess.[5]

By late 1947, with the demilitarization of Japan complete and some progress having been made in dismantling the *zaibatsu*,[6] this policy of creating an enduring and prosperous liberal political and economic order in Japan linked to a burgeoning world economy, present in policy statements from 1944 onward, had come to the fore. It thus paralleled the doctrine of containment, by which these economic concerns were linked not so much with liberalism as with containing the spread of communism. With the United States active in rebuffing Soviet expansion in Western Europe and perceived threats in Persia, Turkey, and Greece, Cold War security had become the dominant theme of US foreign policy.[7] Efforts to revive the Japanese economy and, indeed, US policy toward Asia in general, including Korea, China, and Southeast Asia, were made comprehensible in the simple framework of the global bipolar confrontation with the Soviet Union.

Convinced that Japan would never be able to balance its trade with the United States and as a result it could drain US resources indefinitely, the United States sought alternative export markets and sources of raw materials for the Japanese economy. The question was how to resuscitate Japan's postwar economy without benefit of the raw materials and labor from Northeast Asia that had played such a crucial role in the 1930s. By late 1949, most of this former hinterland (North Korea and Manchuria, as well as the rest of China) was under communist rule.[8] As a result, Southeast Asia assumed great importance in the minds of Japanese and US officials as a potential postwar hinterland for Japan offering markets for Japan's textile and light industrial exports and badly needed industrial raw materials.[9]

Southeast Asia to this point had been very much at the periphery of US strategic concerns. There was no comprehensive US strategy with respect to Southeast Asia until late 1949, when President Truman authorized NSC 48/1, a policy position paper that envisioned a tripartite structure, with Japan situated between the US core and the Southeast Asian periphery.[10] Washington officials expected this structure to revive a three-way trading pattern dating to early in the century, wherein Japan's trade with the United States had been in deficit, its trade with Southeast Asia in surplus, and Southeast Asia's trade with the United States also in surplus.[11]

Southeast Asian leaders were wary of such a Pacific economic order, since it only reflected US priorities with respect to former belligerent, Japan. They accused US officials of advancing a "Japan-centric Asia policy."[12] The chief

Thai negotiator at a 1950 Washington trade conference noted that "apparently it is the United States policy to secure through political pressure what the Japanese Army failed to secure in Asia."[13] These sentiments, however, did not deter US officials, who made purchases of Japanese goods integral to proposed schemes for US and World Bank development assistance to Southeast Asian countries. William Borden has described the proposed aid structure as one in which Japan would supply manufactures while the other recipients (Southeast Asia) would supply foodstuffs and raw materials, and the US dollar would be the medium of exchange for all participants.[14]

The result, as Watanabe Akio notes, was a melding of the old Japanese idea of Asian economic integration with the US strategic objective of containment.[15] The concept was revolutionary in that it foreshadowed a postwar US economic hegemony in Asia unencumbered by territorial possession, in which vast spaces were to be structured by economic arrangements. However, the success of the plan depended upon the United States' ability to persuade other participants to lower barriers to trade and its willingness to lay its economy open to potentially destructive competition, and to accept the consequences of declining economic dependency and upwards mobility on the part of developing-country participants.[16]

The Cold War comes to Asia

With the outbreak of war on the Korean peninsula in 1950, proposals for coordinated aid involving Southeast Asia became a reality and, through 1960, some 10 percent of Japanese exports to Southeast Asia were financed out of US aid to the region.[17]

The Korean War, in Chalmers Johnson's view, was in many ways the equivalent for Japan of the Marshall Plan, because the Korean War boom saved both the government of Prime Minister Yoshida and the United States Occupation administration from near economic disaster.[18] Japan was the principal economic beneficiary of the Korean War. Its attendant economic boom enabled Japan rapidly to increase its production and to double its exports, despite the absence of the important prewar trade with China.[19] In 1951, Japanese exports to Korea and US procurement from Japan accounted for nearly half of all Japanese exports and yielded over one-fourth of total Japanese dollar earnings.[20] US military procurements from Japan in the period 1952–56 amounted to a quarter of American commodity imports, valued at $3.4 billion.[21] American procurement and other military-associated expenditures helped to finance about one-fifth of all Japanese imports during the period 1945–62.[22] Southeast Asia also benefited from Korean War procurements and from commodity price increases that resulted from the efforts of both sides to build strategic stockpiles in anticipation of a heating up of the Cold War. For example, a fourfold increase in the price of rubber and a doubling of the price of tin proved particularly beneficial to British Malaya and Indonesia, the two major sources of both commodities.[23]

Southeast Asia also received Soviet aid beginning in the mid-1950s, about the time that Chinese leaders were announcing their determination at the 1955 Bandung Conference of Nonaligned Nations to woo the governments of the region. Clear indications of US resolve to play an active strategic role in the region emerged in 1950 when, following Chinese and Soviet recognition of the Viet Minh under Ho Chi Minh, the United States moved to recognize Bao Dai in South Vietnam as well as noncommunist regimes in Cambodia and Laos. The Export-Import Bank extended a $100 million loan to Indonesia, and the United States began to dispatch regular economic and military assistance missions to the region. In 1951 the United States concluded mutual security treaties with the Philippines and jointly with Australia and New Zealand. By 1954, the United States had extended $800 million in aid to Indochina, primarily in the form of military supplies.[24]

In 1954, Australia, Britain, France, India, Malaya, New Zealand, Pakistan, the Philippines, Thailand, and the United States concluded the Southeast Asia Collective Defense Treaty establishing the Southeast Asia Treaty Organization. Cambodia, Laos, and South Vietnam were attached to the organization under a separate protocol.[25] As Chinese and Soviet diplomatic activities in the region increased, first Dulles and then Vice-President Nixon traveled to the region in 1956. Despite considerable economic contributions and diplomatic efforts, US influence in Burma, Cambodia, and Indonesia made little headway. The Burmese suspended US aid programs in 1953; the Cambodians in 1965. President Sukarno never cut off US assistance, but he did pronounce:"To hell with your aid."[26]

The Korean War highlighted the strategic importance of Southeast Asia, particularly of Indonesia and Malaya, to the Japanese economy and demonstrated how crucial the region was to the US policy of preventing the political neutralization of Japan.[27] Nevertheless, despite major US efforts on Japan's behalf, Japan's trade with Southeast Asia during the 1950s remained at modest levels in comparison with its global trade. Japanese Prime Minister Yoshida, struck by the lack of purchasing power in the region and besieged by requests for economic aid during a Southeast Asian trip in 1954, concluded that Japan would be better off trading with "rich men, not beggars."[28] Collapsing commodity prices in the aftermath of the Korean armistice were to render the Southeast Asian economies even less desirable as markets for Japanese goods.

Japan's expanding role

Japan lived up to US hopes, at least in its rhetoric, that it would compete with China as a model to attract the hearts and minds of Southeast Asians. As Foreign Minister Shiina Etsusaburo put it: "Communist China is implementing her efforts to lead on the basis of communism, Japan on the basis of democracy and liberalism."[29] Japan became a member of the Economic Commission on Asia and the Far East (ECAFE) in 1954 and entered the United Nations in 1956.[30]

By the early 1950s, Japan, in part at US behest, had embarked on its reparations programs for Southeast Asia. At the same time, Yoshida hoped that in return for political support for US anticommunist policies, Japan could gain US support in the form of a massive $4 billion regional economic assistance program and the creation of an Asian payments union. He expressed Japanese concern about Southeast Asia in a speech in 1953:

> I do not think it is necessary to dwell upon the importance of our relations with Southeast Asia, since we cannot expect much from trade with China. The government desires to extend every possible cooperation for the prosperity of the countries of Southeast Asia in the form of capital, technique, service or otherwise, in order to thus further the relations of reciprocal benefit and common prosperity.[31]

Subsequent Japanese Prime Minister Kishi Nobusuke proposed the creation in 1957 of a Southeast Asia development fund based on a regional development bank. He also called for an Asian focus to Japan's diplomacy as one of three central tenets underlying Japan's postwar international role.

In the late 1950s and 1960s, Japan began to prepare for a larger regional role by developing new institutions of "economic cooperation," enhancing its economic research capabilities, and fostering efforts to create new regional economic institutions. Japanese officials and academics were active in these efforts, particularly when the signing of the Treaty of Rome created the risk of Japan being cut off from European markets. Prime Minister Ikeda Hayato traveled to Southeast Asia in 1963 and developed a conviction that Asian cohesion was needed to foster regional development. As an "advanced elder brother," Japan could play a leadership role.[32] Japan also launched efforts at mediation in conflicts, including those between Indonesia and Malaya and, much later, in the 1970 crisis in Cambodia. During the Vietnam War, Japanese officials talked of a Japanese role in peacekeeping and reconstruction following a settlement of the conflict.[33]

The US commitment to containing communism led policymakers in Washington to send US forces into conflicts in Korea and Vietnam. The United States also established major overseas military bases in Japan, Okinawa (a US territory until 1972), the Philippines, the Republic of Korea, the Republic of Vietnam, and Thailand. US military spending provided a major economic stimulus to many countries in the area. The United States also extended large-scale economic and military assistance to several East Asian countries.

The United States relied on bilateral security guarantees with Japan, South Korea, the Philippines, and Thailand to stabilize the region. Most US institutional efforts in this area concentrated on security institutions, such as the

Southeast Asia Treaty Organization. The United States was less active in fostering regional economic institutions that might have fostered cooperation among countries in the area and reduced transaction costs in concluding economic, technological, and broad cooperation agreements.

Other countries, however, played more active roles in fostering regional economic institutions. Participants at a 1963 meeting of ECAFE discussed the idea of an Asian Development Bank (ADB) and Japanese business and government leaders on hand were prepared with a plan for such an institution. They played the lead role in launching the ADB in 1965 and Japan subscribed to one-fifth ($200 million) the total capital while also supplying the bank's president. The United States provided an equal share of the bank's capital while Japan provided the major share of the bank's special funds.[34]

The most important multilateral institution in Southeast Asia is ASEAN. The United States was an enthusiastic supporter of ASEAN from its inception. Initial Japanese ambivalence toward ASEAN and the 1971 proposal for a Zone of Peace, Freedom, and Neutrality (ZOPFAN)[35] receded following the triumph of communist movements throughout Indochina in 1975. By 1977, Japanese officials attended the first meeting of the ASEAN–Japan forum and, that same year, Prime Minister Fukuda attended the ASEAN Summit in Kuala Lumpur. Fukuda traveled to each of the five ASEAN capitals and in Manila enunciated the Fukuda Doctrine.[36] At that time, Japan agreed to provide $1 billion in loans for five ASEAN regional projects, to discuss a $400 million commodity export earnings stabilization scheme, and to examine its tariff policies in the context of the ongoing Tokyo Round of GATT talks.[37]

On balance, regional institutions such as the ADB, ECAFE, and SEATO have not played a central role in the Southeast Asian region's development or security. The most important organization, ASEAN, established in 1967, has developed into an important institution without any direct participation by either Japan or the United States. By and large, regional economic and security issues have been handled by both Japan and the United States through a complex of bilateral relationships.

With the end of the Cold War, broader regional institutions such as the Pacific Economic Cooperation Council (PECC) and the Asia Pacific Economic Cooperation (APEC) forum appear poised to take on more crucial functions. PECC was established by a joint Australian–Japanese initiative in 1980 to bring together academics, business leaders and government officials (in their unofficial capacities) representing twenty-two nations. From these unofficial beginnings there emerged in 1989 an official organization, APEC, through which Asia Pacific heads of government from all major trading "entities" in North America, Southeast Asia, and the Pacific conferred on issues of regional concern. At annual ministerial or heads of government meetings beginning in 1989, the APEC participants worked towards developing operational mechanisms by which to increase economic openness by expanding markets and lowering trade barriers. The Bogor declaration of 1994 established the intent of members to create "free trade in the Pacific" by fully opening regional trade by the year 2020, thereby creating an Asia Pacific Free Trade Area in the Pacific Basin. Despite substantial obstacles to the working of such arrangements, APEC has demonstrated the potential to make an important contribution to the regional economic context for the ASEAN Four.

Nevertheless, taking the postwar period as a whole, it has been global economic institutions created and promoted by the United States – such as the General Agreement on Tariffs and Trade, the International Monetary Fund, and the World Bank – rather than regional organizations that have played the more important role in shaping economic opportunities for the ASEAN Four.

Having sketched in the broad context of the early postwar years, we now look in more detail at the four events that concern us in the subsequent chapters.

Four events

The first event with which we are concerned is the first oil price shock (of 1973) and the subsequent impact of world economic recession, dubbed "stagflation" (high inflation accompanying slumping world growth, trade, and investment). The oil crisis began in October 1973 with Organization of Petroleum Exporting Countries (OPEC) leaders announcing their intention to restrict the supply of crude oil and embargo those countries supporting Israel, thereby effecting dramatic increases in oil prices. In December 1973, the Persian Gulf leaders of OPEC announced a 125 percent increase in the price of Arabian light crude.[38] This, and subsequent abrupt increases, had the effect of dramatically affecting the supply and cost of energy for all countries and posed particularly acute problems for developing countries that were not oil exporters. It also came on top of a general rise in world prices in the early 1970s that had affected all countries. This was also a period of fixed exchange rates for most developing countries, often dating from the 1950s, and based upon the Bretton Woods system of international financial relations, which precluded continuous adjustment of currency values to respond to external shocks.[39] Nonetheless, the easy availability of cheap foreign loans helped to cushion the impact of the oil price increases for developing countries.

Between 1971 and 1975, the average annual increase in value of developing-country imports registered 24 percent while the rise in volume was only 9 percent.[40] While Indonesia and Malaysia were net energy exporters, the Philippines and Thailand imported 95 and 90 percent of their energy needs respectively.[41] About one-seventh of the latter countries' merchandise exports were consumed in paying for energy needs in 1970, before the price increases; by 1976, this had increased in the case of Thailand to nearly 30 percent.[42] Higher oil costs also affected developing countries indirectly by slowing the pace of world production. The developed market economies grew at average annual rates of 5.2 percent between 1961 and 1965, and 4.6 percent between 1966 and 1970. From 1971 to 1975, however, that rate dropped to 2.8 percent.[43] Meanwhile, the rate of trade growth slumped to 5.8 percent average annual growth between 1972 and 1978 from 9 percent between 1962 and 1972.[44]

Most countries experienced the first oil crisis as an abrupt exogenous economic shock to the terms of trade – the prices of imports rose sharply in relation to the prices of exports – and most responded by hedging rather than adjusting.[45] Anticipating that oil prices would decline, they borrowed to cover trade shortfalls expected to last 2–3 years, taking advantage of the easy credit that accompanied OPEC attempts to recycle petrodollars.[46] The borrowing was generally not excessive; ratios of debt to GNP on average remained more or less the same. In most cases the debt situation was not considered a serious problem, especially since most of new borrowing was going into investment, not consumption. Although in 1975 the story was still mixed, by 1976 the decline in developing-country growth associated with the first oil shock was clearly over. Access to cheap external financing was crucial in enabling developing countries to weather higher energy costs. Indeed, Parvez Hasan suggests that the shock of higher prices was largely offset by negative real interest rates on loans, increasing development assistance flows, and, for some countries, the availability of remittances from nationals working abroad, particularly in the OPEC countries.[47]

Among the ASEAN Four, only Indonesia was a significant oil exporter in 1973,[48] so the effects of the first oil shock were felt differently in Indonesia than they were elsewhere in the region. Indonesia was an OPEC member, but the country's production and share of the world market were much smaller than those of the major oil-producing countries. While Saudi Arabia and Iran produced 8.4 million and 6.1 million barrels per day respectively in 1974, Indonesia produced just 1.4 million. Moreover, with a population more than twice as great as the next largest OPEC member, Nigeria, Indonesia's per capita GNP of $160 was less than half that of the poorest of the remaining members.[49] Hence, the effect of the increased revenue on standards of living was diluted by the large size of the Indonesian population.

The first oil crisis represented a significant external challenge for decision-makers in Thailand, Malaysia, and the Philippines, not simply because it raised their energy import bills and interrupted supply,[50] but also because the anxiety among international investors which the oil crisis engendered led to reduced levels of foreign direct investment and a slump in world trade. The flow of foreign direct investment from the rich countries had about doubled in the early 1970s before stalling between 1973 and 1977. While the flows to developing countries soon recovered, loans played a more prominent role, while direct investment declined in importance.[51]

The sudden economic instability produced in 1974 by the oil price increases called into question expectations of continued global economic expansion and stable prices that had underpinned economic policy planning in each of the

ASEAN Four. As a result, in Kuala Lumpur for example, Malaysia's efforts to redistribute an expanding economic pie among ethnic Chinese, Indian, and Malay populations using the New Economic Policy were stymied when the growth of the pie slowed and new investment from foreign sources to make up for an investment strike by local ethnic Chinese business was not forthcoming.

The second event we consider is the second oil price shock of 1979 and the high interest rates and deepening developing-country indebtedness that followed in its wake. Once oil prices had stabilized at higher nominal levels (falling in real terms) between 1975 and 1978, most developing countries had experienced a period of prolonged growth spurred by high levels of investment financed mainly from international borrowing. Most had not adjusted to the first shock but had instead learned to live with increased balance-of-payments current account deficits and increased debt. The second oil shock in 1979 and the resulting debt crisis that began with Mexico's debt moratorium in 1982 demonstrated the flaw in this strategy.

From an average price in 1979 of $12 a barrel, oil leapt to over $21 the following year and increased again to close to $32 in 1981.[52] This brought with it important direct and indirect impacts for developing countries. In increasing the cost of energy imports it precipitated falling economic growth rates among developing-country energy importers, from an average of 4.9 percent between 1976 and 1980 to 1.4 percent over the next five years. For industrialized countries, the ensuing recession was the sharpest since the 1930s.[53] It also slowed the expansion in world trade, from an average rate of 5.1 percent during the earlier period, to 2.8 percent during the later one. Indeed, global trade actually declined in 1982, a first in the postwar period. Between 1980 and 1983 trade remained nearly stagnant and, for developing countries, it contracted sharply between 1980 and 1982.[54] As most countries' terms of trade declined – and with it their ability to service their external debt – international credit for developing countries dried up and their ability to recycle loans diminished. Debt ratios for short- and long-term debt for most developing countries were markedly worse in 1982 after the Mexican default than in 1979 before the oil price rise. The second oil crisis also exacerbated inflationary conditions in the developing world. Average annual inflation rose from around 10 percent over the late 1960s and early 1970s to over 20 percent in the years after the first round of oil price increases, and climbed steadily after the second price boosts, approaching 50 percent in 1985, before dropping in 1986 and then resuming its climb in 1987.

These extraordinary conditions were much more serious than was the case for the first oil shock, and developing countries were significantly less well placed to meet an external shock in 1979 than they had been in 1973. This in turn was the product of their policy responses to the earlier event, namely that they had chosen debt and then had continued to borrow long after interest rates had begun to climb (the US prime rate reached 21 percent by 1980 and, in real terms, rose still higher to a fifty-year peak in 1982[55] and lenders responding to inflation had started demanding variable rates on new loans in 1977.[56]

The effects of external conditions on developing countries' balance of payments, export markets, growth performance, and external debt put pressure on policymakers to take corrective macroeconomic policy measures. These tended either to produce recessions or, in their absence, to ignite further inflationary pressures. Where policymakers attempted to forestall necessary economic adjustments by borrowing from abroad, the effects generally became more acute in the course of the third event (see below). The ASEAN Four did borrow abroad; their combined bond issues in international capital markets jumped from some $127 million during 1971–75 to over $4.5 billion during 1981–84.[57]

The indirect effects of the two rounds of oil price increases included the transmission of the rich countries' inflation to the developing countries. Widespread use of the dollar as a reserve currency and unit of account meant that inflationary pressures building up in the United States were felt elsewhere as well. Coming on the heels of the collapse of the postwar dollar-based monetary system in 1971 and increasing protectionist pressures in Europe and the United States, the twin oil shocks suggested the end of the postwar economic era and the ushering in of a new one.

Many developing countries mistakenly identified the new era as one serving their economic interests. Ultimately, this was not the case. While the oil-exporting countries were able to create an effective cartel, would-be followers among exporters of other commodities were unable to reproduce OPEC's success.[58] Hopes among developing countries of making effective use of the UN General Assembly and North–South negotiation on a New International Economic Order to address a broad range of economic grievances proved equally illusory.[59] And the belief that developing countries could safely tap the suddenly large pool of savings (petrodollars held in offshore dollar accounts) that bankers were urging on them in the form of loans also proved to be unfounded. Once the value of the dollar began to climb along with interest rates in the early 1980s, debtor countries found that meeting their dollar-denominated debt obligations required the export of ever higher levels of goods. And, following the debt crisis, ushered in by Mexico's default on its loans in August 1982, inflows of new capital for investment to developing countries began to dry up.

The cumulative impact of these shocks was felt by the ASEAN Four in the form of stagnating export growth in the early 1980s (after rapid expansion during most of the 1970s). Between 1980 and 1984, agricultural exports declined for all but Thailand, which managed but a small increase.[60] By 1983, each of the ASEAN Four was experiencing a major current account deficit ranging from 7.5 percent of GDP in Indonesia and Thailand, by way of 9.1 percent in the Philippines, to as high as 11.7 percent in Malaysia.[61] For the Philippines and Thailand, debt-service ratios had climbed to 79 and 50 percent respectively by 1983.[62]

The third event we consider is the slump in world commodity prices between 1984 and 1986, that adversely affected all developing countries but was particularly damaging to the Southeast Asian economies, and the 1986 plunge in oil prices, that was particularly damaging to Indonesia. Using a commodity price index measured relative to industrial countries' export prices (with 1960=100), prices for agricultural raw materials fell from about 100 in 1984 to 86 the following year and 76 in 1986, one of the steepest declines since the mid-1950s.[63] Prices for tin, for example, peaked in 1980, declined slowly, and then collapsed in 1985–86. Rubber prices were at lows in the mid-1980s as were prices for sugar (falling from about 30 to 5 cents a pound between 1980 and 1985) and rice.[64] Overall, the 1980s saw the sharpest drop in commodity prices since the 1930s.[65]

The slump had a number of causes. These included the rising US budget deficit fueled by increased defense spending, and the policies of the US Federal Reserve Board in raising interest rates to finance the deficit and suppress inflation. These had the effect of suppressing demand in the USA and other advanced economies. The strength of the US dollar accentuated the local currency effects of the commodity price falls for developing countries. In the case of particular commodities, especially rubber and tin, spectacularly unsuccessful attempts at market manipulation by individuals and governments, the failure of orderly marketing arrangements, the development of substitutes, and rapid increases in production by new market entrants contributed to downward supply pressures on prices.

The initial conditions prevailing at the start of this event differed from those prevailing at the outset of the preceding event. In particular, by 1984 most developing countries were perforce less reliant on borrowing from abroad than they had been in 1979. Their heavy debt burdens, however, left them vulnerable to terms-of-trade shocks.[66] Nevertheless, the result of commodity price declines was a significant slowdown in the economic expansion of many developing countries, particularly those, like the ASEAN Four, that were heavily dependent on exports of commodities. The terms of trade of our four countries were adversely affected by declining international prices for rubber, tin, palm oil, and some of their other major exports, while slow growth in world trade (affecting markets for developing-country exports) contributed to generally sluggish prospects for commodity exports.

The final external event we consider is rather more difficult to characterize. A dominant feature of the 1980s was reduction in the transfer of resources from developed to developing countries. Following a crisis of confidence among private lenders in the creditworthiness of several key developing countries, notably Mexico, rather than any increase in the cost of international capital (the London Inter-Bank Offer Rate [LIBOR] actually fell in real terms, from 6.5–7 percent in 1982 to 4 percent in 1987),[67] commercial banks reduced their foreign lending and bilateral and multilateral (World Bank and IMF) public sources became more important. Beginning in the mid to late 1980s, the postwar direction of capital flows reversed itself and developing countries as a whole became net capital exporters, as new inflows from the developed world were eclipsed by the size of payments by developing-country debtors on their foreign loans. Gross inflows to developing countries reached a low of some $80 billion in 1986. Subsequent increases were more than offset by outflows.[68] Between 1984 and 1988, developing countries paid a net $143 billion to creditors in industrialized countries.[69]

For the Southeast Asian developing countries, however, 1987 marked the beginning of a boom in intraregional capital flows. Accompanying the broad trend toward capital outflow for most developing countries was a trend within Asia for capital to flow from Japan and the more developed industrializing economies – South Korea, Taiwan, Singapore, and Hong Kong – to the less developed, including China and the ASEAN Four. Most of this took the form of private direct investment. As firms from Japan and the Asian NIEs found themselves no longer able to export competitively from their home markets as a result of increasing costs, these "mobile exporters" moved their production facilities to Bangladesh, China, Mexico, and Southeast Asia.[70] To attract foreign capital, the ASEAN Four changed their domestic economic policies, particularly those regulating direct foreign investment, during the 1980s. James Morley and Shinichi Ichimura suggest that high growth in East Asian countries in the late 1980s may be attributed to their adoption of policies unleashing market forces through deregulation, privatization, and the elimination of constraints on trade and investment.[71]

The boom in Japanese investment to Southeast Asia in the late 1980s was a major boon to the ASEAN Four. Changing relative factor prices in Japan hastened the process of shifting production by mature-technology industries geographically, to Southeast Asia. The image of flying geese in East Asia suggests the passing of technology and production "down the line" to later industrializers like Malaysia and Thailand. This is, however, only part of the story. The shift in production was often accomplished by "mobile exporters" from the formerly dominant producer country.[72] Those firms often entered into joint-ventures or sourcing agreements involving technical assistance with local firms. Many of the firms that relocated within East Asia did so to maintain already established markets, often in the United States. While these firms often did not enjoy technological leadership or produce goods with widely recognized brandnames, by exploiting lower cost labor, East Asian firms could continue to use existing marketing channels and mastery of appropriate process technologies to produce competitively for existing export markets. The spread of manufacturing across East Asia, the rise of new patterns of resource and industry complementarity, and increasing intra-industry trade in part reflected the emergence of new producers and the rising competitiveness of the ASEAN Four and China. The proliferation of export manufacturing in East Asia also resulted,

Table 2.1. *Cumulative direct foreign investment in ASEAN Four from Japan and USA, 1969–93 (US$ million)*

	Indonesia	Malaysia	Philippines	Thailand
To 1969				
Japan	192	36	45	78
USA	228	–	741	123
To 1976[a]				
Japan	2,044 (39)	255[b] (27)	134 (26)	75 (38)
USA	1,000 (19)	108 (11)	175 (33)	30 (15)
To 1980[a]				
Japan	3,372 (36)	226[b] (20)	299 (20)	77 (34)
USA	575 (6)	80 (7)	752 (49)	28 (12)
To 1983				
Japan	7,268	764	721	521
To June 1993				
Japan	13,366	4,585	1,904	5,476

Notes:
[a] Figures in parentheses are percentage shares of total direct foreign investment to recipient country.
[b] Figures for cumulative investment from Japan in Malaysia are from 1977 and 1979 rather than 1976 and 1980.
Sources: Donald R. Sherk, "Foreign Investment in Southeast Asia," in Mark W. Zacher and R. S. Milne (eds.), *Conflict and Stability in Southeast Asia*, Garden City, N.Y.: Anchor Press, 1974, p. 366; Masahide Shibusawa, *Japan and the Asian Pacific Region*, New York: St. Martin's Press, 1984, p. 150; Bret Thorn, "Co-prosperity or Co-recession?" *Manager*, April 1993, p. 44.

however, from changing relative factor prices that encouraged firms to shift their production offshore in order to prolong their abilities to exploit competitive advantages.

In short, East Asia experienced the rapid operation of a series of product cycles.[73] Firms from Japan moved offshore to the East Asian NIEs and, increasingly, to the ASEAN Four. Some Japanese firms that previously had moved to the East Asian NIEs, subsequently relocated to Southeast Asian countries. At the same time, firms from the East Asian NIEs also shifted to the ASEAN Four. The mobility of capital, together with management and technology, drove the expansion of the East Asian economy.[74]

The ASEAN Four also gained from Japan's emergence as a major source of official development assistance (see tables 2.1 and 2.3). Japan had been increasing aid to those countries since the 1950s. Overall, Japanese official development assistance (ODA) increased from $1.14 billion in 1975, to $3.3 billion in

Table 2.2. *Trade between ASEAN Four and Japan and USA 1963–91 (US$ million)*

	Indonesia	Malaysia	Philippines	Thailand
1963 share of total exports[a]				
Japan	8.5	27.9[b]	27.3	18.1
USA	15.8	18.2[b]	45.5	7.4
1970 imports				
Japan	636	419	433	189
USA	144	219	433	95
1974 imports[c]				
Japan	3,969 (53)	714 (17)	932 (35)	631 (26)
USA	1,580 (21)	595 (14)	1,133 (42)	196 (8)
1981 imports				
Japan [d]	12,005	3,010	1,576	1,041
USA	4,084	1,166	1,747	910
1985 imports				
Japan	10,119	4,330	1,243	1,027
USA	4,569	2,300	2,145	1,428
1988 share of total exports[a]				
Japan	10.5[e]	16.9	20.1	15.9
USA	16.2[e]	17.3	35.7	20
1991 imports				
Japan	12,770 (43)	6,471 (19)	2,352 (27)	5,252 (18)
USA	3,241 (11)	6,102 (18)	3,471 (39)	6,122 (22)

Notes:
[a] Percentage
[b] Figures for Malaysia are for 1966.
[c] Figures in parentheses are percentage shares of exporting country's exports.
[d] Japanese figures are for 1982.
[e] Indonesian figures are for 1987.
Sources: Jon Halliday and Gavan McCormack, *Japanese Imperialism Today, "Co-Prosperity in Greater East Asia,"* New York: Monthly Review Press, 1973, p. 55; Shoko Tanaka, *Post-War Japanese Resource Policies and Strategies: The Case of Southeast Asia*, Ithaca: Cornell University East Asia Papers, no. 43, 1986, p. 77; K. S. Nathan and M. Pathmanathan, (eds.), *Trilateralism in Asia, Problems and Prospects in US–Japan–ASEAN Relations*, Kuala Lumpur: Antara Book Company, 1986, p. 98; Masahide Shibusawa, *Japan and the Asian Pacific Region*, New York: St. Martin's Press, 1984, p. 150; Japan External Trade Organization (JETRO), *JETRO White Paper on International Trade (Summary)*, Tokyo: JETRO, 1992, p. 17.

1980, to $8.9 billion in 1989, when for the first time Japan surpassed the United States as the world's largest foreign assistance donor.[75] The ASEAN Four figured prominently in the rapidly expanding Japanese aid budget during the 1980s, as Japan emerged as the region's dominant source of development capital.[76]

Table 2.3. *Official development assistance to ASEAN Four from Japan and USA, 1964–91 (US$ million)*

	Indonesia	Malaysia	Philippines	Thailand
1964–73				
Japan[a]	1,055	167	184	268
1974				
Japan	221 (41)	36 (59)	37 (28)	17 (28)
USA	82 (15)	4 (6)	46 (35)	18 (29)
1987–91				
Japan	8,212	2,001	4,599	4,073
Japan's share of total bilatateral aid (percent)	57	81	59	57
Japan's share of total ODA (percent)	51	78	51	51

Note: [a] Figures in parentheses are percentage shares of total ODA receipts of recipient country.
Sources: Hasegawa Sukehiro, *Japanese Foreign Aid, Policy and Practice*, New York: Praeger Publishers, 1975, p. 64; Shoko Tanaka, *Post-War Japanese Resource Policies and Strategies: The Case of Southeast Asia*, Ithaca: Cornell University East Asia Papers, no. 43, 1986, p. 77; Japan, Ministry of Foreign Affairs, *Official Development Assistance, 1992*, Tokyo: Ministry of Foreign Affairs, 1992, see country data.

Table 2.4. *Aggregate trade with the ASEAN Four: Japan, and USA, 1990 (US$ million)*

	Manufactured imports from ASEAN Four	Capital goods exports to ASEAN Four	Technology exports to ASEAN Four	Cumulative direct investment in ASEAN Four
Japan	5,832	13,485	306	20,784
USA	13,585	6,290	77	8,422
Japan/USA	0.42	2.14	3.97	2.47

Source: Japan External Trade Organization (JETRO), *JETRO White Paper on International Trade (Summary)*, Tokyo: JETRO, 1992, p. 28.

In 1980, Japanese and US net disbursements to the ASEAN Four came to $700 million and $184 million respectively. By 1990, the comparable figures were $2.3 billion and just over $300 million. Indonesia, the Philippines, Thailand, and Malaysia ranked first, third, fourth, and eighth among recipients of Japanese ODA in 1988. That same year only the Philippines was among the major recipients of US assistance and only Indonesia and the Philippines among the principal targets of aid from the group of Development Assistance

Figure 2.1. *Summary of the four events*

Event	Years	Central characteristics (affecting ASEAN Four)
1	1974–75	First oil price shock. Slump in global production and trade. Current account deficits and rising inflation. Stagflation.
2	1979–83	Second oil price shock. Rising debt, high interest rates and strong dollar. Sharper macroeconomic imbalances.
3	1984–86	Commodity shock. Slumping prices, export earnings and domestic demand.
4	1987–	International finance changes course. Restructuring of regional economy with rising capital and trade flows.

Countries as a whole. In some cases, Japanese aid helped to pave the way for foreign investors in the region.

The experience of Indonesia in terms of bilateral aid and tied aid credits indicates how Japan had supplanted the United States by the mid-1980s. In the period 1984–87, Indonesia received $130 million in tied aid from the USA but $1.15 billion from Japan; and $65 million in other bilateral aid from the USA but $2.8 billion from Japan.[77] Of the cumulative total of all Japanese aid during the 1980s, Southeast Asia received about one-third and, by 1990, Japan was supplying 61 percent of total bilateral ODA to the region, the United States just 9 percent.[78]

We selected these four events because of their relative importance, among all the international developments that have impinged on developing countries and the region since the 1950s, in influencing the key economic parameters affecting developing countries. In addition, most of the events (though not all – oil prices and, to a lesser extent, other commodity prices are exceptions) affected all developing countries and, in particular, each of the four countries discussed here. Moreover, to greater or lesser degrees, these events can be pinpointed clearly in time and they compelled decision-makers in each country to develop strategies to respond to them. In short, they represent pivotal events in the international environment that rendered the domestic status quo no longer tenable. As we will argue below and amplify further in the succeeding chapters on individual countries, it is necessary to be sensitive to both global and regional forces when considering the impact of external factors. While some shifts, for example in relative factor costs, are global in nature, others are more regional, as we have noted in relation to our fourth event.

It is important to note that the values for many independent variables did not change for each of the four events. Indeed, more typically, they changed only once over the four periods, although in some cases this varies with the country we are considering. Therefore, in chapters 3 through 6 we focus our discussion on the domestic responses to changes in those external variables most associated with the event in question.

Conclusion

Bruce Cumings suggests of East Asia that the industrial developments of Japan, Korea, and Taiwan should not be considered as discrete phenomena but as part of a single regional and global process.[79] In similar fashion, we can understand the development of the ASEAN Four as part of regional forces and a changing global and regional division of labor, recognizing, however, that, within the framework of incentives shaped by external and domestic factors, policymakers in the ASEAN Four usually have had a range of development policies to choose from.

The point here is that any explanation for the success of the ASEAN Four must take into account the conjunction of interests of the two economic superpowers in Southeast Asia. Most important in terms of opportunity for Southeast Asia has been the United States' postwar commitment to providing a relatively open market for developing-country products. However a necessary complement to the availability of a large open market for Southeast Asian products has been Japan's substantial investment and development assistance commitment to building Southeast Asia's productive capacity. Despite rising levels of intraregional trade (in East Asia it increased as a share of total world trade from 6.5 percent in 1985 to 9.7 percent in 1991, and rapid economic growth in China and expansion in India suggest that the ASEAN Four and other developing economies may be able to benefit in the future from rapid demand expansion elsewhere in the region)[80] and the declining share of exports destined for United States markets, the economies of East and Southeast Asia remain heavily dependent on consumption and savings in other regions.[81]

CHAPTER THREE

Indonesia

Indonesia is the world's fourth most populous nation, with approximately 190 million inhabitants. Its geographic size – 14,000 islands spread across 3,000 miles with a land area of three-quarters of a million square miles[1] – and extensive natural resources have ensured the continuing attention of foreign powers. More importantly for our purposes, Indonesia's natural bounty affords policymakers a broader palette of potential development strategies (closedness, as well as openness) than in resource-poor and energy-dependent Japan or East Asia.

The Indonesian state is authoritarian in character and its officials suspicious both of private business and of foreigners. In the late 1950s, the first president, Sukarno, ordered the confiscation of assets belonging to citizens of the former colonial power, the Netherlands. The armed forces seized control of former Dutch operations after independence. Leaders of the anticolonial struggle did not want to hand former Dutch firms to those seen as Dutch lackeys, namely the immigrant Chinese. More broadly, the quasi-socialist rhetoric of the Indonesian independence movement supported state management of the nationalized foreign (Dutch) firms.[2] Besides, some of the firms were involved in activities of significance for national security, such as oil production and transportation, suggesting that they should appropriately come under the direction of the armed forces.

This example suggests the broad orientation of state actors to the issues of state/private roles in the economy and the degree to which official economic policy should emphasize openness/closedness. The historical experiences of colonialism and of the armed anticolonial struggle following World War II established a predilection for state domination of private-sector economic and political activities. The state's often very active role in seeking to sponsor industrial development has not, however, yielded much fruit.[3] At the same time, state officials have favored public enterprises over partnerships with foreign investors, and the protection of infant industries, especially where these are seen as well-springs of indigenous technological capabilities, over openness to the international economy.

However, in the early 1980s the private sector began to come to the fore in economic terms and to exert a degree of overt influence over policy.[4] With a major reorientation of economic policy initiated in the early 1980s, state officials drew back from a number of strongly interventionist practices. At the same time the private sector overtook the state as the dominant economic actor, and foreign investors and foreign markets played crucial roles in speeding the industrialization of the Indonesian economy.[5] Those officials who favored neo-liberal economic reforms and measures to increase economic openness came into the ascendant, albeit in a bureaucratic milieu in which suspicion of the private sector and of reliance on foreign markets remained as a potent rallying point for those who favored policies emphasizing self-sufficiency and official husbandry of indigenous technological capabilities.

The following section deals with how Indonesian society is organized, the bases of the Indonesian state's power, and the ways in which business firms and state authorities interact. In each case, we emphasize the relevance of each of these characteristics for economic openness.

Political regime

Social organization

The colonial rulers of the Dutch East Indies marginalized traditional Indonesian social institutions and authority and emasculated indigenous commerce. They confiscated most of the best land for plantations, leaving traditional rulers insufficient landholdings to provide the basis for powerful landlord interests after independence.[6]

Agriculture, especially plantation estates, dominated the economy.[7] The Dutch, as did the British in Malaya, imposed a rigid ethnic division of labor that confined the indigenous inhabitants to tilling the fields and providing virtual slave labor for colonial tea, coffee, rubber and palm oil plantations. The small immigrant Chinese population formed a stratum of merchant intermediaries between the indigenous inhabitants and the Dutch, enjoying a profitable yet subservient relationship with the latter. The Dutch themselves controlled not only the plantations but also the trade linking the colony to the industrial economy of Western Europe.

The Dutch were harsh and brutally suppressed periodic social rebellions against their rule. Even under the "Ethical Policy" during the first decades of the twentieth century, when the Dutch undertook to educate a thin stratum of Indonesians to serve as clerks in the colonial administration, the authorities regarded all indigenous religious and ideological movements as likely sources of political instability and suppressed them.[8] This established a pattern of elite dominance and manipulation of social identity and social movements, especially Islamic movements, that has endured throughout the postcolonial period.[9] The vast majority of Indonesians are, at least nominally, Muslims, and Islam has in the past been used as a powerful ideological rallying point for opponents to established authority. Politics has sometimes been more ideological than in neighboring countries because of this historical legacy.

Political containment of social expressions of unrest has been an enduring theme of the three-decade-long rule of Soeharto, Indonesia's second president. Following the failure of parliamentary democracy in the late 1950s, the first president, Sukarno, initiated a movement towards more authoritarian kinds of political structures that Soeharto accelerated, following the widespread political mobilization and enormous social upheaval in 1965–66 surrounding Sukarno's removal from power.[10] Soeharto sidelined political parties, prescribed a narrow realm of acceptable political participation, and channeled this into a network of state-sponsored organizations. This pattern of containment was extended across the political spectrum during the 1970s, with the state either establishing new organizations or designating existing ones as the official representative bodies for particular functional categories. Only in the early 1990s did this authoritarian, corporatist, exclusionary style of politics – reminiscent of Peru or Argentina in the 1970s – begin to change.[11]

Politics and the bases of state power

Colonial officials established the legitimacy of their authority by force of arms and neither invited nor tolerated political participation on the part of their subjects. They granted traditional rulers the trappings but not the substance of authority. The immigrant Chinese who dominated the tiny non-European commercial sector relied on personal ties with the Dutch authorities to anchor their precarious position between ruler and conquered.

The armed struggle for independence (1945–49) mobilized Indonesians politically and influenced the character of the postcolonial state. Sukarno and other leaders of the "revolution" embraced a nationalist ideology and mobilized the population to support the vastly outgunned republican army and irregular bands that waged guerilla war against the Dutch. A small group of nationalist officers and politicians orchestrated the struggle, and developed an ideology – under Soeharto, the *Pancasila*, or "five principles" – to establish the legitimacy of their political leadership. The army's political role – it both fought the war and mobilized people to support it – established the principle of *dwi fungsi*, whereby the military both defended society and was part of society and thus had a legitimate role in developing society.

After the Dutch passed sovereignty to the Republic in 1949, the most important groups in the state were the nationalist politicians, such as Sjahrir, Hatta and Sukarno, the military, and the civil servants (bureaucracy). With Dutch withdrawal, the military seized control of much valuable agricultural land.

Turning now to the character of the postcolonial state, its most obvious feature is that it narrowly concentrates political power, coercing potential competing centers of political power (e.g., Islam) and insulating itself from challenges from organized groups from outside the state apparatus. These characteristics date to the late 1950s and early 1960s, when President Sukarno tried to concentrate state power and undermine groups in society beyond his control. Nevertheless, paradoxically, the state has a rather limited ability to act autonomously in formulating policy. The Indonesian state is weakly authoritarian because it is vulnerable to myriad pressures from elite business linkages and patronage networks that permeate the corridors of power, enabling individuals using clientelist connections to influence policy.[12] Officials within various government agencies often find it difficult or impossible to withhold preferential treatment from individuals who are known to have close ties with important government figures.[13] This was particularly apparent in the mid-1990s, as officials sought favor with Soeharto by giving privileges to his close relatives.[14] Official policies, even when initiated by the technocrats, often reflect the interests of non-state actors.[15]

The Indonesian state, sometimes termed a "bureaucratic polity,"[16] restricts power and political participation to a small elite of military officers, politicians and bureaucrats, and rests on a narrow social base. There are important competing centers of power within the state. Some have described the politics of Indonesia as the politics of bureaucratic pluralism. For the purposes of our exploration of policies of economic openness, the two most important groups within the Indonesian state are the technocrats – economists associated with the University of Indonesia, many of whom were trained in the United States and are dubbed the "Berkeley mafia" after the economics department from which some of their leading figures earned their doctorates in the 1960s – and the technicians or engineers. The technocrats generally control the important macroeconomic policymaking agencies of the government and favor a more open, internationally competitive Indonesian economy. The engineers typically control the line departments and tend to embrace economic nationalist ideas about infant-industry protection and import substitution.[17] Notwithstanding these internal divisions, state officials using open coercion and more subtle patronage are able to wield enormous power over civil society.

Linkages between business and the state

Apart from petty merchants and a declining group of indigenous island traders, Indonesia lacked a modern business class at the time of independence.[18] The local business community was overwhelmingly Chinese and thus the object of disdain and resentment by the indigenous population, comprising mainly peasants and civil servants. Not only were the Chinese not Muslim, but indigenous Indonesians (*pribumi*) perceived them to have been the commercial middlemen of the Dutch. Thus, while they dominated local commerce, they were political outcasts. Resentment of the Chinese has been fundamental to the relationship between the state and business in Indonesia, and to the long tradition of pervasive state intervention in the economy. State leaders have long believed that state intervention in the operations of the marketplace is essential if a satisfactory share of economic benefits is to be enjoyed by the indigenous majority.

This resentment also explains the political weakness of the immigrant Chinese community, which was powerless to protect itself in 1965–66, when hundreds of thousands of Chinese were massacred, often as Indonesian army soldiers stood by, in the bloodbath that followed an attempted coup by military officers suspected of being in alliance with the Indonesian Communist Party. Since then, leading Chinese Indonesian business figures have kept a low political profile and avoided serious involvement in politics in order to minimize the risk of provoking indigenous retaliation against Chinese economic dominance.[19]

Business–state relations involve clientelism. Personal relationships between individual business people and senior political figures have been the dominant pattern of business interest representation. Business organization until the late 1980s was sporadic and fragmented because leading Chinese businessmen had little incentive to support efforts of formal business organizations to shape the prevailing policy environment. They used instead personal bonds with power-brokers to obtain satisfaction from the state.[20] This pattern was established early, in the guise of close business relations between military leaders and Chinese traders employed by republican leaders to sustain the anticolonial struggle. Subsequently, the Chinese sought the protection and patronage of highly placed indigenous politicians and officials, and offered, in return, cash and shares, seats on their boards of directors, or lucrative business opportunities. Chinese businessmen find that their commercial success is closely correlated with how high up in government their patrons rank. Those connected at the highest levels receive subsidies and rent-seeking opportunities that enable them rapidly to accumulate capital for business expansion.[21]

Postwar developments

In the early postwar years, the United States established the global economic system and institutions that would support an open international economy and at the same time contain communism. Many Asian developing economies prospered under these arrangements. After the formal transfer of sovereignty by the Dutch in 1949, Indonesia too was able to share in some of this prosperity by exporting raw materials to developed-country markets. The Korean War boom boosted the prices of some commodities which Indonesia produced (for example, rubber, tin, coffee, and oil) but the lack of a well-developed tax system denied the government the sorts of windfall revenue which accrued to the colonial governments of Malaya and Singapore during this period.[22]

By the early 1960s, politics overshadowed economics. As President Sukarno's ability to manipulate the delicate domestic balancing act between the nationalists, the communists and the army became increasingly tenuous, the economy spun out of control. Rejecting orthodox Western economic principles, Sukarno in 1961 sought to court the personal loyalty of tens of millions of Indonesian peasant farmers by spending heavily on grandiose projects and grossly inflating the economy.[23] Spending in 1961 increased the budget deficit from 2 to 5 percent of GDP. Inflation jumped from 20 percent in 1960 to 95 percent in 1961 and steadily increased thereafter until it averaged 306 percent in 1966 and briefly topped 1000 percent in the second quarter of 1966, at which point store prices changed hourly.

There was much economic dislocation. The crumbling bureaucracy could no longer collect taxes or control pervasive smuggling that evaded import tariffs. Hyperinflation reduced exports and thus the supply of foreign exchange necessary to purchase imports, so trade revenues, on which the Indonesian budget was overwhelmingly dependent, fell. Government revenues plummeted, from 13 percent of GDP in 1960 and 1961 to only 4 percent in 1964–66.

As export earnings fell and foreign loans dried up, so did the ability to import, and import volumes fell to their lowest levels since independence, starving industry of critical inputs. By the mid-1960s, manufacturing was operating at an average of 20 percent of capacity, per capita income was 9 percent less than its 1958 level, and output had shrunk in absolute terms.[24]

This economic nightmare remains seared into the collective memory of Sukarno's successor, Soeharto, and his advisors, as the formative economic event in the country's independent history. It set the scene for the October 1965 military counter-coup and the transfer of power to Soeharto in March 1966.

Soeharto announced in October 1966 a comprehensive five-year (1966–71) stabilization and rehabilitation plan. Its goal was to revive the domestic economy and liberalize international trade.[25] First, policymakers negotiated the rescheduling of principal and interest payments on Indonesia's foreign debt and obtained further concessionary loans to replace the foreign loans that had dried up during the final convulsions of the Sukarno regime.[26] On the advice of an IMF mission, officials ended most price controls, raised interest rates to try to stem the growth of the money supply, and redirected government spending towards desparately needed infrastructure programs.[27]

The opening of trade was an important part of the reforms. This included measures such as adoption of an export bonus scheme (export subsidies), abolition of the import licensing system, simplification of the system of import tariffs, and elimination by 1970 of a tangled web of multiple exchange rates and of exchange controls facing exporters.[28] In 1970, officials adjusted the over-valued exchange rate to bring it closer to the real rate of exchange and fixed the value of the rupiah to that of the dollar.[29] They also raised tariffs in the short run to generate revenue, but this should be seen in the context of a long-term phased reduction in tariff rates.[30]

In parallel with these trade policy reforms, officials eased controls on international capital flows in 1971. They eliminated restrictions on the conversion of foreign exchange, adopting an open capital regime, a move that was unusually farsighted for a developing country at that time. The entire package amounted to what today would be termed a structural adjustment program, including changes in the direction of government spending, policies to restore exports and tax revenues, adjustment of the exchange rate, and simplification of the exchange rate system.[31]

These stabilizing and liberalizing measures had important effects. By improving the country's creditworthiness in the eyes of foreign creditors, they enabled officials to secure international loans to plug budget deficits. They also made vital imports once again available so that production could increase, and with it GDP and government tax receipts.[32]

It is comparatively rare for liberalization programs to yield significant results. The Indonesian liberalization of 1966–71 is one that did.[33] Recovery began in 1968 with exceptional speed. Real GDP grew at 11 percent that year and averaged over 8 percent for the three years 1968–70. Inflation fell to 10 percent in 1969 and 6.5 percent in 1970. Exports recovered, leading to an improved current account balance, which averaged a positive 3 percent of GDP for 1968–70. Government revenues rose to average 9 percent of GDP for 1968–70 (from 4 percent in 1966).[34]

The rapidity of the economic recovery gave credence to those who espoused neoclassical economic ideas, making it more likely that they would be called upon again by the president in times of economic difficulty. It also established well-trained economists within the bureaucracy as important policy players and principal sources of influential advice for the president. The success of their policy recommendations and their solidarity in the face of criticism from elsewhere in the bureaucracy and the army helped insulate them from outside pressures and established a tradition of relative political insulation for agencies such as the Ministry of Finance and the Economic Planning Board.[35]

Challenge and response

Earlier in this book, we introduced a number of possible explanations for how and why domestic policy in the ASEAN Four responds to external events – whether policy becomes more open to cross-border flows of goods, services, and capital, or more closed. We here assess the influence of domestic factors on policy responses in Indonesia. For each external event, we (i) survey how it was felt (its "impact") in Indonesia; (ii) present the major economic changes ("policy record") that occurred around the time of the event; and (iii) explain the source of these policies ("explaining policy choices"). We conclude the chapter with an assessment of our initial hypotheses, in light of our findings for Indonesia.

First oil shock, global recession, easy credit, 1974–75

Impact As Indonesia was an oil exporter, the oil price rise caused dramatic improvement in the terms of trade, a measure of the relative purchasing power of a country's exports over time. With reference to an index with 1987=100, the terms of trade rose from 51 in 1973 to 106 in 1974, and averaged 102 during the years 1974–76. This yielded enormous windfall gains from trade. Merchandise exports increased in value by more than 125 percent in 1974. The current account of the balance of payments went from over half a billion dollars in deficit in 1973 to more than that amount in surplus the following year.[36]

With such stimulation from oil exports, the economy grew rapidly. GDP expanded nearly 60 percent in nominal terms in 1974 (7.7 percent in real terms). Real GDP growth averaged 6.5 percent over the three years 1974–76.[37] Only Nigeria, according to a World Bank study, did better, in terms of the positive terms-of-trade effect on GDP of the oil price rise. The figure for Indonesia exceeded those for other non-OPEC oil exporters, such as Colombia and Morocco, by an entire order of magnitude.[38]

The windfall accrued in the first instance as revenue to the government, which retained ownership over the country's oil reserves. Current revenue increased by 80 percent between 1973 and 1974, and the proportion of government revenues from trade grew very rapidly in comparison to those from domestic sources.[39]

Policy record This windfall revenue reduced the need to borrow, or, put another way, to draw on foreign savings, to support domestic investment. Indonesia's net borrowing abroad over the period 1974–79 was negligible.[40] As a result, total external debt as a proportion of GNP fell from 47 percent in 1973 to 38 percent in 1975.[41] In particular, state officials harnessed oil revenues to clear enormous outstanding foreign liabilities incurred in the course of uncontrolled foreign borrowing by the state oil corporation, Pertamina, during the early 1970s.[42]

In contrast to Nigeria, Indonesian policymakers resisted the temptation to inflate urban consumption in response to the oil revenue windfall. Indonesian policymakers applied much of the revenue gain from the oil price rise to public investment in infrastructure. With a year's lag, gross domestic investment jumped from about 20 percent of GDP, to nearly 25 percent of GDP in 1975 and sustained this new, higher level for the remainder of the decade.[43]

Indonesia may be distinguished from other oil-producing countries at the time by the degree to which policymakers were able to steer oil dollars away from consumption and into investment in agriculture and rural development. This moderated the negative effects on agricultural exports of the rising *de facto* value of the rupiah (precipitated by the massive inflow of foreign exchange from oil) and of inflation (the annual consumer price index increase averaged 26 percent in the period 1974–76).[44] Large state investments in resource-based industries accompanied such rural investments. As a result, non-oil exports, which mostly consisted of agricultural commodities and the products of resource-based industries, accounted for 25 percent of all exports in 1975 but for 43 percent by 1979.[45]

The policy course chosen by Indonesian decisionmakers had the immediate impact of making the economy less open to cross-border flows of goods and services than before. The rapid increase in domestic investment drove up the prices of nontradables (e.g., land, buildings) in relation to those of tradables, and those of imports (e.g., steel, cement) in relation to those of exports, making it more attractive for the individual entrepreneur to speculate in real estate than to invest in improving manufacturing or export agriculture. This, along with sustained current-account surpluses and inflation, drove up the market value of the rupiah (although the nominal exchange rate remained fixed at Rp 415 to the US dollar until late 1978),[46] eroding the international competitiveness of the country's exports.[47]

The policy response to the oil bonanza also encompassed informal administrative practices. While nowhere enshrined as official policy, "administrative friction" – polite words for red tape and corruption – in those parts of the Indonesian government dealing with trade, particularly the customs and trade agencies, and those parts dealing with investment, particularly the Ministry of Industry, resulted in the *ad hoc* aggregation of bureaucratic controls and procedures and their arbitrary enforcement. These institutional barriers to the entry of imports and the export of Indonesian goods, as well as to investment approvals, grew so pervasive as to become serious obstacles to those seeking to trade in goods and services or to invest in Indonesia. There was, in essence, a high effective rate of protection for import substitutes. Consequently, it became more attractive for Indonesians to produce such goods, and less attractive to produce those labor-intensive agricultural commodities in which Indonesia enjoyed an advantage in comparison with producers elsewhere. As a consequence, by 1976, Indonesia imported from neighboring countries some traditional Indonesian export crops, including copra and maize.[48]

In summary, we have established: (i) that the main features of the Indonesian (formal and informal) policy record beginning in 1974 were indeed responses to the world oil price increase; and (ii) that this response left economic policy less open to flows of goods and services and capital than had been the case before 1974. In the next subsection, we turn to the question of why the domestic policy response was towards less openness in this case.

Explaining policy choices Not surprisingly, the oil windfall of 1974–75 increased the policy options for decisionmakers in Indonesia. With the windfall, officials might have stimulated consumer spending or increased government subsidies for urban transportation and staple foods. Alternatively, they could have chosen to increase the salaries and perks of civil servants, or to expand the bureaucracy to provide jobs for political allies. Or they might have held the windfall offshore, investing in foreign assets (e.g., Manhattan real estate).

Instead, official policy focused on reducing Indonesia's outstanding foreign debt and increasing public investment in infrastructure, with particular emphasis on agricultural areas. At the same time, bureaucratic practices increased non-tariff barriers to trade and investment. The causes of the first two differed from the causes of the last of these.

The decision to use government oil revenues to reduce outstanding external debt and to increase public investment in rural infrastructure to some extent reflects the experience of Indonesia in the 1960s. Soeharto's decision to heed the advice of US trained technocrats, beginning in 1966, and their success in orchestrating a sustained recovery from the economic shambles of the late "guided democracy" period under President Sukarno (1963–65), exerted a continuing influence on policy in the mid-1970s. The policy choice to reduce foreign debt and step up investment in infrastructure reflected Soeharto's continued willingness to listen to the advice of the technocrats. But Soeharto did not simply listen to the technocrats out of habit, or gratitude. The technocrats' policy recommendations were in harmony with his background and preferences, namely his personal commitment to the small farmer, rooted in his village upbringing.[49]

Politically, the technocrats were arrayed against others among Soeharto's cabinet ministers and advisors, many of whom were closer to Soeharto personally. Once Soeharto's "new order" government had survived the "trial by fire" of the early years of economic management, these economic nationalists began to gain ascendancy in economic policymaking in the early 1970s.

No economic nationalist was more influential – nor ultimately more destructive – than an exuberant and entreprenuerial general named Ibnu Sutowo, head of the state-owned oil company, Pertamina. Sutowo in the early 1970s appropriated government oil revenues to create what amounted to a vast personal business empire, encompassing manufacturing, shipping, hotels, tourism, and agriculture, not to mention oil exploration and development. Sutowo's personal ties with the president spared him from the oversight of technocratic strongholds at the Department of Finance and the Bank of Indonesia, so Pertamina was able to borrow independently on international markets, using its oil revenues as collateral.

The extent of exposure of the Treasury, as ultimate guarantor of Pertamina's debt, sufficiently alarmed the technocrats as early as 1972 that they won presidential approval for controls to rein in Pertamina's medium- and long-term borrowing.[50] Sutowo responded by resorting to more volatile short-term lending, taking advantage of the easy credit then available on international capital markets as OPEC nations sought to recycle their petrodollars.

When oil demand slackened in 1975, Pertamina found itself with insufficient collateral to sustain this borrowing, thus precipitating a series of spectacular defaults on repayments that triggered repayment calls by international lenders at such a rate that the Indonesian government itself neared default on the national debt. Technocrats once again rode to the rescue, easing Sutowo out as head of Pertamina and forming a cabinet committee that negotiated terms with foreign creditors and aid givers.[51]

The Pertamina crisis is relevant to the policy response to the first oil shock because it was associated with a political struggle between economic nationalists and technocrats which dominated the policymaking of the New Order regime. Nationalists such as Sutowo, favored capital-intensive, import-substituting investments. Technocrats preferred the conservative use of macroeconomic policy tools. They tried to rein in state banks and parastatals (many inherited by the military from the Dutch at independence) and to establish central control of borrowing and budget-based spending.[52] The president clearly felt that the deepening financial crisis, in which Pertamina threatened to ruin the government and reverse many of the gains since 1966, risked a repeat of the 1965 debacle. As he had in 1966, he turned to the technocrats to rescue Indonesia from the debt crisis in 1975.

Despite the ascendancy of technocrats in macroeconomic policymaking, red tape and corruption grew in the Indonesian bureaucracy in the early 1970s. This reflected the opportunities that the oil wealth provided for civil servants and the very limited toehold the technocrats had in the bureaucracy itself. The technocrats essentially represented a very small minority of academic economists who, by their cohesiveness, attractiveness to the foreign aid community, and sheer good fortune, managed to wield influence over macroeconomic policy disproportionate to their numbers. Their ability to influence the day-to-day administration of regulations, tariffs, licenses, and so forth was extremely limited. Deep-seated economic nationalist ideas, such as suspicion of foreign investors and a commitment to maintaining a wide range of public enterprises, persisted throughout the bureaucracy. Hence, the technocrats were able to deliver relative macroeconomic stability, but not enhanced openness. Indeed, macroeconomic policy changes moved in the direction of a less open economy, reducing flows of goods and services and of capital into and out of Indonesia.

In summary, three of the broad potential explanatory variables introduced in chapter 1 are relevant to the explanation of the Indonesian economic policy response to the first oil price rise. This event represented a windfall for state revenues and increased the dependence on trade (oil export) taxes for state revenue. Our hypothesis H1a suggests that reduced capacity to generate state revenues from domestic sources leads to policies that favor a less open economy. Our findings for the first external event bear this out. They also support our idea that windfall revenue gains lead to more closed policies (hypothesis H1c).

Contrary to the prediction of our second hypothesis, increasing dominance of technocrats and macroeconomic policymakers (hypothesis H2) did not yield policies that were more open in this case. As noted above, the result was greater macroeconomic stability rather than a move in the direction of economic openness.

The third explanatory variable relevant here concerns the nature of the political coalition used by the ruler to sustain his rule. Our hypothesis H3a suggests that when the balance within the new-order regime swung away from the economic nationalists toward the technocrats in 1975 we would have expected to see policy favoring greater openness. Again, this was not borne out.

The policy response to the 1974–75 oil price rise created pressures in the Indonesian economy that ultimately forced further policy change in the late 1970s. The growth recorded in Indonesia following the external event amounted to a Keynesian-type stimulation. It precipitated slow erosion of the international competitiveness of Indonesian non-oil exports, especially those of Indonesian agriculture, and resulted from inflation and overvaluation of the rupiah (because of the accumulation of foreign exchange with a fixed nominal rate), which further increased dependence upon oil and discouraged non-oil exports (what is known as the "Dutch disease").[53] In November 1978, policymakers, in what we might view as a response to a response, devalued the rupiah by 51 percent, from 415 rupiah to the dollar to 625. This decision was to prove most significant for Indonesia's ability to respond successfully to the second shock.

Second oil shock and debt crisis, 1979–83

Impact The November 1978 devaluation stimulated the Indonesian economy immediately. In 1979, the volume of exports leapt 25 percent. Indonesia also gained from the terms-of-trade effect of the second oil shock, with export revenues and the current account surplus rising rapidly through 1981.[54] In contrast to other oil exporters, such as Nigeria, Indonesia maintained the volume of its rural and agricultural investment.[55] Nevertheless, at the time of the second oil price rise, Indonesia remained dependent on oil for 57 percent of its export revenues and 25 percent of its GNP.

However, by 1982, a sharp decline in oil prices, deterioration in the non-oil terms of trade (as real appreciation of the rupiah eroded the competitiveness of non-oil exports), and a bout of bad weather contributed to a decline in the volume of Indonesian exports (they fell by 9 percent between 1979 and 1982).

The current account surplus of 1980 turned into a deficit of 8 percent of GDP by 1982.[56]

Policy record In evaluating responses to the second oil shock and the debt crisis, it is worth recalling that the World Bank projected that the price of oil would go on rising at a real annual rate of about 3 percent.[57] Oil exporters expected their good fortune to continue. Oil importers did not anticipate that their predicament of 1979–81 would soon be relieved by falling prices. The relatively sound condition of the Indonesian economy before the shock (with healthy reserves and debt servicing ability) and the firm fiscal control exerted by the technocrats suggested that Indonesia would do very well from a repeat of the first oil price rise.[58]

Accordingly, there was essentially no policy response in Indonesia during the first two years after the second shock. State officials held to the policy in place since 1974 of using windfall oil revenues for public investment. However, with a sharp decline in oil prices in 1982 and deterioration in the non-oil terms of trade and current account deficits, policymakers responded in March 1983. State officials undertook simultaneously a tightening of trade policies (by adopting import quotas and some export restrictions), a repeat of the successful 1978 devaluation (the rupiah was devalued by 38 percent to roll back the real exchange rate to its level after the 1978 devaluation), and cuts in government spending.[59] They adopted this mix of policies in order to reduce import payments and increase the value added for exports, while devaluing to keep the relative prices of tradables and nontradables approximately unchanged, thereby avoiding an anti-export bias.

In this way Indonesia avoided both debt rescheduling and capital flight. While other oil exporters stumbled – Mexico defaulted and Nigeria experienced a 60 percent fall in the dollar value of its exports between 1980 and 1983 – Indonesia negotiated the second oil shock and debt crisis with minimal damage. The dollar value of its exports fell by 14 percent between 1980 and 1983 and the tightening of trade policy in 1983 caused revenues from taxes on trade to decline at an average rate of 7 percent per year in 1984 and 1985.[60] But the devaluation yielded the desired effect – between 1983 and 1985 export volume rose 43 percent.[61] Officials succeeded in restructuring Indonesia's debt around long-term loans, so rising international interest rates had only modest effects on Indonesia's debt service (the ratio of debt service to exports rose from 14 percent in 1981 to a still manageable 20 percent in 1983). Thus the government remained creditworthy and avoided being caught in the international credit crunch. With the exception of 1982, GDP continued to grow through this period and beyond.[62]

Explaining policy choices The notion of "policy response" to the second external event is problematic in the Indonesian case. Policy did not change in response to the second oil price rise. It did however change when oil prices fell in 1982.

The second oil price rise represented less of a windfall than was the case in 1974–75, and the devaluation of November 1978 made policy change less necessary in 1979. The devaluation had already addressed some of the economic problems that were products of the first oil price rise. Policy thereafter held to its earlier course, thus belying any claim that external events always necessitate a domestic policy response.

Nevertheless, our second event encompassed not just the second oil price rise but also the international debt crisis that followed and the drop in oil prices, beginning in 1982. The real price of oil fell 8 percent in 1982 and, with a further 10 percent drop in 1983, fell below the real price that had prevailed before the original 1979 oil price hike.[63]

Thus the policy change reported here, towards a more restrictive trade regime and fiscal conservatism (the effects were modified to some extent by a further devaluation of the rupiah), were responses to an oil price fall toward the end of the event, rather than to the oil price hike. Of our explanatory variables, those best able to explain the policy change are those dealing with state revenues, current account balances and windfalls, and with the shifting policy influence of technocrats. The falling price of oil in 1982 and 1983 placed constraints on state revenues and reduced the relative abundance of foreign exchange. Our hypothesis H1b suggests that this should have triggered efforts by policymakers to increase the supply of foreign exchange. Our hypothesis suggests these efforts are likely to focus on policies favoring a more open economy, especially those encouraging exports. Where restrictive trade regimes in the past have been unsuccessful, it is particularly likely that officials will look for ways to boost exports. However, our findings suggest that, with the exception of the devaluation (which was viewed as a subsidiary, corrective measure, intended to curb some of the worst side-effects of the main policy changes), policy toward trade became more closed.[64] This was the case even though policymakers well understood the effect that the increasingly restrictive trade regime of the early- to mid-1970s had had on the current account balance.

Another part of our first explanatory variable concerns relative sources of government income. Hypothesis H1a suggests that, where the proportion of government revenues that comes from trade declines, we are more likely to see policy responses to external events that change in the direction of greater openness. In the case of the oil price increase in 1979, we find no change in policy. On the other hand, the oil price decline in 1982–83 precipitated a change in policy in the opposite direction to that which we would expect from our hypothesis – policy became less open.

A further aspect of our first explanatory variable is the role of windfalls. From hypothesis H1c we expect policy to become less open in the presence of windfalls from foreign exchange gains. However, the windfall that the Indonesian government reaped from the oil price rise in 1979 did not lead to any percept-ible change in policy. The hypothesis is not supported in this case.

Finally, our second explanatory variable, the relative influence of technocrats over economic policy, is relevant because technocrats led the response to the 1982–83 oil price fall. It was they who embraced fiscal conservatism and it was they who adopted the more restrictive trade regime (albeit in partnership with a devaluation). The findings in this case do not bear out the prediction that as technocrats' influence on policy increases, we are likely to witness policy responses to external events that favor greater economic openness.

In summary, the Indonesian policy response to the second event was to the oil price fall of 1982–83. Subsequent policy changes provide little support for the hypotheses presented at the outset concerning the role of changes in govern-ment revenues and current account balances, on the one hand, and the relative policy influence of technocratic decision-makers, on the other.

Commodity shock, 1984–86

Impact Our third external event encompasses the fall in commodity prices for a number of key commodities in 1985, ones that were particularly important to the ASEAN Four, and the 1986 plunge in oil prices, which was particularly damaging to Indonesia. The biggest impact on Indonesia of this event was the sudden collapse of the price of oil in dollar terms in the first half of 1986, to half the average of 1979.[65] Oil revenues dropped from 75 percent of 1985 mer-chandise exports to 49 percent in 1986 and averaged 49 percent during 1986–89. The dollar value of exports declined by 23 percent in 1986 and the terms of trade, which were marginally lower in 1985 than they had been in 1982, fell by more than 25 percent (they were to remain virtually unchanged through 1989). The current account deficit more than doubled to 5 percent of GNP. This represented a severe adverse shock and the result was a major crisis for Indonesian policymakers.

Policy record Decision-makers might have responded to the commodity shock by adopting a more restrictive trade policy. There was the risk, however, that, in curtailing Indonesians' ability to import, such a policy might have harmed, rather than helped, manufacturing. There was recent historical prece-dent for such an outcome. Import quotas adopted in 1982 had failed to foster a competitive manufacturing sector. Such a course might have precipitated a recession, while in any case being insufficient to bring the current account into balance.

Indonesian officials chose instead a radical structural adjustment and liber-alization of the entire trade regime, beginning in September 1986 and intended to increase the competitiveness of Indonesia's manufactured exports.[66] They enjoyed the strong support of the IMF and the World Bank (the World Bank was among Indonesia's lenders throughout the 1980s).[67] The new trade policy reforms involved a reduction in tariff levels and in the number of products subject to import quotas. They granted exemptions from tariffs for imports needed as inputs for exporting industries. They eliminated most export license requirements.[68] Also, in September 1986, officials devalued the rupiah by 45 percent.[69]

With these policies, Indonesia by the early 1980s had managed to escape the recession that ensnared other oil exporters following the oil slump. Trade liberalization coupled with devaluation doubled non-oil exports between 1985 and 1989, more than compensating for the decline in export revenues resulting from the oil price decline (the total dollar value of exports rose past the 1985 level even though there was no recovery in oil receipts). The volume of manufactured exports rose 80 percent from 1986 to 1988 while their value more than quadrupled between 1985 and 1989.[70] The trade liberalizing reforms reduced the proportion of domestic production protected by import quotas, from 41 percent in 1986 to 29 percent in 1988, and reduced the average import tariff from 29 percent to 19 percent (while consolidating simultaneously the range of tariff rates in effect). The value of imports declined – imports in 1987 were 74 percent of those of 1981 – but exporters were not deprived of vital inputs. Government revenues from trade increased with liberalization at an annual rate of 2 percent in the period 1986–89.[71]

Explaining policy choices To what may we attribute this outward-oriented (and highly successful) economic response to the external shocks of price collapses in both agricultural commodities and oil? Comparison with the experience of the other oil exporters after 1986 suggests that economic conditions prevailing at the outset were important predictors of a response favoring openness.[72] However, it is also true that the decision-makers perceived they had policy choices and that the politics by which policy was made had an important bearing on Indonesia's ability to escape relatively unscathed these disturbances in the international environment.

There is no doubt that the deregulation policies of the mid-1980s reflected the outcomes of political battles within the government itself, battles which were fought in response to a widespread perception of economic crisis precipitated by international price changes as early as the 1983 drop in oil prices.[73] The first of the reforms, the 1983 deregulation of the financial sector, actually predated our event. In the absence of state consensus on reform of the "real" sector, which would have required the concurrence of state agencies and ministers opposed to deregulation, the financial sector, which was both long overdue for reform and well within the domain of the technocrats to control, was the first target for reform. When this first step did not lead to financial disaster, and external conditions became less favorable, the argument was advanced – perhaps exactly as the technocrats had intended – that liberalization of the

financial sector would be futile, and might even risk disaster (because it facilitated capital flight), were it not to be followed by the significant deregulation of
the real sector in order to counter the lack of competitiveness of Indonesia's
manufactured exports in international markets.[74]

The policy debate within the state focused on the deleterious effects of
import licensing. Until October 1986, the month when serious efforts to dis-
mantle the system began, nearly 1,500 important items came under some form
of non-tariff barrier, and such barriers affected some 35 percent of imports (by
value).[75] The system was notorious for the rent-seeking activities it encouraged
and the distributional coalitions within the state that came to dominate the
allocation of import licenses.

Two groups within the state opposed the technocrats, who spearheaded this
drive to reduce barriers to trade. The "engineers," or economic nationalists –
such as Ginandjar Kartasasmita (Junior Minister for Domestic Product
Promotion), B. J. Habibie (Minister of Research and Technology), and Hartato
(Minister of Industry) – favored protection to promote *pribumi* business, while
another group of politicians around the president resisted trade policy change
because it threatened the steady flow of patronage in the form of import quotas
and other favors to the regime's supporters.[76]

When times were lean, as was certainly the case in the period 1984–86,
President Soeharto usually heeded the advice of the technocrats. But the decision of the president to approve the adoption of drastic economic measures in
1985, with the replacement of the Indonesian customs service with a Swiss-
based surveying company, SGS, and in May 1986, with the announcement of
the first of a series of packages of real economy (i.e., trade and industrial)
reforms which were to unfold over five years (including the September 1986
devaluation against the dollar), reflected other factors too. While the groups
within the state that Liddle has described as opposing the technocrats were
unable to orchestrate a political coalition opposing reform, the technocrats were
able to publicize the views of a growing extra-state policy community in support
of the trade and industry reforms. This "public" was as yet extremely limited,
consisting in the main of academic economists, but its views were widely pub-
licized as a result of an increasingly open press.[77] The technocrats succeeded in
marshaling this public in support of their position favoring greater economic
openness and the reduction in barriers to trade and foreign investment, and, by
accentuating the fear of economic crisis within the state, managed to out-
manuever their opponents and have their policy position prevail.[78]

Thus the explanation for the policy response to the 1984–86 commodity
shock supports our hypothesis that the ascendance of technocrats in policy
making will likely lead to a policy response that favors a more open economy
(hypothesis H2).

International finance changes course, 1987–

Impact Indonesia succeeded in the late 1980s and early 1990s in capitalizing on burgeoning international opportunities for labor-intensive manufactures. Oil still accounted for 34 percent of total exports of $40.05 billion in 1994, but non-oil and gas exports such as textiles, electronics, toys, and wood products grew rapidly in the early 1990s, with textiles accounting for 16.4 percent of these in 1994.[79]

Foreign investors from countries such as Japan, South Korea, Taiwan, Hong Kong, the United States and the United Kingdom fueled this growth in non-oil exports. Approved foreign investments in 1994 totaled $23.7 billion, nearly three times the 8.1 billion total for 1993. By far the largest source was Hong Kong, with twice the level of investment ($6 billion) of the next largest source, the UK.[80]

Investors found Indonesia attractive as a low-wage platform for labor-intensive exports destined for the consumers of Japan, the United States and Western Europe. For example, US athletic wear manufacturers Nike and Reebok relocated production from the more developed economies of Taiwan and South Korea, to Indonesia, where wage rates averaged less than $2 a day.[81] The Indonesian government's adoption of a series of investment deregulation packages encouraged such movements.

Policy record Indonesia was well placed by the policy response to the 1986 slump in oil prices to take advantage of the growing trend in the late 1980s of direct foreign investment from Japan and East Asia in search of export platforms for manufactures destined for developed-country markets. Indonesian foreign borrowing during this period exhibited increased reliance on public debt (reflecting declining availability of private foreign bank loans). Indonesia incurred $2.7 billion in new foreign public debt in 1988 but retired nearly a billion dollars of long-term private debt (this contrasted with the average annual inflow of long-term private debt of $1.2 billion during 1980–86). Among official sources, the World Bank was an important lender to Indonesia, providing 44 percent of new foreign public debt in 1988.[82]

Indonesian policy did not so much respond to the flow of investment capital from East Asia as sustain the course of structural adjustment, trade liberalization, and exchange rate devaluation initiated in September 1986. This unarguably increased the openness of the Indonesian economy, increasing non-oil exports, especially manufactures. The reform program unfolded over nearly four years. Though its origins predated regional capital flows from East Asia, it was sustained by these new flows and the growth opportunities they afforded. At the same time, Indonesia contracted several structural adjustment loans from the World Bank in the late 1980s. The familiar conditions associated with these loans encouraged the policy trend toward liberalization.[83]

By the time the reform program had run its course in 1989, Indonesia was

Table 3.1. *Structure of protection in the Indonesian economy, 1987 and 1994*
(percentages)

	Nominal rate of protection		Effective rate of protection [a]		Export share	
	1987	1994	1987	1994	1985	1990
Total	9	6	16	10	21	24
Agriculture	9	5	18	10	2	3
Manufacturing	24	8	39	23	10	23
Food, beverages and tobacco	14	8	35	26	6	11
Textiles, garments and footwear	32	9	102	9	16	42
Non-metal products	17	11	57	31	21	36
Engineering	40	27	152	85	3	7

Note:
[a] Combining tariffs and non-tariff barriers.
Source: World Bank estimates. Presented by Ajay Chhibber, Division Chief, World
Bank, in address to a conference on "Uncovering Indonesia," at the Carlton Hotel,
Washington, D.C., March 15, 1995.

experiencing real GDP growth of 7.3 percent. Much of the massive private
capital inflow (investment accounted for 36 percent of GNP in 1989) went into
the booming export sector, causing a rapid rise in exports. But demand for
investment put pressure on prices and inflation rose accordingly (to 9 percent in
1991).[84]

Explaining policy choices Trade reforms[85] adopted from 1986 through
1991 succeeded in reducing overall levels of trade protection in the Indonesian
economy. The proportion of manufacturing production protected by import
licenses (quotas) declined from 68 percent in 1986 to 32 percent in 1991, and
the weighted average of tariffs levied against imports fell from 28 percent in
1985 to 15 percent by 1991.[86] Table 3.1 shows that, over a slightly different
period, the effective rate of protection – a measure of the protection afforded
not only to final goods, but to the inputs they utilize as well – for manufactures
dropped by almost half between the late 1980s and the mid-1990s.

By the the mid-1990s, however, the rate of reform had slowed. Indonesia's
economy was more protected than those of the other countries of the ASEAN
Four and the rate of reform in countries such as China, Vietnam, and the
Philippines outpaced that of Indonesia.[87] Moreover, as table 3.1 demonstrates,
the *ad hoc* nature of many of the reforms of the late 1980s and early 1990s had
resulted in wide variation in the effective rates of protection accorded different

areas of the economy. Continued restrictions in the domestic market posed obstacles for companies seeking to become internationally competitive. Prices for a range of widely used products, including cement, sugar, rice, and fertilizer, remained subject to administrative control. Government control of the price of sugar, for example, kept production costs in the food-processing industry high by international standards.[88]

Changes in the international environment – including increased competition from other low-cost labor sites such as China and Vietnam, the 1995 APEC proposal to remove barriers to trade among developing-country members by the year 2020, and pressures from the United States to enforce minimum wage and work condition laws which reduce Indonesia's cheap labor advantage[89] – increased external pressures for policy reform in the mid-1990s. The World Bank contributed to these pressures, arguing that not only was it necessary for Indonesia to further reduce its trade protection and the variability of protection but also that such trade reform had to be linked to lifting of the aforementioned restrictions on domestic trade.[90]

The leading foreign investors in Indonesia by this time were no longer trans-national corporations from the advanced countries. Nearly 60 percent of invest-ment approvals in 1994 came from Taiwan, Hong Kong, Singapore, and South Korea.[91] The evolving regional economy, within which Southeast Asian Chinese business networks played an increasingly important role, constrained Indonesian policymakers to respond to the needs of these investors or risk losing them to other sites. Rapid growth and the changing structure of the domestic economy (the increasing importance of manufacture for export and of foreign partners) made Indonesian policymakers more vulnerable to pressures to extend reform still further. At the same time, these economic changes placed constraints on the ways in which policymakers could treat the Indonesian Chinese and on the extent to which state-owned enterprises could be supported.

Within the context of a generally liberalizing trade regime, however, numer-ous policies favoring certain industries with continuing or new levels of trade protection remained. What sustained these policies, and what role did the private sector have in supporting or opposing them?

The truism, that those who gain from trade protections have greater incen-tive to secure such protections than the broader public who stand to lose, is borne out in the case of P. T. Chandra Asri and the protection of olefins. The owners of a private company, appreciating the potential advantages (economic "rent") that could be garnered from high rates of tariff protection, employed political connections successfully in the mid-1990s to have such protections adopted in the case of olefins, against the general trend towards liberalization. The Chandra Asri case demonstrates the bounds of the broader trend towards economic openness.[92]

On February 14, 1996, Minister of Industry and Trade Tunky Ariwibowo acknowledged that the government had quietly imposed a tariff surcharge of

20 percent on imports of olefins ethylene and propylene, the main raw materials for production of polypropylene which is used in the manufacture of plastics.[93] This policy represented a reversal of the minister's September 1995 averral that the government would grant neither tariff protection, tax incentives, nor regulatory protection to Chandra Asri.[94] This appeared to end the Chandra Asri debate. The principal beneficiary of the subsequent imposition of surcharges was the $1.9 billion P. T. Chandra Asri Petrochemical Center (hereafter, Chandra Asri), a company controlled by President Soeharto's second son, Bambang Trihatmodjo, and two business partners, timber tycoon and Soeharto family friend Prajogo Pangestu, and Henry Pribadi.

This policy shift followed by just two weeks the government's unveiling of a series of deregulation packages affecting trade and investment. It suggested a strengthening of clientelistic policy channels at the expense of the technocrats.

Chandra Asri[95] first announced plans to build a petrochemicals plant in West Java in 1991.[96] Chandra Asri's was but one of several proposed mega-projects, worth up to $2.5 billion each, which caused great concern among those technocrats in the Indonesian government who feared their potential to cause Indonesia's foreign debt to spiral out of control. The technocrats responded to these proposals by winning presidential approval for a cabinet committee that would vet all foreign borrowing by state and state-related projects (of which Chandra Asri's was one). This committee, at the behest of then powerful technocrats, rejected the Chandra Asri proposal, arguing that it threatened to add to the country's high foreign debt and would require high levels of protection to be viable.

Within a year, however, Chandra Asri's backers apparently used their family connection to the president to slip effortlessly around this obstacle. The government changed its regulations to permit 100 percent foreign ownership of certain enterprises and the project was reconfigured superficially so that it became nominally foreign-owned. In this way it avoided the oversight of the cabinet committee and the restrictions that had been placed on foreign loans to domestic companies.[97]

In 1994, with commercial operation about a year off, Chandra Asri's principals requested from the government – as technocrats earlier had predicted they would – a 40 percent protective tariff against competition from cheaper olefin imports for a period of eight years.[98] The request for protection highlighted divisions within the Indonesian government over trade reform. The private sector also joined the debate. Industry associations such as the Association of the Plastic Industry of Indonesia, the Formaline and Thermosetting Association, the Association of Plastic Raw Material Producers and the Association of Basic Organic Chemical Producers of Indonesia opposed the proposed tariffs. Downstream, Indonesia's domestic textile producers also worried at the impact more expensive inputs would have on the competitiveness of their products in international markets.[99]

The real issue at stake however transcended the specific company and industry involved. It was the credibility of Indonesia's commitment to trade reform and transparent economic policy, which was paraded during the November 1994 Asia-Pacific Economic Cooperation (APEC) summit in Bogor and firmly embraced by Soeharto in the lead-up to that summit.[100] The important complication specific to the Chandra Asri case was the direct family link between the owners of the plant and Soeharto and the political influence this afforded them.[101]

A striking feature of this case was the role of business industry associations. While private consultations no doubt occurred between businessmen and policymakers, it is significant that the associations, particularly those representing downstream petrochemical and textile industries, went public in opposing the granting of tariff protection. They did so arguing that the costs to a wide range of Indonesian exporters would far exceed the benefits in terms of savings in foreign exchange from producing olefins domestically (rather than importing them). The increasingly assertive public policy role of business associations in Indonesia suggested that there were increasing obstacles to the traditional use of personal ties by businessmen to influence economic policymaking.[102]

Policy change toward greater openness continued in Indonesia with regular announcements such as the package of trade and investment reforms introduced in June 1996.[103] This package included an end to all quota restrictions on imports (non-tariff barriers) and elimination of all import surcharges. In accordance with its commitments under the AFTA (ASEAN Free Trade Area) and APEC agreements, the government specified a timetable for tariff reductions that extended as far as the year 2003, and reaffirmed Indonesia's commitment to final elimination of all tariff restrictions on trade with APEC partners by the year 2020. In addition to making the economy more open to trade, the package for the first time opened opportunities for foreign investors to participate in domestic distribution networks.[104]

Hence, Indonesia showed conflicting trends in the 1990s. Against a broader trend toward greater economic openness, the Chandra Asri case, among others, illustrated the ongoing importance of clientelism, and, in particular, the influence exerted by the children of President Soeharto on policy. This nepotism fomented popular resentment and fueled the first open challenge to Soeharto's presidency, a June 1996 march of thousands in red shirts in the streets of central Jakarta demonstrating in support of the presidential candidacy of Megawati Sukarnoputri, daughter of Indonesia's first president, Sukarno, for the Indonesian Democratic Party (PDI) in the 1998 presidential elections.[105]

In summary, the policy response to the last of our events reflected the continued policy ascendancy of the technocrats in the mid-1990s (hypothesis H2) and the dominance of their preferences regarding policies for greater openness (hypothesis H3). In addition, it reflected the success of the technocratic policy response to the earlier event (1984–86, especially the oil price fall in 1986), and thus reemphasized the importance of path-dependence for the Indonesian case. Nevertheless, in certain policy areas (e.g., science and technology, aircraft, and shipbuilding), and in areas of the economy where the children of Soeharto had considerable interests, policies reducing the openness of the economy still prevailed.

The concluding section of this chapter evaluates the domestic responses to each of the four events covered here and assesses which, if any, of the hypotheses are confirmed by the experience of Indonesia.

Conclusion

The economic crisis confronting the Indonesian economy in 1965–66 was the product of a grand domestic political struggle. The achievement of the technocrats in restoring economic prosperity by 1968 was important for later policy responses to external events. It established the validity of external ideas (neoclassical economic theory) and enhanced the political influence of those who promoted them. Technocrats, or officials whose power lay in their technical competence, were able to assert their autonomy from military and civilian factions, and to gain direct access to, and influence over, the president.

The first oil shock brought windfall gains. Policymakers responded by reducing foreign debt and investing in agriculture. This encouraged production of crops for the domestic market (e.g., rice) as well as those for export (e.g., copra). Subsequently, appreciation of the rupiah, and accumulated layers of institutional, non-tariff barriers to imports established a growing anti-export bias.

The second oil shock repeated the windfall but was closely followed by a debt crisis which increased the cost of foreign borrowing. The Indonesian policy response had elements of both trade tightening (quotas) and efforts to increase openness (a large devaluation), but had the overall effect of making the economy less open.

The aspect of the third external event most damaging to the Indonesian economy was the sudden collapse of global oil prices in 1986. Indonesia's policy response was unambiguously outward looking, combining trade liberalization and a large devaluation, and was associated with a sweeping structural reform (liberalization) program. The response is best explained with reference to factors which contributed to the preeminence of the technocrats, whose recommendations were given added weight by the recommendations and loan conditions of the World Bank.

Indonesian policy did not so much respond to the inflow of East Asian private investment capital in the late 1980s as hold to an already established course of increasing openness. The foreign investment windfall provided the opportunity to extend and sustain structural adjustment and trade liberalization policies mapped out in the wake of the 1986 oil price shock. This contradicts hypothesis H1c, that revenue abundance will result in the favoring of a more closed trade and investment regime.

CHAPTER FOUR

Malaysia

For more than a decade following its independence in 1957, Malaysia was dominated politically by a small multi-ethnic elite that employed economic development to maintain political stability and avoid ethnic strife. This elite controlled a state apparatus that, for historical reasons and in contrast to the cases of Indonesia, the Philippines, and Thailand, was both extensive and relatively competent.

State resources came from import tariffs and from domestic sources, such as corporate income taxes, which were borne most heavily by the non-indigenous, commercial sector – foreign companies and those owned by immigrant Chinese and Indian minorities.[1] These resources were applied to developing the rural sector and improving agricultural productivity as means to improve living conditions for the indigenous, largely rural, Malay community, the largest but least advantaged ethnic group.

This resource allocation was politically consequential: it ensured majority Malay support for the United Malays National Organization (UMNO), the largest of the three ethnic parties in the ruling coalition government. It also succeeded in making it more difficult for groups opposed to the governing elite – including those on the left, whose armed efforts in the guerilla insurgency known as the Emergency were defeated in the early 1950s, and those advocating an Islamic state for the largely Muslim population – from mobilizing popular movements among the poor and rural populations to oppose the ruling elite.

Among the legacies of British colonial rule, which ended in 1957, was a commitment to policies designed to foster private foreign investment. Malaysian policymakers also inherited a tariff structure whose incidence was relatively modest and whose original intent was to supplement government revenues rather than to limit imports. Pressure from British plantation and resource extraction interests that continued to dominate the economy in the first decade after independence and that feared a change in import policies, helped sustain the relative openness of the Malaysian economy.

The watershed event in Malaysia's post-independence history came with the shattering of twelve years of comparatively peaceful ethnic coexistence by Malay–Chinese ethnic violence that engulfed the capital and some of the major provincial centers in May 1969. There followed nearly two years of martial-law rule by a civilian-military council, after which the ruling coalition reinvented itself as a broad national coalition (the National Front), including a wider range of political parties, with the Malay party, UMNO, now clearly in the ascendant. UMNO political leaders in 1971 initiated a new economic policy (NEP) intended to alleviate Malay poverty and redistribute income and wealth to meet twenty-year numerical targets for Malay participation in the modern commercial sector. As part of this new strategy, they sought to attract private foreign investment as the principal means of expanding the "economic pie," so that the Malay "slice" could increase without reducing absolutely the "slices" of any other ethnic group. Despite new protections bestowed on state-sponsored heavy industries (autos, steel, and cement) established in the early 1980s as proxy vehicles for Malay economic advancement, Malaysian economic policy retained its relatively open character. This reflected not only the colonial legacy but also the growing importance of exporting – and the need therefore to keep domestic input costs as low as possible – and the growing importance of foreign capital for high growth, advanced technology industries such as electronics.

The following section introduces the organization of Malaysian society, the character of politics and the sources of the power which state officials wield, and the linkages between business and state officials.

Political regime

Social organization

Malaysia's population[2] of over eighteen million has three main ethnic communities: the indigenous (*bumiputra*) community, consisting mainly of ethnic Malays (accounting for about 48 percent of the population); a sizeable immigrant Chinese community (36 percent); and a smaller Indian population (9 percent).[3] Malays, descended from migrants from Central Asia, are concentrated in rural areas but are also found in large numbers in urban areas and in commercial settings. The Chinese came as traders or, in the nineteenth century, as laborers in tin mines. Their descendants are most numerous in the towns and cities where they still dominate locally owned commerce and smaller-scale manufacturing. Indians were transported from South India by British plantation interests during the rubber boom at the turn of the century as inexpensive labor for the sprawling estates. In the years following World War I, these rubber tappers were joined by traders, businessmen, and professionals contributing to what has become a substantial permanent Indian community population consisting, as is the case with the two other main ethnic groups, of a mixture of rich and poor, workers and employers, rural and urban dwellers.[4]

By the first decade[5] of the century, the British had shaped a social order of distinct ethnic niches, each identified by status and occupational specialization. Among the elite: the Malays were hereditary aristocrats, bureaucrats, and politicians, and, at a lower level, schoolteachers and village headmen; the Chinese were traders, shopkeepers and businessmen; the Indians were professionals and shopkeepers. At the level of the common man, the Malays typically worked the fields; the Chinese labored in the tin mines; and the Indians tapped the rubber trees. Functional or occupational specialization was frequently accompanied by geographic separation – different ethnic groups tended to live in separate areas. Colonial policy thus assigned to elements of each community specific roles in an economic division of labor oriented to the efficient extraction of resources for the British economy. The employment of Malay workers as tin-miners or rubber-tappers, for example, was officially discouraged. The "proper" role for the Malays was as suppliers of food (mainly rice) for the population.[6]

Land in precolonial Malaya[7] was abundant and control of land less important than control over commerce. Traditional authority rested on the ability of Malay rulers to levy taxes on trade passing up and down river valleys to which they controlled access.[8] Local Malay rulers joined British merchants and Chinese traders in undertaking large-scale commercial production of tin (later, rubber). The rulers levied export duties on tin, import taxes on miners' supplies, and received revenue from tax-collecting monopolies in exchange for access to tin deposits. The British supplied the capital and supervised the shipment and marketing of the output on international metals markets.[9]

By the early twentieth century, control of most of the productive land had been ceded to British commercial interests. While traditional rulers nominally reigned (and retained formal control over large tracts of less productive land), their British "advisors" (later "residents") in fact ruled. And the children of the aristocracy were coopted into an expanding colonial civil service. By independence, in contrast to the semifeudal arrangements prevailing in the Philippines, the power of Malay rulers – the landlord class – was greatly reduced. The independence arrangements left the sultans with sources of state-level revenues, and formal ownership of land, but largely ceremonial powers and, most importantly, limited ability to raise revenues from trade. There were no powerful landlord interests with which the central government had to contend in formulating economic policy.

Growth in the economy in the twentieth century was based on agriculture, plantations, and resource extraction. It was facilitated by infrastructure development that was greatly accelerated in the decade following the end of the Pacific War as the colonial authorities confronted and defeated a rurally based communist insurgency. Immigrant settlers, particularly the Chinese, played an important role as commercial intermediaries between the large-scale British trading houses and the non-commercial indigenous Malay population. European commercial interests represented the principal source of investment capital and their orientation toward foreign markets sustained the trade dependence and relative openness of the Malayan economy.

The Malay population as a whole was largely peripheral to the sources of economic growth in the period before independence. The leaders of the Malay political party, UMNO (formed in 1946), drawn from among the lower-level civil servants and village teachers of the colonial civil service, announced their intent to change this. UMNO leaders negotiated directly with the British over a pre-independence agreement and imposed its terms on the remaining Malay hereditary rulers. They then mobilized rural Malays to vote for the alliance of ethnic parties that received power at independence, and preempted competing mobilizations of this population based on class or religious appeals. While retaining British capital as the primary source of private investment capital, UMNO leaders sought to increase the participation of the Malay community in the modern sector, while balancing this against the needs of immigrant capital represented by Chinese and Indian parties in the governing coalition.

The ethnic strife of 1969 suggested that the balance struck thitherto was inadequate to meet Malay aspirations and ensure political stability. By the mid-1970s relations between economic and social forces had been recast, with the Malays clearly in the ascendant, and UMNO directing state policy to foster Malay entrepreneurship and nurturing state institutions as proxies for the Malay community. The political and economic power of the immigrant communities was on the wane.

Politics and the bases of state power

The developmental character of the Malaysian (colonial) state was established early, with heavy investment in irrigation and social and physical infrastructure in rural areas designed to curb a communist insurgency in the 1940s and 1950s. The pattern of conservative monetary and fiscal policy (e.g., balanced budgets) and substantial public investment was sustained after independence, under a series of Chinese ministers of finance, notably Tan Siew Sin. Constraints on the state's ability to orchestrate development included the continuing dependence on British companies' capital, the continued reliance on a limited number of agricultural commodities and raw materials and on foreign markets for most of the country's wealth, and the ethnic division of labor inherited from the colonial British.

Political representation and legitimacy were based upon appeal to the Malay rural voter, whose returns from economic growth were modest. This political rationale dictated the official development strategy during the 1960s – with its focus on rural development and its relatively hands-off approach to commerce and manufacturing. It also shaped the relative openness of state policy toward trade and investment. However, linkages between politics and economics also made inevitable the adoption of the affirmative action program of the NEP. As UMNO developed corporate proxies for Malay entrepreneurship in the 1970s, thereby mobilizing its own funds for electoral campaigns, it grew less dependent on Chinese financial support and Malay leaders were able to pursue policies promoting Malay economic interests at the expense of those of the immigrant communities.

The assertive character of political leadership and the degree of concentration of political power in the hands of Prime Minister Mahathir and the leaders of UMNO – in relation to bureaucrats, coalition partners, the military, business interests, the middle class, and mobilized social groups – reflected the political dominance of the Malay electorate beginning in the 1970s. The party leadership's pursuit of an economic status for Malays commensurate with their political power (an UMNO-led coalition has won every election since independence) created a state whose developmental and interventionist policies were essentially beyond challenge.

While the basic mechanisms for social control rarely included state coercion (a notable exception was the 1987 jailing of over 100 regime opponents) and relied more upon cooptation and collaboration, the political base of Malaysia's elite narrowed considerably after the 1960s. While still taking the form of a multi-ethnic, democratically elected coalition, the government in practice primarily represented the interests of the Malay elite, and the only truly contested democratic election was the party election for positions in the UMNO leadership.[10]

Linkages between business and the state

The state in Malaysia has the upper hand over both local and foreign commercial, industrial, and agricultural capital. This predominance is rooted in early patterns of state intervention under the colonial government and the ethnic character of local business, specifically that it continues to be predominantly Chinese and is thus politically vulnerable. The state has been able to divide and rule, undercutting the British commercial presence while still seeking to attract foreign capital, and at the same time encouraging domestic Chinese business while reminding the Chinese of the potential for xenophobia in the Malay population.

The importance of foreign trade and investment for the Malaysian economy has constrained how far economic policymakers have been prepared to go in closing economic opportunities to outsiders. But these decision-makers have also found foreign investment useful for sustaining the economy while squeezing the Malaysian Chinese.

The character of Malaysian business has changed over time, Malay partners emerging from the shadowy "paper partner" role to becoming fully fledged businessmen in their own right, capable of delivering the political and financial resources for large projects. Malay business activities, often in partnership with Chinese firms and foreign suppliers of technology, extend to the very largest of infrastructural projects, such as the new international airport and the main north–south highway. Malay business groups, such as that controlled by former Finance Minister Daim, now extend their activities to a broad range of financial, commercial, service sector, and infrastructure development activities. They maintain strong political links to UMNO leaders and they act as vehicles for foreign or immigrant Chinese partners to secure political sponsors for new projects.

Postwar developments

The US commitment to containing the communist threat in Asia, and to developing a stable, open, and expanding international economy using new multilateral institutions and trade policies, had an indirect but nonetheless significant impact on Malaysia's potential for future economic development. Initial political conditions in British Malaya[11] after August 1945 were inauspicious for future economic development. Unlike neighbors Thailand and the Philippines, which bound themselves after 1946 to the new regional hegemon, the United States, Malaya reverted to its prewar status as a colony of Britain. This was, however, to prove ultimately more of a blessing than a curse. Now a mere shadow of its former grand self, the British empire began rapidly to contract as the postwar Labour government, reeling under financial hardship, granted independence to India in 1947, and made clear its intention to similarly dispose of Malaya as quickly as possible. Meanwhile, Malayan commodities began to recover in 1946–47 with the beginnings of the steady rise in commodity prices that was to last through the Korean War.

In the meantime, the recurrent crises that engulfed the British economy led to a development with fortuitous – but entirely unintended – consequences for Malaya.[12] In 1947, London issued directives to its colonial governments that they should operate on a self-financing basis and should adopt "a regime of wartime austerity as regards imports." Thus, Britain began to withdraw from Malaya, and in its place US influence grew.

A second aspect of the challenge to Malaya presented by this external event was the impact of the Korean War. The US confrontation with North Korean and Chinese communism led to burgeoning demand on both sides for military procurements to fight the war and to build up stockpiles against the possibility that the war would spread. This resulted in a boom in commodity prices between 1950–53 from which Malaya benefited greatly. The price of rubber, for example, which averaged $0.40 per pound in 1949 reached a high of $2.20 per pound in February 1951. It averaged $1.70 per pound in 1951, more than four times its 1949 price.[13] The price of tin more than doubled in less than a year beginning in the spring of 1950.[14]

A third aspect of this event was the determination of the United States and its allies, Britain and some of the countries of the British Commonwealth, to confront the communist guerrilla insurgency that erupted on the Asian mainland in the late 1940s and overlapped with the Korean War. The Malayan Communist Party initiated the local insurgency in 1948 and fighting was most intense through 1950, resulting in the Malayan Emergency (which was effectively over by 1955 but not officially declared so until 1960).

The budgetary and trade self-sufficiency imposed on Malaya in 1947 by the Colonial Office in response to the fragility of the British postwar recovery encouraged a colonial Malayan policy response of fiscal conservatism. The Colonial Office under the new Labour government in London insisted that its colonial administrations generate more revenue than they had before by way of taxes. Thus, dispite the vociferous opposition of (largely British) business interests, the governor of Malaya introduced legislation in December 1947 by which an income tax was established in the colony, and adopted a sliding-scale duty on exports of rubber and tin, the colony's two largest exports. Subsequently, the colonial government also revised the corporate tax structure so as to generate more revenue. As we will show, these measures were to prove most beneficial to Malaya's future economic development.

Postwar expansion in world trade – facilitated by the US commitment to an open global trading order and to providing open access to the US market – and growing demand for commodities (rubber for the postwar auto industry and tin for canning and industrial machinery) were enormously profitable for Malayan producers. The profit earned per pound in the Malayan rubber industry rose by a factor of eight between 1949 and 1951, from less than seven Malayan cents to over fifty.[15] Therefore, the first consequence of the Colonial Office directive was to increase the capacity of the colonial government to generate revenue far beyond that anticipated at the outset. Government revenue at the height of the Korean War boom in 1953 reached nearly three-quarters of a billion Malayan dollars, more than three times its level in 1948, before the tax took effect (M$235.5 million). Income and corporate taxes together accounted for 30 percent of total revenues in 1952 and 1953, and government revenues overall accounted for a higher proportion of GDP than in any other country of the region.[16]

The second unintended consequence was to keep most of the profits from the key Korean boom years of 1950–53 in Malaya. Although British companies repatriated some of their profits as dividends, the restrictions imposed on origins of imports meant that even in the absence of capital controls much of that earned from rubber and tin that would hitherto have likely been spent on imports was invested or spent locally, or went in taxes. The colonial government, implementing instructions from London, severely restricted imports from non-sterling areas (including Japan and the United States – and later even from Britain itself). This raised wages and encouraged a limited amount of import substitution. But it also resulted in an acute shortage of important machinery and parts which hampered economic growth and created friction between the colonial administration and the British business community in Malaya.[17]

At the same time, the Korean War commodities boom presented the colonial government in Kuala Lumpur with unprecedented opportunity. The by now fairly well developed tax system yielded greatly enhanced revenues from domestic sources and from exports, and discouraged reliance on tariffs on imports as a revenue source. The government deficit which stood at M$13.4 million at the beginning of 1950, reflecting the high level of expenditure necessary to fight the Emergency, had by the end of 1951 turned into a surplus of M$289.9 million.[18] Long before independence, Malaya's government had developed a significant capacity to generate revenues from the local economy.

The way colonial administrators allocated the windfall revenues from rising commodity prices also proved to be consequential for the future growth of the Malayan economy. They embarked upon a massive expansion of the colony's economic and social infrastructure in order to counter the internal security threat posed by the communist insurgency. Initial attempts to confront the guerillas militarily had failed because of their base of support among rural Malayan Chinese communities. In 1950, the government launched a new strategy that focused on the civilian support population and expanded the scope of civil administration.[19]

Under the leadership of the new British Conservative government, with Lieutenant-General Gerald Templer as High Commissioner, the administration policy in early 1952 opened the floodgates of the huge accumulated government surplus from the Korean War boom for use in developing the economic and social infrastructure and thereby in fighting the guerillas on all fronts.[20] Railway lines were laid, and roads were built and improved. More electric power stations were constructed. Healthcare spending doubled between 1950 and 1954, and the number of school students more than doubled between 1950 and 1958. With all this development, the civil administration expanded enormously.[21] By 1959, the total of administrative employees at federal, state, and local levels had increased by nearly 200 percent over 1948, from 48,000 to 140,000.[22] Templer's strategy had succeeded. By 1955, the insurgency had been largely quelled.

At independence, the new Malayan government enjoyed three very important legacies of the early Cold War years. Responding to declining British official commitment, the Korean War commodities boom, and an internal communist guerilla insurgency, colonial administrators had expanded the government's ability to generate revenues from the Malayan economy (and thus maintain a relatively open trade regime), expanded the scope of economic and social infrastructure, and increased the size and capacity of the government administrative apparatus. Together these provided the basis for the rapid accumulation of capital and the relatively high growth rates recorded by Malaya during the 1960s.[23]

Although a favorable basis for future growth had been established as a result of policies adopted in the 1950s, the Malayan economy at independence shared many of the weaknesses of those of other newly independent nations. It was raw material-dependent, foreign-dominated, lacking in diversity, and dualistic, a rural–urban dualism being compounded in the Malayan case by a native-born/non-native division.[24]

The maintenance of a stable, open, and expanding international economy enabled Malaysia to continue to prosper as an exporter of commodities as prices rose through the 1960s (albeit with ups and downs). As had been the case in the preceding decade, when colonial administrators had sought the hearts and minds of the rural population, the now independent government of Malaysia focused its economic policies on developing the rural-agricultural sector.[25] These included infrastructural development designed to increase agricultural output,[26] programs designed to improve living conditions in rural villages and towns,[27] and efforts to increase Malay participation in the modern economy by assisting Malay entrepreneurs in such areas as transportation, construction, and the timber industry. For example, transport licenses for buses, trucks, and taxis were required by the 1958 Road Traffic Ordinance to be issued in proportion to the ethnic composition of the population in each state; in many states, a Malay contractor could receive a government contract if the tendered price did not exceed that of the most competitive non-Malay tender by more than 10 percent; and at least half of all timber concessions were granted to Malays.[28] The government set up a state-owned bank, Bank Bumiputra, to provide financing for Malay businessmen who felt they were not served by Chinese or foreign banks.[29]

In the area of industrial development, the government recognized the need to expand Malaysia's industrial capacity in order to reduce dependence on tin and rubber production, but chose to let the private sector take the lead.[30] Policy focused on improving general economic conditions and offering mostly non-selective inducements to invest.[31] The Pioneer Industries (Relief from Income Tax) Ordinance of 1958 granted various degrees of "relief" from the 40 percent company tax to new industries deemed essential to Malaysian economic growth.[32] The ordinance represented the response of a 1957 government-appointed Industrial Development Working Party, to a 1955 World Bank mission's report[33] which had urged that the relatively open, free-enterprise character of the economy be protected, but that diversification of production be promoted by a variety of measures, including depreciation allowances and limited tariff protection. The working party seconded most of the Bank's recommendations, but added tax relief as a vehicle to encourage foreign investment.[34]

Tariffs, which officials had used hitherto to generate revenue, were now used in some cases as a means of fostering import-substituting industry. However, the Tariff Advisory Committee of the Ministry of Commerce and Industry, established in 1961 to recommend tariff changes to attract new industries, advised reductions in tariffs for imported industrial materials, rather than tariff increases for finished products (reflecting a primary government concern at the time to avoid creating a high-cost economy).[35] And powerful plantation and mercantile interests, fearing rising costs of production, were able to block extension of tariff protection to new industries.[36] The average effective rate of protection for manufacturing stood at 15 percent in 1962, but subsequently rose to 45 percent in 1966 and 55 percent in 1972. David Lim has argued that this was still quite low in comparison with other similar economies.[37]

The government also established new institutions to foster development of industry. Malaysian Industrial Development Finance (MIDF) was established in 1960 to provide debt or equity financing for promising smaller local industrial ventures, using funds borrowed from public and private sources.[38] A subsidiary of MIDF, Malaysian Industrial Estates (MIE), helped industries establish themselves in "industrial estates" developed by local development agencies.[39] Overall, while the government worked to improve basic infrastructure, developed new industrial sites, offered general financial inducements, and to a limited extent used tariffs to attract import-substituting foreign investment, these measures were adopted within a broadly *laissez-faire* policy environment toward industry.[40]

Malaysian government policy in the 1960s reflected not only the dominant ideas of economists in the United States and multilateral institutions at that time, but also the character of the interethnic elite coalition represented by the Alliance electoral coalition. Malay leaders of the dominant party, the United Malays National Organization (UMNO), recognized that the Chinese and Indian communities' acceptance of their political hegemony was conditional on the state not interfering in private commerce and industry, beyond the performance of traditional regulatory functions.[41]

A good illustration of how the interethnic arrangement restrained some UMNO leaders from adopting pro-Malay economic policies that might encroach on non-Malay commercial and industrial interests is provided by the experience of Abdul Aziz bin Ishak. In the early 1960s, Aziz, UMNO Minister of Agriculture and Cooperatives, sought to transfer the ownership of rice mills in the state of Perak from private Chinese entrepreneurs to Malay-dominated, government-funded, rural cooperatives by summarily revoking the licenses of some 350 Chinese rice millers. Vehement protests by the affected Chinese soon led UMNO's partner, the Malayslan Chinese Association (MCA), to become involved. Concerned that capitulation on the issue would result in a loss of confidence by Chinese businessmen in their ability to protect Chinese economic interests, MCA leaders threatened to withdraw their support from the Alliance.

Malay leaders, concluding that the Minister had gone too far in encroaching on Chinese business interests, acquiesced to the MCA's demands. In late 1962, Aziz was dismissed from the cabinet for "unconstitutional practices," namely, for violating the guarantee, under Article 152 of the Constitution, that the government would protect the "legitimate interests" of non-Malays.[42]

The example illustrates a conviction on the part of Malay leaders that inter-communal cooperation was a necessary condition for regime survival.[43] Although politically dominant, with the capacity arbitrarily to impose state poli-cies on the private sector, they were prepared to make important concessions to non-Malay concerns and to limit the extent to which government encroached on private sector commercial and industrial activities in the interests of pre-serving communal peace.[44]

Moreover, industrial development policies entailed political costs for UMNO leaders for, in the eyes of many Malays, they suggested that the state was favor-ing urban commercial (predominantly non-Malay) interests.[45] These Malay political concerns of UMNO leaders also explain why official measures affect-ing industry favored foreign capital, despite the fact that the Malaysian economy was already heavily foreign-dominated (especially in the critical mining and plantation sectors).[46] Well after independence, foreign (largely European, and particularly British) capital remained important, especially in sectors such as mining, plantations, and banks. Local (mainly Chinese) entrepreneurs had, by the late 1950s, created only limited concentrations of wealth to rival these heavily capitalized European operations.[47] Foreign planta-tion and mining interests lobbied successfully against the use of tariffs as a primary means of encouraging local manufacturing. The state encouraged expansion of foreign-owned industry because this allowed it to strengthen the industrial sector while avoiding any appearance of showing favor toward domestic non-Malays. Thus the constraints inherent in the interethnic settle-ment and in the nature of political relations between ethnic groups militated against the Alliance government adopting anything other than a market-led approach to industrial development.

This disincentive to direct state involvement in the commercial and industrial sector had its complement in incentives for the state to involve itself in the development of agriculture. The concentration of Malays in rural areas and UMNO's concern to establish its legitimacy with them as the Malay political party in the face of challenges from competing parties, such as the Islamic party, PMIP, encouraged Malay leaders to focus state development efforts in the rural-agricultural sector.[48]

Challenge and response

We here analyze the response of Malaysian policymakers to the four external events. Our treatment of policy in each case emphasizes how policy changed from that prevailing before the event, and why. For each event, we discuss the domestic impact of the external event, the policy record, and those factors most important for explaining the relevant domestic policy choices.

First oil shock, global recession, easy credit, 1974–75

Impact The first oil shock was felt in Malaysia as a source of windfall gains. As an oil producer, Malaysia, like Indonesia, experienced the oil shock very differently from the Philippines and Thailand, as a windfall opportunity rather than as a severe policy constraint. Malaysian oil production in 1974 was just 100,000 barrels per day (Indonesia's was 1.4 million; Saudi Arabia's 8.4 million),[49] but this was sufficient to afford Malaysia, like Argentina and Colombia, the luxury of virtual energy self-sufficiency, importing only a negligible proportion of its energy needs.[50] Because other import prices rose alongside oil (the value of merchandise imports rose 70 percent in 1974, while the value of merchandise exports rose 40 percent) the terms of trade in real terms declined by nearly 20 percent in 1975.[51] The current account (before transfers) of the balance of payments moved from surplus in 1973 into deficit during 1974–75 (averaging the equivalent of 5.5 percent of GDP) before rebounding to a surplus equivalent to 5 percent of GDP in 1976.[52] Growth in real GDP slowed, from over 8 percent in 1974 to less than 1 percent in 1975, but subsequently recovered.[53]

The oil shock had an adverse indirect effect on Malaysia's economy because it caused declines in world trade and investment. Higher oil prices led to stagflation in the developed economies during the mid-1970s and reduced direct foreign investment in developing countries (even as private bank lending increased with the availability of recycled petrodollars). While oil reserves rendered Malaysia's economy initially resilient to the direct trade effects of the oil shock, it was particularly vulnerable to a decline in foreign investment. Malaysia was adjacent to the latest "dominos" to fall to communist victories in Indochina in 1975, and therefore perhaps at risk itself, and had a recent history of ethnic unrest. Direct foreign investment fell by nearly 40 percent, from $570 million in 1974 to $350 million in 1975, and did not reach its 1974 level again until 1979.[54]

Malaysia's leaders needed foreign investment for domestic political reasons. The oil shock came just as the political situation in Malaysia was stabilizing after the 1969 ethnic riots and as the effects of the NEP were beginning to be felt. The assumption of an expanding economic pie was critical to the NEP's redistributive formula. Declining foreign investment, paralleling a dramatic decline in domestic private investment as Malaysian Chinese businessmen responded to the uncertainties of their future roles, threatened the expanding pie.

Trade figures show the effects on the Malaysian economy of global recession in late 1974 and 1975, precipitated by the oil crisis. As consumer confidence in the advanced industrialized countries plunged, markets for developing-country goods contracted. Malaysia's merchandise exports fell 10 percent in 1975 and only as developed-country markets recovered did it leap ahead again by nearly 40 percent in 1976. The value of total merchandise trade followed a similar pattern. It reached the equivalent of 85 percent of GDP in 1974, dropping to 76 percent in 1975, before recovering to nearly 80 percent in 1976.[55]

Policy record Malaysian economic policy[56] responded not to the oil shock itself but to the subsequent decline in private investment, domestic and foreign. Policymakers in the early 1970s were concerned principally with achieving the NEP's redistributive goals. The state adopted a higher profile as an economic actor in its own right. It established numerous new public corporations and extended the range of operations of many established in the 1960s, creating what were in essence proxies for Malay business that were eventually to be divested into private (Malay) hands.[57] Over the five-year period ending in 1975, development budget allocations for government corporations averaged more than ten times those of the previous five years.[58]

Government leaders sought to bring business into voluntary compliance with ethnic targets for employees and business partners. When this failed, officials adopted laws and regulations that required firms seeking tax concessions, export incentives or protection from foreign competition to employ at least 30 percent Malays at all levels. A proportion of licenses and government contracts was also reserved for Malays and Malay-owned firms.[59] The primary target of these measures was Chinese business which, for the most part, continued to use family-based employment and ownership practices which officials felt were an obstacle to Malay economic advancement. In 1975 the government adopted the Industrial Coordination Act (ICA) that created a licensing system for most industries and made granting of a license conditional upon compliance with NEP guidelines.

When private domestic investment lagged, the government turned to international capital markets for capital to support domestic investments. Net long-term foreign loans increased from $220 million in 1974 to over $750 million in 1975, and accumulated long-term debt increased from $1.1 billion in 1974 to $1.8 billion in 1975 (the proportion from private banks increased from 22 to 27 percent).[60]

At the same time, officials tried to increase Malaysia's attractiveness to foreign investors by a variety of means: establishing "one-stop" investment approval at the Malaysian Industrial Development Authority (MIDA, formerly the Federal Industrial Development Authority); expanding incentives for export production in free trade zones; developing industrial estates and licensed manufacturing warehouses; and instituting labor laws that barred unions from key export industries such as electronics.[61] However, the intrusive and restrictive nature of the 1975 ICA and the passage that same year of the Petroleum Development (Amendment) Act (PDA), which threatened foreign oil companies with nationalization of their oil exploration and production facilities, made the challenge of attracting direct foreign investment more difficult.[62] The ICA increased restrictions on foreign investors and limited their ability to retain 100 percent ownership of investments in Malaysia. It also increased the scope of bureaucratic authority (over employment practices and shareholding structures) and widened the opportunities for corrupt practices. This made Malaysia appear less attractive to foreign investors in comparison with neighboring countries. The PDA, adopted without prior consultation with foreign oil companies, required them to forfeit to the state-owned oil company, Petronas, majority ownership in all production, transportation, and refining of Malaysian oil and gas. In addition, the Act gave Petronas control of all marketing and distribution of Malaysian oil, through joint ventures with foreign partners.[63] The oil companies vehemently opposed the measure. While the government eventually backed down, amending the measure to exclude the most objectionable of its provisions, its adoption of the PDA suggested that future policy might move in an economic nationalist direction. Together, the policy changes embodied in the ICA and the PDA reduced Malaysia's openness to direct foreign investment, which grew in 1976 at less than one third the 10 percent rate targeted by the government.[64]

With few alternatives, the government itself took up some of the slack, using statutory bodies to invest in shares required by law to be offered to Malays in any public offering of corporate stock. In a short time, the scale of government holdings of corporate stock soon became very large indeed. State intervention also extended to activities of the ruling party; UMNO leaders turned the Fleet Group into a corporate vehicle for the party itself and began accumulating stock from Malay share issues and taking advantage of ownership quotas to develop its own "stable" of companies.[65] However, this had the unintended effect of making non-Malay business even more anxious about its future, and this further discouraged private domestic investment.[66]

In summary, the economic policy record associated with the first external event was mixed in terms of the extent to which new policies were responses to the event, and in terms of whether policy became more open or more closed to the international economy. Regarding responsiveness, the central policy change in 1974–75, adoption of the ICA, was not a response to the oil shock, although the government's ability to sustain the ICA in the face of dramatically declining private investment depended on statutory agencies picking up some of the investment slack, which in turn was dependent on availability of petrodollars on international capital markets and on growing revenues from Malaysia's exports of oil. Regarding openness, the ICA and the PDA together made Malaysia less open to the flow of direct foreign investment, although the effect was ameliorated to some degree by incentives adopted subsequently to counter the fall-off in direct foreign investment. Nevertheless, to the extent that policy became significantly less open during 1974–75, the effect was limited largely to measures affecting flows of private capital and the change was only indirectly a response to the external event that is the focus of this section. In terms of openness to trade in goods and services, there were no major policy changes during 1974–75.

Explaining policy choices The principal factor motivating policy changes in the mid-1970s was official concern for the political ramifications of the domestic crisis precipitated by the 1969 ethnic riots. This is best reflected in the adoption of the ICA. UMNO's political leaders wanted to accommodate rising Malay economic aspirations by institutionalizing the NEP. To the extent that state officials responded to the external event, their principal motivation in doing so was concern for the effect of external developments on their ability to achieve their domestic political objectives. The oil price rise contributed to policy change, but only indirectly. Malaysia's oil exports provided revenues that made it easier for the government to borrow abroad on international capital markets and enabled statutory bodies to use resources mobilized abroad to make up for slumping private foreign and domestic investment.

By 1975, the Malay share of manufacturing jobs had increased to 32 percent, from 25 percent in 1970, and Malays comprised 17 percent of managers (compared with 11 percent in 1971). They held almost 30 percent of institutional credit (up from 14 percent in 1971) and their share of all capital stood at 8 percent.[67] The NEP was nonetheless a source of frustration. Malay entrepreneurs were becoming more numerous than in the 1960s, but in many cases their activities were limited to "paper partnerships" which afforded non-Malay partners access to licenses and quotas but excluded Malays from hands-on, management experience.[68] A shortage of experienced Malay managers made it difficult for many firms to meet the 30 percent target for Malays in their management staff.

Responding to the ICA, most Chinese entrepreneurs (that is, most domestic businessmen) simply stopped investing, or redirected their investments into non-productive uses such as real estate speculation or financial instruments.[69] This, combined with the decline in direct foreign investment following the oil shock, precipitated a marked decline in overall private investment, about 60 percent of which was attributable to domestic investors.[70] Domestic private investment in commercial and industrial enterprise in 1977, for example, fell well short of the M$22 billion target projected for that year by the Third Malaysia Plan.[71]

The government responded by increasing its foreign borrowing and using the proceeds to finance public investment and to develop state institutions that would act as proxies for Malay entrepreneurship in the short term. Officials also responded with incentives to foreign investors.

In summary, we may explain the main policy initiatives of this period with reference to UMNO leaders' domestic political agenda of economic redistribution. The external event – in particular, the oil price rise and subsequent availability of cheap international credit – facilitated these policy objectives by making it possible for policymakers to generate resources (export revenues and official loans) that could be used to sustain the economy as private investment lagged. The external event did not cause these domestic policy changes. However these policy changes did have "openness" effects, causing official policy on average to be less open to flows of direct foreign investment.

Second oil shock and debt crisis, 1979–83

Impact The second oil "shock" is a misnomer in the Malaysian case. While most developing-country decision-makers – including those in neighboring Thailand and the Philippines – found their policy choices narrowed by international economic developments stemming from the fall of the Shah of Iran in 1979, for Malaysia, now a substantial, non-OPEC oil and gas producer, the event was one of increased opportunity.[72] In the early 1980s, buoyed by increased government revenues from oil exports, the Malaysian government undertook a large-scale program of state-led industrial deepening.

The second round of rapid oil price increases brought not a shock but windfall trade and revenue gains to the Malaysian economy. The terms of trade improved, averaging 15 percent growth in real terms in 1979 and 1980 (before falling slightly in 1981 and sharply in 1982, as oil prices sank from their earlier peak). Partly as a result, the value of merchandise exports grew by 50 percent in 1979 alone[73] and foreign trade became more important to the economy. Whereas total merchandise trade was the equivalent of 81 percent of GDP in 1978, by 1983 it stood at more that 90 percent.[74]

The oil price rise increased the value of resources that were scarce internationally, but relatively abundant in Malaysia, and the principal Malaysian beneficiaries were those controlling oil and gas resources. Petronas, the state oil company, owned all production from Malaysia, allocating production shares to international oil companies that did the exploration and extraction. Therefore the government was able to capture most of the windfall gains, affording policymakers a wider palette of potential policy options in the economy as a whole. Windfall gains made possible a turn toward state-managed, import-substituting, capital-intensive, industrial projects, modeled superficially on the Korean heavy and chemical industries policy of the early 1970s.

Policy record Minister of Trade and Industry Dr. Mahathir Mohamad[75] announced in November 1980 a policy initiative which the government claimed would:

> reduc[e] the [country's] dependence on foreign countries for the supply of machinery and intermediate inputs, exploit[] forward and backward linkages in industrial development, creat[e] spin-off effects for the growth of small and medium-scale industries, and develop[] the technological capability of the manufacturing sector.[76]

The heavy industries policy aimed to create a stratum of "second-stage" (capital-intensive), import-substituting industries. State-run enterprises were placed in the vanguard of a state-led industrial deepening effort to provide the underpinnings for new private sector intermediate and consumer goods industries.[77]

The policy's centerpiece was the state-owned Heavy Industries Corporation of Malaysia (HICOM), chartered "to plan, identify, initiate, invest [in], implement and manage projects in the field of heavy industries."[78] HICOM developed a series of joint-ventures with foreign partners in iron and steel, automobiles, cement, and small internal combustion engines, with the support of state development expenditures in the first five years (1981–86) estimated at between 6 and 8 billion Malaysian dollars, or the equivalent of the allocation for all social programs (which totaled M$6.4 billion).[79] In autos, Malaysia's "national car," the Proton Saga, was heavily promoted as an example of what Malaysians could achieve in the industrial realm, given state leadership and foreign technology (in this case, that of Mitsubishi). On the East Coast, natural gas reserves discovered in the early 1970s were tapped to fire a M$1.2 billion iron and steel plant, completed in 1985.[80] HICOM commissioned a major new cement plant on an island off the West Coast state of Kedah. And in small (up to 200 c.c.) engine manufacture, HICOM undertook ventures with partners Honda, Suzuki, and Yamaha, each involving a 30 percent HICOM share in investments in the M$8–10 million range.[81] The heavy industries policy also incorporated a number of energy refining and utilizing projects, including Petronas production facilities for the processing and export of natural gas.[82]

Explaining policy choices Economic policies adopted by Malaysian decisionmakers during the period dominated by the second oil shock and the debt crisis of the early 1980s were conditioned by earlier policy choices. The first event – the oil price rise of 1974–75 – brought windfall gains that the government used to develop infrastructure and to foster public agencies to act as proxies for the Malay community.

In part because of these policy choices – and in part because of improving prices for other commodity exports in the late 1970s – economic conditions on the eve of the second oil price hike were already auspicious for Malaysian growth in the early 1980s. Despite the slump in economic growth and investment in the mid-1970s, Malaysia recorded average real annual GDP growth of 7.9 percent over the decade of the 1970s, the highest among the ASEAN Four.[83] Malaysia's manufacturing sector had grown significantly faster (admittedly from a low base), averaging 12.4 percent annual growth, or about the same as for Indonesia and slightly better than for Thailand (11.4 percent).[84]

By 1979, the share of Malaysian manufacturing in GDP had nearly doubled (from 9 percent in 1960 to 16 percent), while industry as a whole accounted for 33 percent of GDP (up from 18 percent in 1960).[85] Against the backdrop of a generally robust domestic economy, the 1979 revenue windfall provided Malaysian decision-makers the means with which to pursue the next stage of the economic redistribution agenda that had been initiated a decade before.

The heavy industries policy was not an offshoot of the second oil shock. It owed its parentage to Mahathir, who became trade and industry minister in 1978, and its conception, stimulated by the economic recovery in the late 1970s, predated the oil price rise by at least a year. On the other hand, the windfall gains from oil revenues afforded Mahathir the luxury of structuring the leap into heavy industries with minimal attention to cost-effectiveness. The oil shock provided Malay leaders like Mahathir a window of opportunity to focus on non-economic goals, giving priority to redistribution of wealth and ownership.

The redistributive agenda of the NEP had not been completed by the end of the 1970s, although considerable progress had been registered. Malay economic aspirations were on the rise, stimulated in part by the very success of state investment agencies like Perbadanan National (National Corporation, or Pernas) in accumulating enormous amounts of savings very rapidly. State regulation of business hiring and the distribution of shareholding to give Malays more economic power appeared inadequate to satisfy these aspirations. Even though forced to comply with the provisions of the Industrial Coordination Act, Chinese and Indian business appeared able to circumvent Malay demands for a "fair" share of the country's economic wealth. Foreign-owned business, while contributing to industrial expansion in general, also seemed to offer comparatively little to the Malay community. Foreign firms in free trade zones, for example, absorbed only limited quantities of local materials – in general, less than 5 percent of value added – and established few linkages with the local economy, beyond employment of low-skilled labor.[86]

Mahathir, in announcing the new policy, pointed to the Japanese "economic miracle" and the achievements of South Korea, and argued that Malaysia ought to follow their lead. But Mahathir's perception of Malaysia's earlier experience of industrialization was central to the form the new strategy took. He was convinced that domestic business was unable (or unwilling) to undertake large-scale projects with heavy capital requirements and long gestation periods. With high regard for the capabilities of state-led enterprises and suspicious of private sector industrial abilities, Mahathir embraced elements of the South Korean import-substituting, export-promoting "model." South Korea appealed perhaps not simply because of its industrial record but also because it was the only NIE whose people were not ethnically Chinese. Championing a non-Chinese exemplar thus enabled Mahathir to embrace a NIE "model" while avoiding the charge that he was perpetuating the unacceptable (for many Malays) domestic economic dominance of the Malaysian Chinese.[87] Moreover, the state-led character of Korean industrial "deepening" was attractive because it suggested a leading role in the Malaysian case for officialdom, which was predominantly Malay.

There were also political considerations at work. As one senior official observed, "The projects we're going into aren't purely economic projects. They have quasi-political, economic and strategic considerations."[88] Under pressure from some sections of the Malay community to more aggressively pursue NEP goals using direct state action, Mahathir and the UMNO leadership found in the heavy industries policy an attractive vehicle with which to hasten the redistribution of economic power as envisioned under the NEP. The scale of the heavy industries projects also reflected ethnic political considerations. Existing small- and medium-scale domestic industry was primarily in the hands of Chinese business and it made little sense politically to favor them when the Malay community was already anxious about how little ground it was gaining on the non-Malays.[89]

In summary, the heavy industries initiative, the principal economic policy change that paralleled our second external event, had three main causes. It was conceived before the external event as a vehicle for launching Malaysia as a newly industrializing country and satisfying rising Malay economic aspirations. Thus it was meant simultaneously to achieve an economic goal, of forcing the pace of industrialization, and a social and political one, of improving the economic position of Malays relative to non-Malays. Ultimately, the particular form that the initiative took (the government as majority stockholder, with government officials as managers), the comparatively large scale of the undertakings, and the government's ability to launch them, relied upon a third causal factor: they were all made possible by the revenue windfall associated with the second oil shock.

The heavy industries policy led Malaysia's economy to be less open to flows of goods and services. The protective barriers (tariffs and non-tariff barriers) thrown up around the new industries reduced the flow of less expensive foreign cars and steel, for example, while increasing domestic prices for such items. Costs of production for exporting manufacturing industries went up and exports declined, encouraged by recessionary conditions in the United States. There were foreign partners in each of the HICOM projects, but the government provided the lion's share of the capital, and the increased costs imposed on other industries by inflated prices for cars and steel products discouraged new foreign investment in those industries.

In short, our second event, by generating windfall revenue gains for the government, contributed to a new direction in policy, although the principal motivation for this new direction lay elsewhere, in a domestic political agenda. The policy initiative did have implications for the relative openness of the Malaysian economy. The heavy industries policy represented "second-stage" (capital-intensive), import-substituting industrialization.[90] While the Malaysian economy remained relatively open by most developing-country standards (see table 1.6), the policy change was toward a less, not more, open economy in the early 1980s.

Commodity shock, 1984–86

Impact The resource-abundant Malaysian economy, having weathered the two oil shocks relatively unscathed, suffered greatly from the mid-1980s commodity shock. The adverse effect on economic growth of slumping prices across the board for the commodities Malaysia produced in abundance, such as rubber, tin, and palm oil, was compounded in Malaysia's case by a rapid decline in oil prices in 1986. Rubber lost about one-quarter of its value between 1983 and 1985, and its price remained low in 1986, with recovery beginning only in 1987. The price of tin dropped between 40 and 55 percent (depending on the grade) between 1984 and 1986. Palm oil lost nearly two-thirds of its value between 1984 and 1986.[91] The index of Malaysia's export prices declined by 28 percent between 1984 and 1986. As a result, Malaysia's real terms of trade recorded an average annual decline of 15 percent in 1985 and 1986.[92] The value of merchandise exports fell by 17 percent between 1984 and 1986 and trade as a proportion of GDP fell from 90 percent in 1984 to 88.6 percent in 1986.[93] With trade as such an important component of the economy (more than twice as important as in any of the other ASEAN Four), these trade effects inevitably affected economic growth. Real GDP declined for the first time in over a decade, registering a 1 percent fall in 1985, and GNP per capita fell 1.5 percent in 1985 and 1986.[94] This real contraction in the economy caused government revenues (including tax revenues and revenues from exports such as oil) to decline. The government budget balance went from nearly M$3 billion in surplus in 1985 to a barely positive balance of M$14 million in 1986. Policymakers increased foreign borrowing and cumulative external debt grew by 8 percent in 1986, reaching a peak of US$23 billion in 1987 before dropping back to US$18.5 billion the following year.[95]

These broad macroeconomic developments caused particular problems for some sectors and industries. None was more vulnerable than the state's new heavy industries. The timing of the commodity shock could hardly have been worse for them. Just as they brought their first products (cars, steel, etc.) to market, demand fell. As a result, with virtually every major HICOM unit in the red, from its auto-making division (Proton), to its steel subsidiary (Perwaja Trengganu), and its cement operation (Kedah Cement), the corporation suffered operating losses for the 1986/87 year of M$249.6 million (US$100 million) – an increase of 71 percent over the previous year – and after-tax losses of M$117.8 million (US$47.3 million).[96] Beside these losses, there were also drains on state coffers associated with extensive foreign loans incurred by these state enterprises. At the end of 1988, federal government liabilities stood at M$5.5 billion (US$2.2 billion), of which two-thirds, or M$3.7 billion (US$1.5 billion), took the form of contingent liabilities stemming from government-backed foreign loans. Thirty-seven percent, or M$15.3 (US$6.1) billion of the total public sector debt of M$41.6 (US$16.7) billion, was attributable to these public enterprise loans.[97] The mid-1980s commodity shock represented the most severe economic setback for Malaysia since independence.

The commodity shock also had political ramifications. The sinking economy emboldened those among UMNO's leaders who sought to curtail Mahathir's dominance. Tengku Razaleigh and Musa Hitam launched a challenge to Mahathir's presidency at the 1987 party convention that came very close to unseating him. The commodity shock also weakened the non-Malay political parties in the governing coalition. The collapse of large Chinese conglomerates such as Promet, whose principals were important sources of political support for UMNO's largest partner party, the MCA, and the demise of Multi-Purpose Holdings, which had been nurtured as the corporate arm of the MCA, undermined the financial foundations of the MCA. This, and similar developments at the Malaysian Indian Congress (MIC), encouraged UMNO to look elsewhere for electoral funds and thus to become less reliant on the MCA and MIC to sustain its three-decade-long monopoly on power. This accelerated the decline in influence of non-Malay business on economic policy.

Policy record For a decade and a half, economic policy had been oriented towards a domestic political agenda and had been increasingly state-centered. The mid-1980s commodity shock and the recession that Malaysia experienced in its wake precipitated a policy watershed. Between 1986 and 1988, Malaysian policymakers reduced the state's direct involvement in managing businesses and downplayed laws and regulations intended to further the political agenda of the NEP. They reemphasized industrial exports and strengthened incentives to attract foreign investors to locate export industries in Malaysia. Economic policy in the wake of the commodity shock thus became much more open to inflows of foreign investment capital and to flows of goods and services.

The most obvious change was in government policy toward the heavy industries. To prevent their dragging down the economy as a whole, the government abandoned its eight-year commitment to the vanguard role of state (and Malay) management of the heavy industries. Cabinet ministers, including Mahathir himself, citing heavy losses and mismanagement, argued that the appropriate criteria for success of the heavy industries were competitiveness, profitability, and exports.[98] Malay civil servant managers were replaced by private sector managers, in most cases executives of foreign joint-venture partners, and almost without exception non-Malay, something quite unthinkable in the early days of the NEP.[99] Malay managers of the major HICOM subsidiaries quickly found themselves supplanted by non-Malays, including foreigners.

At the same time, faced with a contracting domestic market, HICOM became more oriented to exporting its products to foreign markets. HICOM's prestige projects, while still enjoying tariff protection, no longer produced only import substitutes. Proton began aggressively to seek export markets. After 1987, HICOM experienced a modest revival in sales and profits. Proton, for example, nearly quadrupled its production rate, from around 24,000 autos in 1988 to 88,000 in 1991, increased its capacity to 100,000 units, captured domestic market share (autos of under 1600 c.c.) of 72 percent, and increased its annual exports, from about 3,000 units in 1989 to 34,000 units in 1991.

A further change in policy was never announced. UMNO leaders, as they turned away from state-run companies and offered more contracts to the private sector, favored companies linked to the party through nominee owners. While more government projects were offered to private sector firms, the contracts were often no-bid contracts, and the winners of the contracts were often UMNO-linked. Privatization and the reduced state role appeared to open up government contract opportunities for foreign investors. But, with the opaque character of the process by which contracts were allocated, such opportunities were often illusory. In fact this policy change represented a turn toward less openness to international capital flows (foreign investors typically are wary of "smoky, back-room, deals" and clientelistic relations as the principal basis for allocation of government contracts).

Nevertheless, in other areas, policymakers sought to remove the disincentives to potential foreign investment that emerged in the 1970s and were associated with the redistributive agenda of the NEP and the ICA. The government amended the ICA in October 1986 to apply only to investments of roughly US$1 million or more (the threshold was previously less than US$400,000) or to plants employing seventy-five or more full-time workers.[100] The amendment also eased domestic equity requirements and limitations on the number of expatriate employees that could be hired by foreign companies seeking manufacturing licenses. Foreign investors could own 100 percent of new projects that exported most of their production or sold it to factories in free trade zones that did, and that employed at least 350 full-time Malaysian workers.[101] Moreover, the Promotion of Investments Act (1986) strengthened incentives available to foreign investors.[102]

In summary, the policy changes that accompanied the commodity shock had a long "tail," extending beyond 1986 to at least 1988, and were in general designed to enhance the openness of the economy to flows of goods and services (they placed greater emphasis on exports) and to increase the attractiveness of Malaysia to private sector investors, including those from abroad. However, some of the policy practices, such as that which became more prevalent following the party elections of 1987 of allocating an increasing share of government contracts to UMNO-linked companies, had the effect of discouraging the inflow of private direct investment.

Explaining policy choices The mid-1980s commodity shock challenged the emphasis of earlier policies on distribution rather than growth, and on the primacy of state-led rather than private sector initiated industrialization. When the economy contracted in 1985, it threatened the "expanding pie" which policymakers considered essential if redistribution of income and wealth was to proceed without pain to any community. It also threatened the domestic markets upon which the import-substituting state-run heavy industries depended.

The commodity shock constrained the government's ability to use economic policy to pursue social and economic goals simultaneously. The "fat" of the late 1970s – the product of windfall revenues from oil and gas – which had provided the spare resources for the heavy industries initiative, no longer existed. The changes seen at HICOM reflected the economic imperative imposed by external events. Economically, they marked a new government emphasis on market signals and the profit criterion for evaluating state enterprise performance. No longer were projects undertaken that could not be justified by strictly economic criteria. The government passed management control – if not equity control – of state industries to foreigners, and non-Malays if necessary, to ensure the profitability of potentially embarrassing white elephants.[103]

A political disjuncture in the late 1980s helps to explain the policy response. This was the unprecedented rift that emerged in Malay politics in 1987 leading to a political challenge to Mahathir's leadership within the dominant party, UMNO, in the 1987 party elections, and to Mahathir's bare survival as party president and prime minister, posts he had held since 1981.[104]

In the end, Mahathir survived the challenge. Intraparty splits, and the resulting political vulnerability felt by Mahathir and the surviving UMNO leadership, precipitated subsequent efforts to still extraparty opposition by imposing exclusionary politics at the national level. In October 1987, Mahathir resurrected the draconian Internal Security Act (ISA) – a vestige of British efforts to suppress communist insurgence in the 1950s – and imprisoned more than a hundred opponents without trial. The government justified the clampdown by alluding to the May 1969 ethnic riots and emphasizing the importance of political stability to avert capital flight.[105] But it seems clear that the arrests were part of Mahathir's political offensive against opponents to his leadership both inside and outside UMNO.

Subsequently, the government amended the ISA in 1989 to eliminate judicial review of ISA detentions. This was followed by measures which precluded judicial review of executive decisions governing the administration and running of political parties.[106] The sharp political disjuncture represented by the intraparty challenge to Mahathir's rule, itself precipitated by the external event, was important for policy because it represented a defeat for the traditional roots of the party that lay in rural areas. The reformulated UMNO (UMNO *baru*, or "new" UMNO) that emerged following the challenge to Mahathir, drew upon the rising Malay business community for funds to contest the 1990 general election. Traditional local party leaders in rural districts, especially village headmen and teachers, became less important, as "money politics" took over. This support from Malay business interests required a payback, and this took the form of preferential access to government contracts and first options on privatizations of government services. The Malay business support for Mahathir demonstrated that the NEP and state-led industrialization had indeed made progress in nurturing a Malay business class. It also suggested that economic policies designed to create proxies for the Malay community, such as state-led industrialization efforts, were no longer necessary.

So policy changed in the wake of the commodity shock, away from state-led development and in the direction of greater emphasis on the private sector. This presented greater opportunities for foreign investors, in partnership with politically connected Malay entrepreneurs, to invest in privatized contracts and offerings (e.g., formerly state-owned utilities, maintenance facilities, etc.). It had the effect of making the economy more open to the inflow of foreign capital.

The above-mentioned political disjuncture accentuated the declining political importance of the Chinese business community. While still dominant in locally owned business, the Chinese, who had once been virtually the sole source of election financing for the governing coalition, no longer held the power of the purse strings over UMNO. This was apparent in the 1987 UMNO party elections, which were clearly much more important to Mahathir and his supporters than the general elections, and in which the financial support came largely from the Malay business community.

The rapid proliferation of companies owned by, controlled by, or in some other way related to the ruling party has freed UMNO from its long-standing dependence on the MCA for electoral campaign financing and thereby weakened ties that bind the coalition parties together.[107] Moreover, as UMNO-linked companies have grown stronger, strain between the two ethnic elites has risen to levels unprecedented since the informal "settlement" of the ethnic question in 1957.[108] The Malay elite's coming to full financial maturity, after decades of subservient status, has in effect led to a *de facto* recasting of the relationship between the communal elites. The non-Malay political elites have been marginalized as the balance of both political and economic power now rests with the Malay elite, and this, in turn, has encouraged representation of non-Malay business interests directly to Malay government leaders, thereby bypassing the increasingly irrelevant Chinese and Indian political parties. Consequently, as non-Malay business has withheld real support from the MCA and the MIC, these parties have lapsed into quarrelsome infighting, prompting UMNO leaders sometimes to step in, if only to ensure that the illusion of a multi-ethnic coalition government is perpetuated.[109]

While the 1987 political disjuncture led to greater openness in economic policy – in terms of making greater opportunities available for foreign investors – it also accentuated clientelistic relations between political leaders and business, making the process of allocating government contracts more opaque and therefore less open to foreign investors. In other words, there were more opportunities, but these were less transparently allocated, thus placing a premium on client-like ties linking businessmen with leading Malay patrons associated with the now long-lived Mahathir administration. In the past, such relations were subsidiary to the representation of business interests through the coalition partner parties, the MCA and the MIC. Today, however, direct personal access is perceived to be a *sine qua non* for obtaining lucrative partnerships in privatized government operations and infrastructural projects. The existence of these personal ties indicates that policymakers in Malaysia are by no means completely insulated from policy pressures from business. Business, however, is clearly the client in this hierarchical structure; the Malay political elite controlling the state apparatus holds most of the cards. Meanwhile, the relative influence of technocrats within the civil service has declined, as policy has become more politicized with the political ramifications of the economic downturn.

The result has been a corporate empire blessed with unrestricted access to state-issued licenses and Malay preferences that is under the direct control of the governing party, UMNO, and is used to raise funds for constituent and electoral purposes.[110] Government leaders have used Malay preferences from the NEP to justify the awarding of contracts to UMNO-linked enterprises and individuals, creating in the process a large and influential group of domestic, *bumiputra* companies that are the vehicles for ensuring continued UMNO political dominance.

Summarizing the effect of the political disjuncture represented by the 1987 leadership challenge on economic policy: it encouraged policy to be more open to foreign investment because it downplayed the importance of state-led enterprises (now potentially "white elephants," and superfluous, since Malay entrepreneurship had already been jump-started); and it improved opportunities for foreign investors. There were now more contracts, and more potential joint-venture partners in the form of Malay business players. But it also made the actual allocation of government contracts and privatized opportunities more political, reduced the policy influence of technocrats in the civil service, and accentuated the importance of clientelistic ties to UMNO leaders. The overall effect was thus greater openness, but with the caveat that foreign investors had to work much harder to develop personal relations that would lead ultimately to business opportunities.

International finance changes course, 1987–

Impact Malaysia was well positioned to capitalize on the flow of investment from Northeast to Southeast Asia that began in the late 1980s. As international currencies realigned and the costs of production in Japan, Taiwan, and South Korea escalated, investors in these countries relocated production of manufactured exports to Southeast Asia. In fact, the realignment of global currencies, beginning in the mid-1980s with the depreciation of the US dollar against the Japanese yen, contributed to a change in international capital flows favoring

Southeast Asia whose beginnings can be traced to even before 1985. Then, pressures we usually associate with the product cycle led to increased Japanese and East Asian investment interest in export-oriented industries in Southeast Asia. Land- and labor-intensive (and often polluting) industries with lower technology content moved from the industrialized economies of Japan and East Asia to the neighboring region where land and labor were relatively abundant, leaving newer, higher technology products to be manufactured in Japan or East Asia.

Malaysia was attractive as an investment site, for electrical and electronics industries in particular, because of its relatively well-developed infrastructure, relatively educated workforce, and already established electronics plants (for example, those of Motorola, National Semiconductor, and Matsushita). In addition, despite UMNO's internal upheavals, Malaysia was considered a low political risk investment site (especially when compared with the Philippines, for example). The flow of net long-term direct investment into Malaysia grew from less than half a billion dollars in 1986 and 1987 to $1.7 billion in 1989, and $2.3 billion in 1990.[111]

The currency realignment and product cycle effects represented both opportunity and constraint for Malaysian decision-makers. In the short run, yen appreciation increased the already heavy debt burden of state-owned enterprises, since much of this debt was denominated in yen. Total long-term debt reached a peak of $20.5 billion in 1987 (before falling off to $17 billion in 1988 and $14 billion in 1989). The proportion of such debt accounted for by public enterprises such as HICOM, which had stood at 12 percent in 1977, grew to a peak of over one-fifth of total long-term debt in 1987.[112] Thus, with 1985–87 declines against the yen of 40 percent in the case of the Malaysian dollar, the debt situation of these enterprises worsened precipitously, coinciding with a downturn in their sales and contributing to the reevaluation of their economic roles discussed in relation to the previous event.[113]

The trend towards the integration of the Japanese and East Asian economies with the economies of the Southeast Asian region accelerated in the early to mid-1990s, especially as yen appreciation continued (peaking at less than 80 yen to the US dollar in 1995). As a Sanyo Electric vice-chairman observed, "Japanese industry can no longer afford to stay in Japan. We have to escape from Japan . . . at this rate, only our head office will be left in Japan."[114]

Malaysia felt the impact of these changes in the flow of international capital as a windfall direct investment gain. By the early 1990s, the flow of net long-term direct investment had become a virtual torrent; the net inflow in 1992 alone amounted to $4.5 billion.[115] And companies like Hitachi and Matsushita, which previously had moved offshore only low value-added products (while reserving product design and higher value-added production for their Japanese production sites), now began moving higher value-added production, for example of computer peripherals such as disk drives, as well as increasingly sophisticated research and development to Malaysia to take advantage of lower costs there.

This change in international capital flows contributed to a period of unprecedented economic growth in Malaysia; for eight years, beginning in 1988, real GDP growth averaged over 8 percent annually.[116] The value of exports of goods and services grew in the early 1990s (1990–93) at an average rate of 17 percent annually.[117]

Policy record Had Malaysian policymakers not responded to the investment windfall, the economy would still have become more open. However, the policy record through the mid-1990s suggests that policy did indeed respond to the external event, in particular because of official policymakers' perceptions that Malaysia needed to compete with the increasingly attractive incentive packages offered Northeast Asian investors by neighboring countries such as Thailand. In contrast to the policy response to the windfall of the second oil shock, a decade before, which focused on state-led, import-substituting industrialization serving social redistributive goals, the policy response in this case emphasized markets and privatization, and the result was an economy more open to the flow of goods and services and to the inflow of investment capital.

The government cashed in on its sunk investment in the heavy industries by privatizing part of its 70 percent stake in the auto-making subsidiary Proton.[118] Government policy focused on encouraging private sector industry, and sought foreign participation in particular as a means to expand capital- and technology-intensive industries and increase manufactured exports.

To attract foreign investors, the government adopted laws to limit the ability of national labor unions to press for higher wages and improved employee working conditions. With increasing numbers of Japanese companies investing in Malaysia in the late 1980s, the government moved to overhaul Malaysian labor laws to encourage Japanese-style enterprise unions and weaken existing large national unions.[119] Existing national unions were forced to bow to enterprise unions in industries where they competed for members.[120]

The government also relaxed conditions for foreign investors by further raising the threshold above which Malay equity and employment requirements were of concern in granting licenses. This more liberal treatment of the redistributive requirements of the Industrial Coordination Act – in keeping with the adoption of the National Development Policy (NDP), which abandoned the prescriptive, ethnic-based targets of the NEP (1970–90) which it superseded – had begun earlier in response to the commodity shock. The government also expanded provision of short-term export credits to enhance the international competitiveness of export products manufactured in Malaysia.[121] Tax rates on corporate profits were lowered in 1989 (the highest reduced from 40 percent to 35 percent) and a 5 percent development tax on company profits was rescinded. In regard to trade openness, the government in 1990 reduced tariffs across the board, with especially large reductions in tariffs on business equipment to reduce the high cost of inputs associated with protected domestic manufacturers.[122]

Explaining policy choices Several factors contributed to the Malaysian policy response to our fourth external event that favored economic openness, exports, and more foreign investment. First was path-dependence – policy choices made in the mid-1980s in response to the commodity shock set the course for the policy response to the later event. For example, reduced emphasis on the numerical targets of the Industrial Coordination Act, and on ethnic quotas in general, began in 1986 when the economy was reeling under the effects of significantly reduced commodity prices and a pronounced fall in revenues from Malaysia's oil exports. This departure from the social redistributive agenda of the 1970s accelerated in the late 1980s. Foreign investors found the incentives and conditions they faced in Malaysia converging with those of neighbors Indonesia and Thailand (specifically, ethnic requirements became less important for investment approvals).

Faced with a windfall of foreign investment flows from Northeast Asia, Malaysian officials opted to emphasize the private sector role, in contrast to policies in the late 1970s. The record of success with Malay entrepreneurship raised the prospect of achieving by private means what state officials in the early 1980s felt was only possible by public means, namely establishing a stratum of Malay entrepreneurs capable of competing at the highest levels with Malaysian Chinese and Indian magnates. Government leaders by the early 1990s embraced economic openness as the best avenue for improving opportunities for Malays, and foreign investment as the best vehicle by which to improve the technological sophistication of the Malaysian economy.

A reemphasis on the private sector[123] was feasible politically, because the principal beneficiaries were foreigners and members of an expanding, Malay business elite with symbiotic ties to leaders within UMNO. For foreigners to benefit was no liability for an UMNO leadership whose nationalist rhetoric historically had tended to the ethnic rather than the xenophobic. Likewise, that rising Malays and UMNO-controlled companies benefited was non-problematic politically because it bolstered the party's financial security and thus its political future while advancing the long-standing NEP goal of nurturing a Malay commercial and managerial class.

Political developments were not primary causes of the policy changes described in the previous subsection. After weathering the 1987 challenge to his leadership of UMNO and the 1990 election challenge to the National Front coalition, Mahathir's political dominance within the party and the government was virtually unassailable.

The final section of this chapter reviews the policy record associated with each of our four external events and draws conclusions about the relevance to this policy record of the five broad sets of variables set out in chapter 1.

Conclusion

The most significant findings presented here for Malaysia are that economic policy responded fully to external economic changes in the direction of increased economic openness for two of the four events and responded partially for the other two. Political disjunctures in 1969 and 1978 were critical in shaping subsequent policy responses to external events (hypothesis H3b).

For most of our external events, the variables we laid out in chapter 1 showed no change, or changed for reasons unrelated to the external events, and therefore cannot be part of any explanation for how or why policy changed the way it did in response to the external event. And not infrequently, the major economic policy initiatives that paralleled an external event were motivated entirely by domestic considerations. Nevertheless, the findings for Malaysia substantially support our initial assertion that the countries of this study have tended to respond to changes in their external economic environments with policies that favor greater integration into the international economy, rather than with those that tend to close their economies off to flows of goods and services and capital.

The main policy initiatives observed around the first external event, the first oil shock, were (with a single notable exception) not responses to that event. The adoption of the Industrial Coordination Act and the promotion of statutory bodies as proxies for Malay entrepreneurs were both intended to advance the domestic redistributive agenda that emerged with the NEP. It would have been impossible to sustain them, however, were it not for the government's increased foreign borrowing and incentives offered to foreign investors, which were in turn responses to the investment slump that the ICA had precipitated. Although the latter of these measures contributed to greater policy openness (to foreign loan and investment capital), together these policy changes resulted in a significantly less open economy. And they were ultimately all linked to the political disjuncture represented by the ethnic riots of 1969 and the adoption of the NEP. Nevertheless, the important thing to note about these policies is that they were not responses to the external event, and therefore explaining their character is a moot point.

The main policy initiative taken in the wake of the second external event, the second oil "shock," was Prime Minister Mahathir's embracing of the heavy industries policy and championing of state-led, Malay-run capital-intensive industries. The trade protections and high costs associated with these undertakings rendered the economy significantly less open to the international economy. However, as with most of the policy initiatives reported for the first event, this policy change was not a response to the external event. It represented instead a continuation of the domestic policy agenda to advance Malay entrepreneurship. The windfall gains from the second oil shock, however, enabled policymakers to sustain the high levels of capital investment needed to bring these industries into production. The heavy industries initiative was associated with a reduction in the relative policy influence of technocrats within the official bureaucracy.

The commodity shock of the mid-1980s was associated with an economic downturn that in turn led to three policy responses. The state reduced its direct involvement in the economy, offered incentives to try to win back foreign investors, and tried to reorient the state-run import-substituting industries toward exports. All of these policy responses increased the openness of the economy. The choice of these responses was influenced by the demonstration effects of neighbors Singapore, Indonesia, and Thailand pursuing exports and foreign investors using liberalizing reforms. The reduction in the state's role was also influenced by the political disjuncture of the leadership challenge to Mahathir in the UMNO 1987 party elections. This challenge, while ultimately unsuccessful, encouraged Mahathir to view the Malay entrepreneurial elite as capable of prospering outside the cocoon of state enterprises. It also precipitated a change in the governing coalition, reducing the influence of the Chinese minority in politics and rendering Malay business increasingly important as a source of political funds. Hence Mahathir and others, former champions of state-led industrialization, now embraced a market orientation because they felt the Malay entrepreneur could prosper.

One official practice that became increasingly common after the commodity shock was the favoring of "crony" and UMNO-linked companies with privatization opportunities and government contracts. This was again a product of the political upheaval and reflected a turn toward greater clientelism and a reduced policy role for technocrats. It amounted to a policy which, by its opaqueness, made the economy more closed to outside investors. However, this practice was only indirectly a response to the commodity shock, and was more directly relevant to the new political environment that followed 1987.

The final event we consider here, the changing flows of international capital, precipitated four policy responses, all of which left the economy more open. Government officials undertook broad liberalization measures in the domestic economy, including an increased program of privatization; they lessened the restrictions included in the ICA; they offered more extensive export incentives for foreign investors; and they reduced obstacles to imports by reducing tariff levels across the board.

We identify path-dependence as a factor contributing to these policies (their shape was influenced by policies undertaken after the earlier external event, the commodity shock). The liberalizing measures and the rollback of ICA conditions also reflect the influence of the 1987 political disjuncture, the change in the character of the governing coalition, and the tendency toward increased clientelism (which meant that Malays could benefit from political connections even in a liberalized economy).

In conclusion, the policy changes adopted in the wake of each of the four external events varied, both in terms of the extent to which they were indeed responses to the event – in the case of the first two events, most were not, while in the case of the third and fourth, most were – and in terms of the variables that best explain the character of the policy response. The variables that appear most regularly in explanations of policy responses in the Malaysian case are path-dependence and political disjunctures, which changed the perceptions of policymakers.

CHAPTER FIVE

The Philippines

The Philippines has been the East Asian capitalist laggard. Its economic performance after the 1950s, and particularly after the early 1980s, was consistently less impressive than that of the other commodity-rich economies of
Southeast Asia. The country squandered an early head-start in its industrialization and, beginning in the 1960s, steadily lost ground relative to other East
Asian developing countries. Yet, neither in the late 1940s nor in the early 1970s
did observers expect the Philippines to fare less well economically than other
regional economies. Its inferior performance resulted in considerable part from
public policies, including ones that limited the economy's openness, that were
motivated largely by distributional concerns and had the effect of retarding economic efficiency. In no other case considered in this book was the disjuncture
between the interests of the dominant few and the policy requirements of sustained economic growth so sharp.

From 1950 to 1965, the Philippine government, a fairly stable democracy
with regular alteration of parties in office, had controlled the Huk rural insurgency while keeping military spending at modest levels. Until the late 1950s, the
country had one of the highest rates of economic growth in East Asia. In 1965,
President Ferdinand Marcos, a gifted politician and lawyer, came to office
apparently determined to overcome those obstacles that had begun to hinder
Philippine economic growth in the late 1950s and to launch an economic take-
off. He appeared to some to be Manila's Park Chung Hee (the South Korean
president who helped to launch his country's rapid growth in the early 1980s).

Neither changes in leadership nor in regime type, however, fundamentally
altered the Philippines' course. Under the martial law declared in 1972, Marcos
enhanced the role of technocrats in policymaking, reduced street crime,
improved revenue collection, rationalized the bureaucracy, upgraded infrastructure, attracted foreign capital, weakened the rural oligarchs who constituted the traditional Filipino elite, and aimed to create strong domestic firms.

Manila became cleaner and more attractive and, for a time, Marcos enjoyed strong and widespread support.[1] And yet, as Gary Hawes notes, in spite of resource wealth, foreign aid and investment, and strong political leadership, the Philippines slipped behind other economies in the region.[2] Whether under democratic or authoritarian regimes, particular characteristics of Philippine economy and society persisted in producing poor economic results after the 1950s. And the economy's openness to trade rose little over the 1970s and the first half of the 1980s (see table 1.6).

Philippine manufacturing, much of it developed under an inadvertent import-substituting industrialization regime that later became firmly entrenched, was uncompetitive and unable to generate jobs or foreign exchange. Rigidities in the economy proved too great to overcome a series of external shocks.[3] Looking at investment capital output ratios (a crude index of efficiency that measures the amount of capital input necessary to yield a given marginal output) between 1964 and 1982, Shinichi Ichimura found a significantly higher value (lower efficiency) for the Philippines than for the other countries in our study (Indonesia 3.2, Malaysia 3.4, Thailand 3.5, the Philippines 4.0).[4] More disturbing was the rise in the Philippine index from 3.9 between 1965 and 1973 to 5.4 between 1974 and 1983.[5]

Especially important in explaining the Philippines' weakening economic performance was the role of the Filipino elite. The Philippine oligarchy stands out as Asia's oldest surviving dominant economic class, the only significant landlord class that survived into the postwar period, and a truly formidable and durable "distributional coalition."[6] Even under martial law and despite Marcos' determination to weaken the political power of opposition elites, he in fact was unable to move against those elites' interests. And Marcos failed to mobilize domestically the resources he needed to finance the ambitions he entertained for the country.

While Marcos failed to break the deeply entrenched structure of the Philippines' political economy, nonetheless he survived in office for over two decades. He did this with the help of foreign savings. External resources enhanced the powers of the state but, more crucially, made it possible for Marcos to continue in office without taking on directly the interests of the country's elite. One result of this dependence on foreign savings was rapidly growing foreign debt in the 1980s.

The Philippine state never enjoyed great autonomy from the Filipino socio-economic elite and, therefore, was rarely able to control it. Wolters argues that provincial elites stymied the emergence of a strong central state and state officials were unable to establish monopolies over violence and taxation.[7] In the Philippines, social elites used patron–client links to extract resources from the state.[8] State officials generally failed in their schemes to squeeze resources from society to finance their economic development plans.

The Philippine state was never able to wheedle significant levels of revenue from the elite. This inability limited the size of the state, produced chronic government deficits, and forced reliance on indirect taxation and foreign savings. Paul Hutchcroft describes as "booty capitalism"[9] the Philippine political structure in which the national elite uses the state to further its own interests.

Economic development requires an effective match between the domestic economy and policies, and the dominant features of the international political economy. The East Asian NIEs, for example, used open markets and US economic and military assistance to launch rapid economic growth in the 1960s. During the same period, however, rent-seeking behavior increasingly dominated the Philippines' economy. And the economy grew more closed, rather than more open. Two decades later, as Thailand adjusted in the early 1980s to the oil price shocks of the 1970s, the Philippine state's capacity to force necessary adjustments began to diminish. In the short term, adjustment was not necessary as the state had lavish access to external savings. However, by the time Indonesia, Malaysia, and Thailand were exploiting the regional economic conditions facilitating expansion of manufactured exports in the late 1980s, the Philippine economy had become so mired in debt that it could not sustain economic expansion. Similarly, in the 1990s, even with greatly increased economic openness, the lack of physical infrastructure, a legacy of years of constrained budgets, emerged as an important bottleneck for economic growth.

Until the mid-1980s, US support ensured that Marcos was able to fend off pressures for economic reform. This help included both payments for the use of military bases and other economic and military assistance. Indirectly, the United States also furthered the Philippines' cause by pressuring international financial institutions and Japan to extend assistance. As a result, not until the effects of the second round of oil price increases, tight money policies, and a strong dollar had ballooned the Philippine debt in the early 1980s, did the Philippine economy incur the full costs of the state's long failure to force economic adjustment.

In the following section, we describe briefly the nature of social organization in the Philippines, limitations on the state's capacity to extract resources from society or to force economic adjustment, and the nature of private sector links with the state. This discussion serves to illuminate the third section of this chapter in which we examine and try to understand Philippine responses to external constraints and opportunities.

Political regime

Social organization

Sugar was the main Philippine export by the nineteenth century, along with hemp and tobacco. The sugar industry boosted the fortunes of many immigrant Chinese and sugar exporters emerged as the first strong supporters of Philippine nationalism. Chinese and European immigrants, often of mixed blood, dominated this group. Without a "usable past," status in the Philippines tended to be defined largely in terms of wealth rather than according to traditional roles. As Steinberg notes, the mestizos consequently established a fluid social hierarchy based upon wealth and conspicuous consumption.[10]

Social fluidities produced in the Philippines a distinctive form of clientage, according to Lucian Pye. The Filipino elite, he suggests, constitutes "a dynamic society of people" among whom bonds of loyalty are transient. This fluid pattern contrasts with "a stable hierarchy of patrons" found in other societies marked by clientage networks rooted in traditional institutions. Leaders in the Philippines, Pye argues, lack those Confucian obligations that in other East Asian settings helped to constrain venality, foster institutionalized patterns of behavior, and encourage leaders to act benevolently.[11]

Filipinos launched their independence with economic, political, and social structures that differentiated them from other Asians. In particular, the Philippines retained a large landowner class and decentralized political power. Nowhere else in the region did a powerful landlord class survive well into the postwar period and only in the Philippines did the state remain weak, with political power diffused geographically among landed families. These features contributed to the oligarchy's persistent ability to resist land reform or property taxation, to the small size of government, and to the economy's vulnerability to political business cycles.[12]

Would-be reformers in Manila not only confronted entrenched oligarchic interests, but also had to contend with political institutions designed along US lines that were intended to curb state power. The strength of legal institutions designed to limit the arbitrary exercise of authority often worked against official efforts to reform the economy. In addition, beginning in the late 1950s and intensifying thereafter, populist currents also limited the executive's relative capacity to transform existing institutions.

Most observers long believed that significant economic restructuring would require a political leadership able to amass the unprecedented level of political power necessary to break the grip of the Philippines' estimated 400 leading families.[13] Marcos may have shared this view. He certainly managed to mobilize enormous resources by looting the economy after he neutralized his political opponents. Marcos, however, faced great obstacles in changing existing economic, social, and political structures: a populist political culture with the most educated population in Southeast Asia, an elite accustomed to democratic norms,[14] and the region's only surviving landed oligarchy. These traits continued to bedevil the reform initiatives of successive Filipino leaders.

Politics and the bases of state power

Following the Spanish–American War, the United States became the new colonial power in the Philippines in 1898. Under US control, the Philippines built on the Spanish legacy of an entrenched oligarchy, but a weak state.[15] The United States organized elections for local office as early as 1901, and the first national elections in 1907, and by 1916 Filipinos controlled the legislature.[16] Filipinos established the Nacionalista Party in 1907, the oldest in Southeast Asia.[17] At an early stage, US officials managed to coopt most of the Filipino elite. Elite Filipinos, generally from landed families and often trained in law, tried to serve their economic interests through careers in politics. In no other country in East or Southeast Asia was the draw of talent into the service of the state as weak. The Americans, in short, taught Filipinos the importance of electoral politics, but little about building an effective state apparatus.[18]

Colonial administrations spent comparatively little on either the bureaucracy or the army. A relatively large share of total government spending went to education and health. Congress passed the Payne–Aldrich Tariff Act and the Philippine Tariff Act in 1909, allowing US goods duty-free entry to the Philippines. Filipino goods also had duty-free access to the US market.[19]

The 1934 Tydings–McDuffie Act created a Philippine Commonwealth to last ten years beginning late in 1935 after which the Philippines would be independent. By 1935, all literate adult Filipinos had the right to vote.[20] Despite the emergence of a constitutionally strong presidency, an independent press and judiciary, and a relatively professional civil service that accepted subordination to political leadership,[21] the advent of democracy did not prevent the entrenchment of oligarchic rule. Democracy and mass education, more than in any other Asian colony, produced participatory popular politics behind which power-brokers continued to hold sway through networks of patron–client relations.[22]

During the Philippines' constitutional convention, Manuel Quezon pushed successfully for a strong presidency at the head of a unitary state. Legislators, therefore, had an interest in currying good relations with the president. Despite the constitutional powers of the presidency, however, the 24-member Senate and the 110-member House constituted one of the developing world's most powerful legislatures.[23] Hence, the president was far from omnipotent.

The executive branch as a whole did not attract the best and brightest Filipinos. After independence, the professionalism of the civil service diminished. In 1964, more than 80 percent of the membership of the national civil service had gained their jobs without competitive examinations, through recourse to "temporary" appointment. Most of these had solid educational backgrounds; indeed, the vast majority had college degrees.[24] Civil servants, however, were beholden to patrons outside the civil service who got them their jobs. These bureaucrats would be less apt to identify with the civil service and the state. As a result, they helped to ensure its susceptibility to control by powerful social groups.[25]

After independence, the Filipino state grew rapidly. Between 1930 and 1960 the bureaucracy increased in size more than tenfold; by the early 1990s it had expanded another 250 percent. The budget grew more than eightfold between 1930 and 1960, doubling again in the years to 1972. Yet over the 1970s, average government expenditure stood at little more than 13 percent of GDP,[26] and even by the mid-1990s, state expenditure accounted for well under one-fifth of gross domestic product.[27] The state's limited capacity to extract revenue from society curbed the former's growth and contributed to chronic public sector deficits.

Postwar Philippine elections built on unstable patronage networks. The need for access to the state treasury encouraged stiff political competition, party-switching and very costly elections.[28] Politicians used inflated promises to win elections marred by fraud. One observer of Elpidio Quirino's (Liberal Party) victory in the 1949 election noted the prevalence of electoral fraud, including the apparent ease with which the dead gained access to the voting booth.[29] Once in office, politicians often were unable to deliver on their promises and the disappointed legislators stood ready to defect from the winning party before the next election. The logic of minimum winning coalitions probably helped to sustain this dynamic as successful coalitions shed unnecessary allies in order to reduce the number of players among whom a finite public trough had to be apportioned.[30]

The suspension of democracy in 1972 did nothing to strengthen its institutions. Following Marcos' overthrow in 1986, Corazon Aquino's subsequent restoration of democracy, and Fidel V. Ramos' assumption of the presidency in 1992, many of these electoral and partisan patterns resurfaced. While Philippine democracy showed some evidence of stabilizing under President Ramos in the mid-1990s, party-switching remained common.[31] Politics continued to be characterized by a combination of populism and local elite domination. Despite the victories in Senate elections in May 1995 of several younger representatives of the managerial class over prominent politicians,[32] local notables continued to dominate in House and local elections. The state's ability to implement critical economic reforms remained in doubt.

Philippine politics, particularly since the late 1960s, have been marked by relatively sharp political polarization, considerable mass mobilization, and comparatively easy access to the political process. This picture emerges particularly clearly when the Philippines is contrasted with other polities in the East Asian region. And this political context helped to frustrate leaders' efforts to restructure the economy.

The Philippines under Marcos was an example of a "weak" authoritarian regime, distinguished both from East Asian developmental states and from Latin bureaucratic-authoritarian regimes. Weak authoritarian regimes are characterized by porous borders between public and private spheres; limited power accorded to technocrats; cronies linked to the executive who has a personal stake in their operations; and dependence on broad networks of instrumental, patron–client networks, particularly where electoral politics continue to play an important role as was true in the Philippines (as Marcos reopened politics after 1978, cronyism and patronage grew).[33] Furthermore, in the Philippines, no matter how much autonomy from groups outside and inside the state technocrats might achieve, they gained none *vis-à-vis* Marcos himself; hence, the economy's vulnerability to predation.[34]

Further impeding state efforts to forge effective political coalitions and guide economic restructuring, the legal system long ensured that privileged Filipinos had means of blunting state initiatives. In 1994, for example, the state faced severe budgetary pressures. The International Monetary Fund's willingness to provide a Standby Loan hinged on the state increasing its revenue collection. The Ramos government managed to extend the value-added tax to services not previously covered, but the Supreme Court then suspended that extension, ruling on behalf of plaintiffs challenging the new legislation. Clearly, the state's pluralism and the ease with which Filipinos gained access to it could frustrate rapid and concerted public action.

Linkages between business and the state

Until the 1950s, the economy was agriculturally based. Thereafter, import controls and higher tariffs enabled the emergence of significant import-substituting industrialization. At the same time, the state severely curtailed the Chinese role in distribution as well as in other economic sectors. "Filipino First" (anti-Chinese) legislation included the Import Control Act of 1950 restricting Chinese access to foreign exchange, the 1954 Retail Trade Nationalization Act, and the Rice and Corn Nationalization Act excluding the Chinese from certain economic sectors.[35] Gradually, the government also made greater efforts to promote Philippine industries. Kunio Yoshihara argues that in part because of such policies, the Philippines emerged as perhaps the only capitalist Southeast Asian economy in which indigenous (Filipino) capital played a role more important than that of Chinese capital. Even in banking, more private institutions were in the hands of indigenous entrepreneurs than in Chinese ones.[36] As a result, early nationalist economic initiatives concentrated on promoting the indigenous private sector rather than the state sector. Greater emphasis on state enterprises emerged during the Marcos years, however, in part as an effort to undermine his political opponents.

While granting that the Philippines of the 1950s was an enterprise economy, Frank Golay insisted that the state played the central role in distributing favors and regulating market incentives.[37] The state's most dramatic expansion during Marcos' twenty-year tenure was in agriculture and the financial sector. As a result of banks defaulting to the Development Bank of the Philippines and the Philippine National Bank in the 1980s, the state role in finance expanded dramatically.[38] In agriculture, officials monopolized the distribution of sugar through the Philippine Sugar Commission. They worked through the Coconut

Producers Federation (COCOFED) to establish United Coconut Oil Mills (UNICOM) and extended its control over most of the country's mills.[39] Government agricultural monopolies created enormous new rent-seeking opportunities that several Marcos cronies skillfully exploited. Herminio Disini, for example, set up his Philippine Tobacco Filter Corporation in 1970, gained special tariff privileges from Marcos in 1975, and used his ensuing fortune to launch a business empire.[40] The Aquino and Ramos governments subsequently dismantled state monopolies in agriculture and restructured the financial sector.

Postwar developments

In this section, as in chapters 3, 4, and 6, we sketch postwar development before the first oil shocks of the 1970s. This discussion helps to lay down a baseline for understanding the effects of external impacts and domestic responses in the four events we study in the succeeding section.

The Philippines suffered greater damage during World War II than other Southeast Asian countries. It was not until about 1950 that the economy regained prewar production levels. Nonetheless, the Philippines would seem to have been well positioned to achieve strong economic growth in the postwar context of a stable and open international economy with growing levels of international trade. As a result of its former colonial ties to the United States, the country had duty-free access to that market for most of its exports. Philippine exports gained from rising prices for commodities and the country was a major recipient of US economic assistance.[41]

Filipino leaders learned early how to turn to the United States for assistance when the economy seemed headed for significant instability.[42] Newly elected Filipino presidents regularly traveled hat-in-hand to the United States in search of aid.[43] Between 1946 and 1949, foreign savings outstripped domestic savings and even for the period up to 1958 the former amounted to nearly two-thirds the latter.[44] In addition to the $620 million for war reconstruction from the United States, the US Veterans Administration also paid some $1.7 billion to Filipino veterans between 1945 and 1956. Other US funds provided the government with budgetary relief and Philippine officials made use of a variety of *ad hoc* war-related revenues to meet their obligations in the early postwar years.[45] When Filipinos became more worried about security issues following the communist victory in China in 1949, they were able to secure a mutual security treaty with the United States in 1951. Following a 1956 reparations agreement with Japan, Filipino leaders were able to draw on a further source of external savings (although this came almost entirely in the form of Japanese goods and services).

United States assistance to the Philippines proved in some respects a poisoned apple because it allowed continuing commitment to flawed economic policies. Other US policies were more transparently problematic from the

Filipino viewpoint. The US Congress tied its assistance to the Philippines to the latter's adoption of a bilateral trade agreement (the Bell Trade Act) that required the Philippine Congress to amend its new constitution. Under the terms of the Act, US exporters gained duty-free access to the Philippines until 1954, the peso remained tied to the dollar, the Philippines committed itself to refrain from using exchange controls (without the permission of the US president) or export taxes, and US citizens gained "parity rights" (nondiscrimination) in the Philippines – treatment as Filipino citizens in getting access to local natural resources and utilities.[46]

Previously, in 1947, the Philippines and the United States had signed a Military Bases Agreement. Subic Bay naval base and the 130,000-acre Clark Field, as well as dozens of other smaller facilities, became particularly important following massive US intervention in the Vietnam War in the 1960s.[47] Philippine cities played host to tens of thousands of GIs on rest and recreation rotations. American military-related spending increased by a factor of three during the war. Relative to other countries in the region, however, the overall impact of the war on the Philippines' GNP was small.[48]

Into the 1970s, the Philippines managed a solid economic performance, albeit one that constantly raised concerns about its sustainability. On the one hand, production expanded steadily, outstripping a rapidly growing population. Through the 1950s, Philippine agricultural and mineral exports helped to finance import-substituting industrialization. Industry grew at an average annual rate of 8 percent between 1949 and 1957.[49] On the other hand, by the late 1950s the import-substituting industrialization strategy, still provoking periodic balance-of-payments crises, no longer appeared sustainable in the long run. Economic growth slowed during the 1960s and Marcos was unable to sustain the early economic promise of his rule, despite expanding access to foreign resources. In fact, exports continued to expand briskly through the early 1960s until Marcos' 1965 election. They moved from 11 percent of GDP in 1961 to 18 percent in 1966. Thereafter, the economy's external orientation declined again through the rest of the decade.[50]

The most fundamental weakness that beset the Philippine economy after the war resulted from commitment to a set of bad economic policies. A small economy pursuing an import-substituting industrialization policy inevitably would be hampered by fiscal policies and landholding patterns that produced sharp income inequities and minimized the size of the domestic market for all but the cheapest necessities. As early as 1962 under President Macapagal, leaders tried unsuccessfully to move toward an export strategy.[51] Initially, commitments to the United States prevented the Philippines from adopting protective tariffs against US imports and compelled recourse to import and foreign exchange controls to protect local industry and the country's balance of payments.

The Philippines was able to sustain these misguided policies over a long

Table 5.1. *Comparative export performance of the Philippines, 1952–57*

	1952	1954	1956	1957
World (1937–38=100)	131	141	173	187
Ceylon (1938–40=100)	134	142	144	137
Cuba (1935–39=100)	152	140	182	n.a.
Malaya (1938=100)	156	158	180	186
Philippines (1937–40=100)	95	97	118	109

Source: Frank H. Golay, *The Philippines: Public Policy and National Economic Development,* Ithaca: Cornell University Press, 1961, p. 122.

period of time owing to the easy availability of foreign savings with which policymakers could finance high levels of imports. Golay argued that access to foreign savings was linked directly to external economic imbalances.[52] He characterized Philippine policies on balance of payments as combining reliance on foreigners and intermittent deflationary policies, suggested that Philippine officials were largely unconcerned to promote export manufacturing, and maintained that they doubted that local manufacturers had the capacity to export.[53] During the entire import-substituting phase, the Philippines used import and exchange controls to manage balance of payments disequilibria. The comparatively weak export performance during the 1950s that resulted from adherence to these policies is evident in table 5.1. All of the economies shown in this table were commodity exporters and all, like the Philippines, benefited from high commodity prices, at least until the end of the Korean War.

By the early 1950s, Philippine officials were using import and exchange controls as substitutes for tariffs to control imports. The Laurel–Langley Agreement of 1955 initiated the phasing out of prohibitions against trade tariffs.[54] Philippine manufacturers increasingly were able to gain protection for their enterprises and state officials shifted industrial promotion toward the private sector and away from public enterprises.[55] The Philippine import-substituting phase of industrialization was under way, although not as part of a coherent development strategy.[56] By 1965, the average tariff level on consumer goods imports was some 70 percent.[57]

The commitment to an import-substituting industrialization policy, however, was not firm. Facing major balance-of-payments problems and an overvalued peso, Diosdado Macapagal, when he became president in 1962, pushed the Philippines toward an export promotion policy by loosening foreign exchange controls, devaluing the peso, restructuring trade tariffs, and providing incentives for foreign investment in the Philippines.[58,59] The results, however, were not encouraging: there were declines in real wages, bankruptcies, and slower growth in manufacturing (5 percent average annual expansion over the 1960s). For the period between 1960 and 1970, Philippine exports grew at an average annual rate of 7.3 percent against an average rate of growth of 6.5 percent for all developing countries and 9.5 percent for total world trade (as noted above, export growth was far stronger in the early 1960s than in the later part of the decade).[60] Filipino leaders did not decisively reorient the economy toward export-driven growth during this period. The 1957 protective tariff structure remained largely unchanged.[61] In consequence, the Philippines developed a strikingly uneven manufacturing sector and economic growth slowed. The average annual rate of economic growth for the Philippines between 1965 and 1973 was 4.2 percent. The comparable figures for Thailand, Malaysia, and Indonesia were 6.9, 8, and 11.1 percent respectively.[62]

State policies obstructed flows of capital as well as goods and services. In addition to the foreign exchange controls discussed above, Philippine authorities used a tax on foreign exchange sales that impeded foreign capital inflows. The government adopted more direct controls on Japanese capital, limiting investment opportunities beyond manufacturing and, until 1967, preventing trading companies from establishing branch offices.[63] With strong anti-Japanese feeling after the war, the Philippines did not approve the first Japanese investment until 1967. In the early 1970s, Japanese investment in the Philippines was still far less than in Indonesia or Thailand.[64] With the declaration of martial law in 1972, Marcos took steps to attract foreign capital, including a decree ratifying the Treaty of Amity, Commerce, and Navigation with Japan.

President Marcos moved to strengthen ties to foreign capital in part in response to foreign pressures. By 1967 chronic budget and current account difficulties had led his government to reintroduce exchange and trade controls. The IMF extended further assistance to the Philippines in 1969 and 1970, but required Philippine officials to adopt a stabilization package that devalued the peso, liberalized foreign investment regulation, and began to phase out import controls.

Philippine leaders did not enjoy the support of a coherent political base favoring a single economic strategy. Economic conflicts divided rural from urban interests as well as import-competing and export-oriented producers. As early as the 1930s, the Philippines had a business faction whose interests opposed policies of economic openness. This group became stronger in the 1950s and 1960s, clashing increasingly with the oligarch's concerns to export sugar and other cash crops. The clashes often centered on efforts by exporting interests to weaken the import and foreign exchange controls imposed in 1950. These controls, meanwhile, afforded windfall profits for certain importers, bureaucrats, and politicians fortunate enough to get access to the necessary licenses.[65]

Socioeconomic diversification worked against the emergence of a coherent political base supporting open economic policies. Over the 1950s, the Philippines saw a growing middle class, rising economic nationalism, and wider political participation. These trends, in turn, required politicians to mobilize larger numbers of voters and led to the diversification of elite economic interests. In the 1950s, the landed elite shifted to urban production to some degree, but generally in areas such as real estate and banking. The class of industrialists, emerging under a regime of tariff and other protection, drew primarily from Chinese merchants.[66] By the late 1950s, conflict between the "sugar bloc" and industrialists was acute.[67]

These tensions grew more acute through the 1960s. Added to these sources of conflict were economic stagnation and the rise of the political left (largely students and workers),[68] rising unemployment among college graduates, a breakdown in patron–client relations, rural insurgency,[69] legislative gridlock blocking reform, and the failure to attract investment from local or foreign capital. By the early 1970s, these forces engendered a sense of crisis and eventually encouraged Marcos to declare martial law. These pressures also induced a policy shift away from conservative macroeconomic policies.

The escalating tensions of the late 1960s led to an atmosphere of political crisis. In this context, Benigno Aquino, one of Marcos' most prominent political opponents, began telling journalists that he would declare martial law if elected in 1972.[70] Marcos, however, preempted him by declaring martial law before the 1972 elections. David Wurfel sees Marcos' decision as resulting from a confluence of three conflicts: (i) between elites and masses; (ii) between foreign and local capital (exacerbated by the imminent expiry, in 1974, of parity rights); and (iii) between Marcos, on the one hand, and Aquino and Eugenio Lopez, a sugar baron and former vice-president, on the other.[71]

The Philippines, then, experienced recurrent economic crises and relied on external aid to overcome them. The state had little capacity to mobilize resources at home. Golay argues that the regular fiscal imbalances induced crises not because of their severity so much as because of the government's unwillingness to address them.[72] In 1949, the government relied on import tariffs for over half its revenue. The imposition of import controls the following year to deal with a balance-of-payments crisis reduced the amount of trade revenue by about 17 percent.[73] The state's dependence on trade taxes (see table 5.2) is extraordinary when we recall that the vast majority of imports, those coming from the United States, were not subject to any tariffs.[74] The Philippine tariff in effect since 1909 (before officials implemented a new one in 1957) was crafted to produce maximum revenue consistent with the duty-free status of US goods.[75] Through the 1950s and 1960s, Philippine state expenditure as a share of GNP was about half what it was in many other Asian developing countries (the tax/GDP ratio was under 7 percent in 1971).[76]

Trade taxes became decreasingly important as a source of income over the 1960s. In part, this simply reflected the fact that trade levels were too low to generate significant revenue. In addition, reforms backed by international financial institutions resulted in lower tariff levels. In the 1960s, trade taxes accounted for a lower share of total revenue in the Philippines than in Thailand.[77]

Table 5.2. *Philippine revenue and expenditure, 1948–57 (million pesos)*

Fiscal year	Import revenue	Total revenue	Total expenditure
1948–49	199	362	467
1949–50	164	329	534
1950–51	177	443	523
1951–52	349	655	635
1952–53	283	601	660
1953–54	322	644	787
1954–55	312	681	854
1955–56	401	738	980
1956–57	375	821	1057

Source: Frank H. Golay, *The Philippines Public Policy and National Economic Development,* Ithaca: Cornell University Press, 1961, p. 195.

Throughout the 1960s, the Philippines continued to have a low national savings rate, averaging 17 percent between 1965 and 1972 and resulting in an average annual savings shortfall of nearly 4 percent of GDP.[78] Foreign aid offset these shortfalls. Between 1962 and 1969, the Philippines was the fourth largest recipient of Japanese foreign aid and ranked twenty-fifth among recipients of US assistance.[79] By the late 1960s, private inflows assumed a more significant role. Between 1969 and 1971, official development assistance inflows accounted for an average of only 29 percent of foreign capital inflows while total foreign capital inflows amounted on average to nearly 3 percent of GNP.[80] Total private OECD resource flows to the Philippines in 1970 exceeded those going to Indonesia, Malaysia, and Thailand.[81]

In summary, the Philippine state's weaknesses hindered efforts to meet emerging development challenges. Golay expressed doubt in the early 1960s that a nonauthoritarian state could produce economic growth in the Philippines.[82] Lindsey also concluded, based on the Philippine case, that states in capitalist economies could not stimulate industrialization in the face of opposition from the dominant social class. The oligarchy's disinterest in capital accumulation in the manufacturing sector, Lindsey held, left the state with the options of assuming such a role itself or of inviting in foreign firms. Increasingly, in the 1970s, the Philippine state would pursue both options.[83]

Challenge and response

As in all the chapters dealing with individual countries, we present, for each of four events, three subsections. We begin by discussing the specific impact the event had on the Philippines. We then go on to describe the policy response to external challenges. Finally, we attempt to account for the policy record.

First oil shock, global recession, easy credit, 1974–75

Impact The first oil shock was a significant blow to the Philippine economy, aggravating already serious balance-of-payments difficulties. The oil import bill shot up from $187 million in 1973 and continued to rise through the decade, reaching over $2 billion by 1982. Some estimates suggest the negative impact of the oil price increases was over 9 percent of GNP (ignoring the positive effects of access to foreign loans at negative real interest rates).[84] The gap between savings and investment, an average of 3.8 percent of GDP between 1965 and 1972, rose to 4.7 percent from 1973 to 1978.[85] Growing foreign aid to the Philippines did not increase enough to compensate for this sharp shift in its current account balance.[86] Foreign borrowing began to grow.

Nonetheless, the negative impact on the economy during this first event was balanced by some positive developments. Enhanced earnings from commodity exports offset higher prices for oil imports. The Philippines' terms of trade remained positive during this initial period.[87] The economy managed per capita income growth through most of the 1970s. Gross domestic product expanded by 8.8 percent in 1973, 3.4 percent in 1974, 5.5 percent in 1975, and 8.8 percent in 1976. The Philippines sustained healthy rates of growth in agriculture using subsidized credit, fertilizers, and increased infrastructure.[88] Merchandise exports expanded erratically, from $1.8 billion in 1973, to $2.7 billion in 1974, $2.3 billion in 1975, $2.6 billion in 1976, and $3.1 billion in 1977.[89]

Looking over a longer time period, the economy showed evidence of significant structural shifts, most prominently in its exports. Overall, between 1967 and 1979, exports as a percentage of GDP increased from 11 to 15.3 percent.[90] During that same interval, industrial exports as a share of total exports climbed from 8.1 to 23.6 percent.[91] The share of agriculture in GDP fell by only 1 percent between 1970 and 1978, while manufacturing rose 2 percent and other industry increased nearly 3 percent.[92]

Policy record In response to the oil price rises, Filipino officials modestly increased their borrowing from private foreign sources[93] in order to cushion the adjustment shock. They also followed expansionary fiscal and monetary policies that resulted in the overvaluation of the peso.[94] Ranis and Mahmood characterize the policy response to the oil shock as an aggressive use of expansionary policies attempting to offset the worsening in external economic conditions.[95] With loans available at low or negative real interest rates, this strategy appeared at the time to be sound. The ratio of public investment to GDP rose sharply, from about 2 percent in 1973 to close to 10 percent in 1976.[96] Nonetheless, the state's role in the Philippine economy remained sufficiently limited for the World Bank in 1976 to suggest that public authorities establish more public corporations, including in industries such as fertilizers, steel, and shipbuilding.[97] The number of state-owned firms did in fact expand from 70 in 1972 to some 300 by the mid-1980s.

In general, President Marcos used neither the oil shocks nor martial law to launch a sharp policy reorientation (although, as noted above, officials did liberalize the foreign direct investment regime). Indeed, the economy's outward orientation decreased after 1972 and tariff revisions the following year increased protection for local producers as well as taxing exports. Higher tariffs promoted those industries which were more capital-intensive and contributed to declining total factor productivity throughout the 1970s.[98]

During the Marcos years, at least until 1983, the government fairly steadily expanded its roles in setting wages, interest rates, and foreign exchange and other prices. It also played a growing role in protecting domestic producers, creating monopolies, and providing exemptions.[99] Its ability to raise revenue also grew, though not as fast as spending. Marcos centralized planning and accorded technocrats a greater role in policy formulation. Under the Integrated Reorganization Plan, he expanded the powers of technocrats working through the National Economic Development Authority which replaced the National Economic Council. Further centralizing policy control, in December 1975 Marcos abolished a Cabinet Coordinating Conference that previously had screened and coordinated government proposals.[100] The first external shock, then, followed closely on Marcos' declaration of martial law and together these factors led to a growing state role and, at least in terms of trade, a more closed economy (the foreign investment regime grew more open). Some of these effects grew more evident during the second event considered below. Their most important impacts, however, were not felt until the third event in the mid-1980s.

Explaining policy choices By the time of the first oil price increases, many of the positive achievements of Marcos' early years in power were in danger of being reversed. Increasingly, Marcos used what power he could muster to undermine his political opponents. The needs of the economy received little sustained high-level attention. Nonetheless, the economy's performance continued strong, even if growing macroeconomic imbalances signaled future dangers. The Philippines was able to draw on external savings to finance rising levels of investment that, for almost another decade, sustained economic expansion.

Marcos' decision to declare martial law appears to have been aimed both at the oligarchs and the rising left. One view has it that Marcos declared martial law in an effort to launch a Philippine "export platform" but that, following the oil price increases, global economic conditions were no longer conducive to success in such an enterprise. This view holds that slower global economic expansion, rising industrialized-country protectionism, and the head-start of the East Asian NIEs foreclosed possibilities for would-be emulators.[101] Stauffer sees Marcos siding with export-oriented Filipinos and international creditors against "nationalist" Filipinos, thereby helping to cleave the elite and polarize Filipino politics.[102] Within a context of a strong Filipino tradition of economic nationalism that barred foreigners from natural resource industries, retail operations, public utilities, importing, and banking, Marcos was concerned that still stronger discrimination would be enshrined under the new constitution being considered in 1972. Supreme Court rulings, meanwhile, were challenging the rights of foreign capital in the Philippines. Marcos moved, according to this analysis, to head off such steps. This suggests that Marcos was trying to forge a coalition favoring economic openness. Our third hypothesis argues that had he been successful, the first oil shock might have induced greater economic openness.

An alternative explanation for Marcos' declaration of martial law gives greater weight to his own political concerns and sees Marcos using state marketing organizations to undermine his political opponents whose interests were tied to commodities such as copra and sugar. This concentration of political power in his own hands, however, did not provide Marcos with political space to select economic policies autonomously or to delegate decision authority to his technocrats. Even under martial law, Marcos was forced to rely on a patronage system operating through patron–client networks. At the top of this hierarchy were Marcos' cronies, some of whom benefited from new rent-seeking opportunities. For example, beginning in the mid-1970s, the state deposited coconut levy funds interest-free in the United Coconut Planters Bank. This private bank was part of crony Eduardo Cojuangco's empire. These deposits helped to boost his bank from the nineteenth rank in 1976 to the fourth largest in 1983.[103] The Development Bank of the Philippines was also a popular instrument for extending state credit to Marcos' cronies.[104]

Ultimately, it is not possible to know what Marcos was thinking or the goals toward which he hoped to use his enhanced powers. In any event, to strengthen his grip over Philippine society, Marcos turned to the military.[105] He tried to eliminate national level competitors, increased the state's presence at local levels, depended increasingly on the civil bureaucracy and the military, and continued his reliance on external sources of funds.[106] These steps hint at a possible effort to enhance the state's powers by creating a supportive political coalition, including actors both within and outside the state. Clearly, however, Marcos failed to use the sharp political disjuncture (his declaration of martial law) to consolidate a stable political base.

Marcos and his technocrats failed to establish significantly greater control over the state apparatus. The newly created Economic Development Authority, for example, never achieved policy dominance. Both the Ministry of Trade and Industry and the Board of Investments continued their policy influence and their links to manufacturing interests dependent on ongoing state protection. Far from corporatist arrangements linking relatively unified state and private sector interests, Philippine politics continued to exhibit sharp divisions within both spheres. The result was that rent-seekers had ample opportunities to seek their fortunes. Neither could technocrats challenge Marcos' personal control over the budget. And Imelda Marcos, partly in her role as Minister of Human Settlements, controlled public and private funds equal to half the government budget.[107] Hence, there were clear limits to the Marcos' delegation of policy-making control to technocrats.

In short, the state commitment to an export strategy remained uncertain. The concentration of state power in Marcos' hands increasingly became an end in itself and was not linked to any coherent economic strategy. Ongoing con-flicts within the Marcos government and the need to maintain political support impeded such commitment, to the extent that it ever existed. (Even among Filipino technocrats, many remained adherents of policies aimed at deepening the Philippines' industrial structure through further import substitution while ending protection for consumer goods industries.)

Referring to our hypotheses, developments during this period did not predict a move toward greater economic openness, although technocratic influence over policymaking probably did increase. The consolidation of Marcos' polit-ical power (and the economy's shortage of local savings) helps us to explain Marcos' decision to increase the economy's openness to foreign capital.

Second oil shock and debt crisis, 1979–83

Impact In the early 1980s, when US macroeconomic policies favored a low-debt, outward-looking economic strategy, the Philippines was accumulating large debts in pursuit of an inward-looking strategy.[108] United States deficit spending sucked in imports from elsewhere, but the inflow from the Philippines did not rise sharply. A strong dollar and rising interest rates, however, did greatly expand the Philippine external debt. Higher oil prices in the late 1970s placed severe adjustment costs on the Philippine economy, amounting to over 6 percent of GNP, according to one estimate, or as much as 10 percent by another.[109] The Philippines' terms of trade suffered a modest decline over the early 1980s.[110] The current account deficit worsened steadily following the second oil price rises, growing from 5.4 percent of GDP in 1978 to 6.3 percent in 1981 and an alarming 9.1 percent the following year.[111] Yet, it was only some years after the second round of oil price increases that the accumulated effects of a failure to adjust to price shifts began to be evident in the Philippine economy. Gross domestic product continued to expand at over 5 percent during 1979 and 1980, then fell to about 3.5 percent over the following two years, before falling to 1.8 percent in 1983. Thereafter, the economy experienced a very sharp contraction.

Policy record Although the Philippine strategy of adjustment to the first oil price hikes – increasing external borrowing to finance higher levels of state investment – no longer appeared tenable by the time of the second oil price increases, heavy external borrowing continued and, indeed, increased. Growth in direct investment inflows came to a halt in 1979 and did not recover until 1987. Official net inflows rose modestly, while borrowing from private sources rose sharply in 1978, 1979, and again in 1981.[112] Long-term loans began to increase sharply in 1976 and continued to expand through 1983, averaging near $1.5 billion a year from 1979 to 1983.[113] Late in 1979, the Filipino government announced plans for eleven large industrial projects, including copper and aluminum smelters, fertilizer and petrochemical plants, a pulp and paper mill, the manufacture of diesel engines, and an integrated steel project, as part of efforts to stimulate further industrial deepening. Officials' concern to strengthen industry reflected in part a feeling that export-oriented industries did little to reduce import requirements. Local value added in the garment industry, for example, was 44 percent; the figure was far lower in the electronics industry.[114]

The government also maintained substantial levels of investment in agriculture. Between 1973 and 1981, the Marcos government channeled some $1 billion to the rural sector. Agricultural programs helped to produce higher yields in corn and rice, but only with higher imports of fertilizers that became much more expensive with oil price increases. Government expenditure increased from 14.8 to 15.7 percent of GNP between 1978 and 1982 while revenue declined from 13.6 to 11.4 percent. For the years 1974–80, the average national investment rate, 29.5 percent of GDP, was the highest among the ASEAN Four, but economic efficiency, as measured by the incremental capital–output ratio, was considerably lower than in the other three.[115]

Aggravating the effects of public sector mismanagement of the economy was the growing fiscal burden associated with the insolvency of industrial and financial firms, both private and state-owned, that became the burden of state entities. Many public sector holding companies, particularly the Ministry of Trade and Industry's National Development Company, had a host of subsidiaries. These were not subject to regularized central government supervision and holding companies could relatively easily launch new enterprises and incur new debts. These subsidiaries were exempt from the personnel rules of the regular civil service. And they provided incomes to government officials and cabinet members.[116] As a consequence, the number of state-owned enterprises increased from 70 in 1972 to 245 in 1984.[117] The state enterprise sector as a whole yielded low rates of return on investment, in many cases negative, and required a steady flow of transfers from the national budget, amounting to some 35 percent of 1984 government revenue, or 4 percent of GNP. Nonperforming assets targeted for privatization by mid-1986 had a book value of some $7 billion. Estimates indicated that only about one-fifth that figure could be recovered.[118]

Despite clear signals of the urgency of macroeconomic reform, Philippine officials did not respond. As a result, the Philippines failed to achieve any significant growth in exports as a share of GDP, to reduce government and current account deficits, or to reduce the savings–investment gap. Gross domestic investment did not increase between 1979 and 1981. It increased in the following two years before collapsing in the mid-1980s. In 1981 and 1982, public budget deficits reached new highs.

Between 1980 and 1985, Philippine exports expanded by less than 1 percent. While exports for all developing countries and total world trade during that period grew by an average annual rate of only 1.8 and 2.9 percent respectively, other Asian developing countries increased their exports at much higher rates.[119] A World Bank study suggested that much of Philippine manufacturing was subtracting rather than adding value. Exports as a share of GNP, which stood at 15 percent in 1970, had declined to 10 percent by 1983.[120] The composition of Philippine exports continued to move away from agricultural toward manufactured goods (the share of raw materials in total exports dropped from 24.6 to 18.4 percent between 1978 and 1982, almost entirely because of adverse commodity price trends).[121] For the period between 1980 and 1985, however, industry's share in total production declined considerably, from 39 to 35 percent.

In the area of trade, however, Philippine authorities moved toward greater openness during this period. Following the second round of oil price rises, officials launched significant tariff reforms. Between 1980 and 1985, they lowered tariffs, with an average nominal tariff by the latter date of 28 percent (from 43 percent in 1980). They also reduced the number of goods covered by quantitative restrictions by half (37 percent of all goods had been covered in 1980).[122] And in 1983 and 1984, tax changes further reduced discrimination against imports. A foreign exchange crisis in 1983, however, largely put an end to this episode of liberalization. By October of that year, officials had imposed foreign exchange controls.[123] Without accompanying changes in macroeconomic policies, these moves toward greater openness in the trade regime had little short-term impact.

By the late 1970s the World Bank was increasingly intent on encouraging economic reforms in the Philippines. Short-term public debt doubled between 1970 and 1975 while the external public debt went up by 214 percent over the same period, and then quadrupled to $10.5 billion in 1980.[124] The economic crisis worsened dramatically in January 1981 when Dewey Dee, a businessman, fled the Philippines, leaving behind debts close to $100 million. Dee's departure left behind ripple effects that undermined other companies. The government then began a series of rescue operations of insolvent firms. Initially, the Philippines was able to continue to borrow, but with its earlier (frequently ill-considered) investments doing poorly, capital flight, and a variety of sectoral problems, including one in the finance industry, a full-blown foreign exchange crisis seemed increasingly probable.

It came in 1983. The government faced rising tensions with the IMF in 1982 as a result of its financial mismanagement. As a result, that year, for only the second year since 1962, the Philippines had no standby agreement in place.[125] With falling international reserves, collapsing external lending, and a ballooning current account deficit, the Philippines in October 1983 declared a moratorium on its debt payments to commercial banks and imposed import controls.[126] Coping with the foreign exchange crisis required severe contractionary measures that, in turn, produced a sharp depression from 1984 to 1986. In short, by the end of the second event, Filipinos were accruing the full costs of a decade of policy errors.

Explaining policy choices By the time the second round of oil price rises hit the Philippines, state officials were decreasingly effective in pushing for reforms and economic policy lacked clear direction. Cumulating policy errors increasingly offset Marcos' early martial law achievements. Increasingly his concern was to forge a new political base, particularly after he returned the Philippines to elections in 1978. Partly consistent with our first hypothesis, *ad hoc* economic (mis)management continued to be possible, thanks to ongoing Philippine access to foreign capital (although this hardly constituted a "windfall").

After closing down Congress in 1972, Marcos ruled by plebiscite until the Interim National Assembly elections in 1978 when his electoral vehicle, the Kilusang Bagong Lipuna (New Society Movement, KBL), came close to sweeping all positions. While ending martial law on January 17, 1981, Marcos retained enormous powers, including the power to issue decrees. Filipinos approved by ballot a new constitution providing for a president and a prime minister.[127] Marcos' attention remained riveted on efforts to shore up his political base.

To sustain patterns of reform and his own tenure, Marcos continued to attack his potential political opponents. Marcos generally used legal cover for his actions even as he subordinated the judiciary, compelling the Supreme Court to bend to his will, and cowed the press.[128] The autonomy he thereby gained from the traditional oligarchs in the 1970s, however, he lost to his cronies in the 1980s. Reliance on foreign credits was supposed to free Marcos from the oligarchy.[129] Ultimately, however, Marcos' efforts to forge new, stable bases of political support proved ephemeral and he was forced to construct a new patronage network along traditional lines. International financial institutions continued to push for trade reforms. However, after bruising battles within the bureaucracy the Marcos government achieved only minor tariff reforms during this period. The dominant political coalition still favored protection of local industry and was able to deflect moves to devalue the peso. As for Marcos himself, some estimates suggest he embezzled between $5 and $10 billion.[130] The evidence indicates that Marcos failed to forge the kind of political coalition, suggested by our third hypothesis, that might have encouraged greater economic openness.

Marcos used his economic powers to expand the range of state services, but did not provide a matching capability to extract resources to pay for them. During the 1970s, state spending as a share of GDP increased rapidly and continued to exceed revenue collection. The deficit jumped from 350 million pesos in 1979 to 14.4 billion in 1982, before subsiding to 7.5 billion in 1983.[131] Tax exemptions provided to shore up political support eroded the corporate income tax base.[132] Trade taxes continued to be a fairly significant source of revenue, climbing sharply in the early 1980s.[133]

The sense of policy disarray and plunder of the state by Marcos and his cronies is evident in a variety of policy arenas. Overall, the record from these years suggests that the top-level leadership was consumed with issues other than development strategy. Sectoral crises swamped macroeconomic reform goals. In 1983, for example, Philippine officials promised devaluation of the peso, budget cuts (including five of the eleven big projects), and removal of some price controls. But, as a result of government assistance to insolvent financial institutions and further investment in state-owned enterprises, expansionary monetary policies continued. When the government also reimposed trade and exchange controls, the international financial institutions for the first time canceled a program of loans. During the 1983 financial crisis, external creditors discovered that half the largest nonperforming accounts were Marcos "behest loans."[134] In supporting his cronies, Marcos himself was largely responsible for the Philippine macroeconomic mess of the mid-1980s.

Political opposition and Marcos' growing weakness help to explain why Marcos did not overthrow the Philippine import-substituting industrialization regime. Instead, Marcos moved only against his rivals.[135] His cronies were more closely tied to production for the local market than for export markets.[136] With external funds available in such abundance, Marcos was not compelled to launch a serious export push that would require breaking up the export monopolies.[137] By the time an export strategy became an economic requirement, Marcos' base of political support had narrowed to the point where sustaining the old trade regime had become a political necessity. In sum, Marcos failed to find a means of bringing into balance the needs of the economy and the means to ensure his own survival.

Technocratic influence increased under Marcos, in part as a result of technocrats' links with international financial institutions. Our second hypothesis predicts that this would lead in the direction of economic openness in response to the second oil shock. The technocrats, however, remained highly dependent on Marcos, and his political concerns limited the extent to which he delegated policymaking authority. In the end, the technocrats served Marcos by helping to hoodwink international lenders. Technocrats overreported foreign exchange holdings to international financial institutions in 1983, and understated the 1985 budget deficit. By the early 1980s, the Philippines was in the grip of several mutually reinforcing vicious circles. Concern for survival, rather than strategy, dominated the thinking of Marcos and his technocrats and cronies. Political realities – the threat of collapse – overrode economic necessities. Economic recovery would require a new strategy that could exploit external opportunities. At a time when the country was avowedly aiming at increasing the competitiveness of its exports, however, state officials allowed the peso to appreciate. The economy was poorly positioned to survive falling commodity prices in the 1980s.

Commodity shock, 1984–86

Impact The Philippine economy collapsed in the mid-1980s, more because of cumulative economic problems than because of the impact of external changes. The country's terms of trade did not change much during this time. Falling oil import costs offset lower commodity export prices. Indeed, between the end of 1984 and the end of 1988, the terms of trade rose by over 50 percent.[138] The sluggishness of Philippine exports also reflected domestic problems more than it did any shift in global or regional trade patterns. Following the government's failure to meet budget targets, the IMF refused the Philippines access to the second tranche of a loan in April 1985. By this time the United States, long the Philippines' ace in the hole, was taking a harder line and the international financial institutions were insisting on the reform of the agricultural monopolies.

With the effects of previous errors being felt and severe contractionary policies in operation, the economy experienced a sharp downturn. In both 1984 and 1985, GDP fell 7.3 percent, before recovering with growth rates of 3.4 and 4.8 percent over the following two years. Merchandise trade as a share of GDP fell to 32 percent in 1985 from 42 percent five years earlier.[139] Unemployment and underemployment combined reached 40 percent in 1984.[140] Farm production contracted between 1983 and 1985, while the industrial sector shrank 4.6 percent in 1984 and a further 6 percent in 1985.[141] Between 1982 and 1986, real per capita income fell by 16 percent.[142] This sharp curtailment of economic activity at least ameliorated the economy's external imbalances. The current account deficit contracted from 5 percent of GDP in 1984 to 2.5 percent in 1986, and 1.7 percent the following year.

Policy record A 1983 foreign exchange crisis forced officials to adopt draconian economic measures that curbed mounting inflation but sent the economy into a tailspin. Gross domestic investment dropped from a range of 27 to 30 percent of GDP between 1980 and 1983, to 22 percent in 1984 and between 15 and 16 percent the following two years.[143]

In October 1983, two months after Benigno Aquino's assassination, the government adopted the following economic measures: a devaluation of 21 percent, tightened exchange controls and higher tariffs, and a ninety-day moratorium (the first of several) on debt repayments. In October 1984 the government produced a package promising tax reforms, closer scrutiny of state-owned enterprises and reductions in their deficits, restructuring of the Philippine National Bank, the Development Bank of the Philippines, and the Philippines Export Guarantee Corporation, and agricultural policy reform. Between 1981 and 1985, public investment as a share of GNP declined from 8 to below 4 percent.[144] With the debt-service ratio at 40 percent by 1982, officials devalued the peso four times between October 1982 and June 1984, reducing its value by half.[145] Philippine trade contracted over 1984 and 1985. Then, late in 1985, a big increase in the money supply leading up to the December 1985 elections produced a surge in inflation.[146] Further capital flight resulted.

The Philippine economy was unable to respond to the emerging opportunities in the global and regional economies. Political crisis and the encrustation of decades of failed economic policies combined to preclude the flexibility that would have been necessary to adjust to the severe circumstances that faced all developing countries during this event. Between 1978 and 1985, the composition of Philippine GDP changed very little, suggesting a period of structural stagnation.[147] While the economy had begun to recover by 1986, growth brought a surge in imports and renewed balance-of-payments problems.[148]

Explaining policy choices Marcos was able to defer fundamental economic adjustment until the mid-1980s, owing to his access to balance-of-payments deficit financing. Government revenue, helped by inflation, continued its rapid expansion, climbing from 46 billion pesos in 1983 to 79 billion in 1986. These gains, however, were offset by more rapid spending increases as the government deficit grew from 7 billion pesos in 1983 to 31 billion in 1986.[149] Net long-term capital flows to the Philippines continued at high levels until 1986. Net inflows in 1983 registered $1,464 million, then dropped to $308 the following year, jumped to $3,059 during the 1985 election year, and fell back to $1,215 million in 1986.

Given Marcos' dependence on external sources of finance, no relationship was more important to him than that with the United States. Marcos managed the relationship well. By 1981, the Philippines was receiving $700 million from four multilateral lenders and an additional $200 million from Japan.[150] The 1983 agreement extending US access to Philippine bases provided Marcos with a major fillip: $900 million, part of it in grants and the remainder at concessional interest rates. David Wurfel suggests that Marcos' key foreign policy goal was to gain foreign support for domestic economic expansion.[151] He succeeded famously.

By the mid-1980s, however, external creditors were putting increasing pressure on Marcos to follow through on promised economic reforms. The facilitative external conditions that made it possible to postpone a turn to economic openness began to shift. Political factors at home, however, continued to obstruct greater openness. In the midst of simultaneous economic and political crises, it became increasingly difficult for Marcos to push economic reforms that undermined elements of his shrinking support base. Facing a severe economic crisis and declining exports, Marcos needed IMF approval. Of more immediate concern, however, was the fact he needed the support of his cronies.[152] Marcos' inability to deliver on policy commitments led the IMF to refuse to release the third tranche of a loan in 1985. Marcos had lost the external support on which so much of his economic and political strategy depended.

The assassination of Benigno Aquino in August 1983 served as a turning point leading to less US support for Marcos and growing strength in the domestic political opposition, which managed a strong showing in the May 1984 and December 1985 elections. Severe economic conditions hurt the shrinking Filipino business elite (corporate ownership had become increasingly concentrated in a small number of families)[153] and paved the way for Marcos' downfall. Marcos eventually fled the country and Corazon Aquino assumed power in 1986.

International finance changes course, 1987–

Impact As oil prices fell further and the East Asian economy moved into high gear in the late 1980s with capital flowing from Northeast to Southeast Asia, the Philippines was initially poorly placed to exploit the opportunities that emerged. Net long-term capital inflows fell to $564 million in 1987, rose slightly the following year, and then began to expand rapidly, reaching $1.7 billion by 1990 and well over $2.5 billion in 1992.[154] By the 1990s, reform in the Philippine economy coupled with growing inflows of direct investment promised a major burst in economic growth and structural changes in the economy. At the same time, however, state officials continued to contend with their own weaknesses and ongoing political instability.

Foreign capital (and returning Filipino capital) began to flow into the Philippines in the second half of the 1980s.[155] By the late 1980s investment from Hong Kong and Taiwan into the Philippines was booming. As one Filipino wag remarked, "Coup attempts may come and go. I stop investing when the Chinese do."[156] Net direct foreign investment grew sixfold between 1986 and 1989.[157]

The Persian Gulf War in 1990–91 damaged the economy, dampening tourism and leading to the loss of overseas contract workers' remittances (in 1990, these two accounted for some $2.6 billion).[158] Some 60,000 Filipinos had been working in Iraq and Kuwait.[159] The Philippines also forfeited a major source of foreign exchange, $480 million a year, when negotiations with the United States over the cost of leasing its Clark and Subic Bay bases collapsed.[160] The United States left these bases in 1992. However, active Taiwanese recruitment of Filipino workers, mostly in construction, partly offset these losses.[161] In total, overseas workers remitted over $2 billion in 1993 amounting to 2.3 percent of GNP.[162]

Increases in public expenditure again fueled strong economic growth in the early Aquino years. From 1987 to 1989, GDP expanded by between 5 and 6 percent annually, before slowing to near zero over the subsequent four years, and then rising to about 5 percent in the mid-1990s, during Ramos' tenure. The economy benefited from favorable movement in its terms of trade, including low oil prices and relatively high prices for copra and sugar.[163] Nonetheless, current account deficits which remained below 2 percent of GDP in 1987 and 1988, began to climb again, reaching near 7 percent of GDP in 1990, and, after falling sharply for two years, increased again in 1993.

Policy record The Aquino and Ramos governments benefited from some of the Marcos era reforms stipulated in the IMF's 1984 Standby Agreement. Building on this start, the NEDA released in May 1986 its Yellow Book, a relatively coherent statement on economic policy promising a market orientation and calling for institutional reforms, export orientation, the ending of rural monopolies, tax reform, trade liberalization, privatization, and income redistribution. In December that year, NEDA announced its Medium-Term Philippine Development Plan (1987–92).

The Aquino administration enjoyed considerable policy success in the areas of tax reform, dismantling monopolies, adopting a new investment code, and trade liberalization. The government reduced trade protection, dismantled the marketing monopolies for coconuts and sugar, ended price controls and export taxes on agricultural goods, and deregulated exchange and interest rates.[164] Success was harder to achieve in the areas of land reform and privatization of state-owned firms. With the benefit of a severe depression, the government brought the current account into balance in 1985 and registered a large surplus in 1986. Thereafter, deficits again began to expand.

The economy picked up late in 1986 and in 1987, in part through export expansion but also because the government was priming the pump. Investment levels remained low (an average of 15 percent of GNP between 1985 and 1988) and state officials continued to face difficult fiscal burdens. In 1987, the fourteen largest non-financial state enterprises incurred combined losses near $600 million.[165] As a result of continuing high levels of debt, authorities were unable to raise spending on infrastructure. This led to bottlenecks, particularly in electrical supply. Persistent deficits and IMF pressures pushed Ramos to adopt a privatization plan in the early 1990s that pioneered the extensive use of privately financed build-operate-transfer schemes.[166] Nonetheless, by the mid-1990s, some observers suggested that the lack of infrastructure was hindering the economy's potential for more rapid expansion.[167]

One of the government's most pressing problems in the late 1980s concerned the enormous losses, amounting to close to $13 billion by the end of 1991, burdening the central bank. The central bank had incurred these losses in the course of handling transactions for Marcos cronies and assuming the foreign debt liabilities of the Philippine National Bank and the Development Bank of the Philippines. As a result, the government was forced to subsidize the central bank and maintain high interest rates. This discouraged bank lending to industry and further devaluation of the peso which would increase the peso burden the central bank faced in meeting foreign liabilities.[168] Nevertheless, by the mid-1990s, reform and sustained economic growth had alleviated these financial sector problems.

In the early 1990s, the government adopted more liberal regulations governing foreign capital. The new regulations removed Board of Investment discretion in approving investment. President Ramos carried forward the removal of foreign exchange controls, on both current and capital accounts, by the end of 1993 and the liberalization of regulations governing foreign investment in the Philippines.[169] Ramos also enhanced the independence of the central bank.

After a period of sluggish economic growth, the economy picked up after 1993. Even in 1993, the local stock market did extremely well in response to lower inflation, progress in reducing government budget deficits (below 2 percent of GNP in 1992 and, with the help of creative book-keeping, a surplus in 1994)[170] and interest rates, and expectations of an economic turnaround. And, in fact, the economy performed well in subsequent years.

The government moved firmly to liberalize the trade regime beginning in the late 1980s. Under the 1984 agreement with the IMF, the Marcos government promised to remove quotas and licenses covering the import of some 1,200 types of goods. In 1986, President Aquino decided to remove these controls on two-thirds of the items, leaving intermediate goods protected and thereby hurting producers of finished goods. In 1988, the government removed the remaining controls and shifted to tariffs, ranging between 10 and 50 percent.[171] In total, the Aquino government removed controls on nearly 1,500 items during the late 1980s. After long and arduous negotiations, the government adopted a new code in 1991 that reduced and simplified the tariff structure.[172] Ramos began to implement a new series of tariff reductions in 1995 with the goal of a very low (5 percent) uniform tariff by 2004. Membership of the ASEAN Free Trade Area gave additional impetus to these moves. In a short period, the Philippines moved from having the highest to having among the lowest tariffs within ASEAN.[173]

On a variety of measures, the Philippine economy grew significantly more open during the late 1980s and early 1990s. While non-tariff barriers remained pervasive,[174] the Philippine economy became, by some measures,[175] the most open among the ASEAN Four to foreign capital. The Foreign Investment Act of 1991 adopted a negative list system of sectors closed to foreign investors and subsequent regulatory changes further limited those restrictions.[176] Tariffs fell sharply, continuing into the mid-1990s, and trade as a share of GDP jumped from 32 percent in 1985 to 54 percent in 1993.[177]

The prolonged stand-off between those forces favoring openness and those wanting protection was finally settled in the 1990s in favor of the former group. Decades of protection left the economy relatively weak. The structure of industry revealed the effects of the lack of competition. Industrial concentration in the Philippines in the 1990s was higher than in other developing countries such as Brazil, Mexico, and South Korea, and generally lacked the small and medium-sized firms that could serve as subcontractors to larger firms.[178] The World Bank noted that over the twenty-year period beginning in the early 1970s, urban employment's share of total employment had increased only 3 percent, against 27 percent in South Korea and 20 percent in Malaysia.[179] Victories by forces favoring trade openness in the 1990s promised stronger competitive pressures and greater structural shifts with a reallocation of resources.

Explaining policy choices Not long after taking office, Aquino faced rural insurgency and military insurrection. Newly mobilized popular forces were eager to advance their policy agendas. Aquino dissolved the National Assembly and purged regional and local governments, the judiciary, and the armed forces, placing her supporters in these positions. She also seized the assets of Marcos' supporters. For eighteen months, Aquino ruled by presidential decree. By the time of her 1988 election, she had established links with business at the expense of Bayan, an umbrella organization of leftist, single-issue groups.

By 1990, many investors were seeing good prospects for profit in the Philippines despite political instability (a 1989 coup attempt lasted nine days before its collapse), bad infrastructure, the weakness of the presidency and the inefficiency of the bureaucracy. Business profit margins, however, remained high. Investors also noted some of the positive legacies of the Marcos era, including improved physical infrastructure and the liberalization of naturalization that encouraged Chinese capital to make longer-term commitments, moving from commerce into the industrial and service sectors. Indeed, Chinese Filipinos in business gave strong support to Aquino through the Federation of Filipino-Chinese Chambers of Commerce and Industry with its 160 trade-association members.[180] These trends appeared to strengthen under Ramos. Increasingly, there emerged signs of the coalescence of an effective political constituency (Philexport) favoring an export-oriented economy. Local resistance to foreign capital diminished as local firms became joint-venture partners, often with Asian capital. The result, then, was the promise for the first time in half a century of an effective export-oriented political coalition in the Philippines.

Chinese capital both inside and outside the Philippines played increasingly important roles beginning in the late 1980s. Taiwanese investors bought control of a Philippine bank in the early 1990s. The local landscape began to feature more figures like John Gokongwei, a Chinese Filipino who began in the corn starch business and subsequently diversified his interests into an enormous business empire including communications, petrochemicals, and a host of other sectors. In the mid-1990s, observers were struck by the symbolism of the Metro Pacific Group's (with links to the Sino-Indonesian-based Salim Group) successful outbidding of the Ayala Group (a traditional and powerful family of the Philippine oligarchy) for Fort Bonifacio in Manila.[181] Chinese capital, in this case, was victorious over the old oligarchs.

Even if we accept that Filipinos had shifted toward an export strategy in the 1990s and that the influence of Chinese business groups had increased, this did not signal the emergence of a consensus favoring cautious macroeconomic policies. And there was little evidence of institutional arrangements that could deliver such policies. Neither was there evidence of a significantly more effective Philippine state.

Given the Philippines' economic difficulties and the inadequacy of local savings, attracting foreign capital remained a central concern. The government also needed to stabilize the economy and to increase savings, in part by reducing public sector deficits. The move by the Aquino government to enforce a 27 percent increase in oil prices in 1989 helped to trigger a coup effort by 400 soldiers in mutiny among the business offices and hotels of the Makati district. Indeed, instability threatened to undermine efforts at economic stabilization. Bombings in Manila continued into 1990 and a major rebellion exploded in Mindanao late that year.[182] Even under Ramos' relatively stable leadership in the 1990s, crime, kidnappings, and lingering secessionist struggles posed serious problems.

The state's weakness, even in areas that elsewhere are seen as exclusive preserves of the state (e.g. organized violence, managing the money supply), continued to prompt concerns about the Philippine economy. In the early 1990s the state still was unable to control organized violence. The Red Scorpion Group, originally created by the military to combat the New People's Army's urban guerilla faction, went into the kidnapping business. Both kidnappings and murder for business purposes grew during the early 1990s.[183]

The Aquino and Ramos governments also failed on occasion to implement the reform agenda in the face of concerted popular opposition. In September 1990, with debt servicing still consuming some 40 percent of the budget,[184] the Aquino government tried to raise oil prices 32 percent, but with offsetting lower taxes on oil and oil products. The major labor unions demanded a reduction of the price increase and, in addition, an increase of 42 percent in the minimum wage, calling a national strike in support of their demands in October. The Aquino government eventually settled on a smaller price increase.

In 1990, after extensive talks within the executive branch, including the Department of Trade, protector of domestic-market oriented firms, President Aquino promulgated a new tariff code while Congress was in recess. However, following howls of protest from various quarters, such as the Philippine Chambers of Commerce and Industry, the government first suspended the bill for sixty days and then withdrew it. Only after another year of negotiations between the executive and legislative branches did the government adopt a new tariff code that, while less open than the one first proposed, nonetheless was significantly more open than the trade bill previously in force.[185]

Demonstrations and strikes in February 1994 in response to a later announcement of a 22 percent increase in fuel prices again showed the Philippine governments' difficulties in pursuing reform. In the 1994 case, President Ramos faced a court challenge to this move and rescinded the announced price increases. That move, in turn, prompted the IMF to cancel negotiations aimed at providing the Philippines with a $650 million credit facility.[186] The IMF's 1994 approval of the Philippines' three-year economic program had been contingent on the state securing additional revenue. When Ramos failed in his effort to raise oil prices, he turned to the value-added tax and secured Congressional approval for extending the tax to services. Congress, however, began to grant a variety of exemptions to the tax and a legal challenge to the new tax kept it tied up in the courts.[187] This saga continued into 1996, little affected by Ramos' strong victory in 1995 elections for the House and Senate.[188] In an address to Congress in 1994, Ramos called on the politicians to resist the "populist pressures being generated within our paternalistic political culture" and warned of the dangers of a "pork-barrel state."[189]

How have our hypotheses fared in explaining policy shifts in the Philippines in response to the fourth external event? One hypothesis argued that economic openness would likely result from foreign exchange shortages, particularly following prolonged periods of ineffective import-substituting policies. The likelihood of such a result was particularly great in the Philippines given its regular dependence on international financial institutions and bilateral foreign assistance. In fact, however, many earlier moves toward openness clearly were designed more to impress foreign creditors than fundamentally to reorient the economy. Fundamental economic shifts came only in the mid-1980s, before and after Marcos left office, during the third and fourth events. We also found some evidence that concerns for lost revenue helped to strengthen the hand of opponents to tariff changes during 1990 and 1991.[190]

Several of the other hypotheses are of limited relevance to the Philippine case. For example, the country never enjoyed a foreign exchange windfall (unless we choose to describe its continuing access to bilateral and multilateral assistance in those terms). Similarly, technocrats never enjoyed significant policy autonomy. That would be possible only under a leader enjoying greater security of tenure than any Filipino appears to have enjoyed. However, it is possible, perhaps even likely, that regional demonstration effects during the fourth event had a major impact on Filipinos. Unfortunately, this is difficult to support empirically. After all, as early as the late 1960s Filipino leaders were looking approvingly at South Korea's economic performance and policies. Furthermore, it is difficult in this instance to disentangle demonstration effects

from shifts in structural incentives that resulted from the large flows of manufacturing investment from Northeast to Southeast Asia.

Conclusion

Several of the variables we laid out in chapter 1 help us in explaining the policy
choices officials and politicians have made in the Philippines over the past half-
century. Historical and social structural influences left the Philippines with a
very powerful oligarchy and a weak state, with the former able to check the
growth in the power of the latter. The ministries responsible for macroeconomic
policymaking were unable to control those agencies, captured by private interests outside the state, that allocated particular privileges and benefits. Both the
rural elite, with its export interests, and the urban manufacturing elite, with its
concern to protect local markets from foreign competition, were stronger politically than their counterparts in Indonesia, Malaysia, and Thailand. In short,
what most sharply distinguishes the Philippines from those three countries is the
power of societal groups relative to the state.

The power of the oligarchs prevented the state from expanding its revenue
base or pursuing policies designed to transform the existing economic and social
orders. Access to external patronage to finance balance-of-payments deficits,
however, allowed the Philippines to defer critical economic adjustments until
the late 1980s. The first hypotheses concerning the impact of foreign exchange
shortages and windfalls raise the impossible-to-answer question of whether
leaders would have redirected the economy earlier than they did had they not
enjoyed such regular access to foreign savings. As noted above, fears of revenue
shortfalls played at least some role in creating opposition to tariff reductions.

Clearly, political disjunctures have proved important and stimulated economic reform efforts. In particular, Quezon after independence, Marcos after
declaring martial law, Aquino after Marcos' overthrow, and Ramos after his
election had greater opportunities to move against entrenched elite groups.
Ramos proved most successful in using his power to change the course of the
Philippine economy. While Ramos clearly proved himself an adept politician
able to widen the policy space at his disposal, the demonstration effects and
structural factors noted above also seem to have played key roles. Finally, in
looking at the flows of direct foreign manufacturing investment into the
Philippines, it may be possible to argue that new transnational coalitions took
on increasing importance in shifting the country toward an open economic
strategy.

Throughout the postwar years the Philippines faced problems of corruption,
internal insurrection, and inconsistent economic growth. Efforts to reform the
economy were frustrated by an inability to create enduring and effective
governing institutions. The presidency appeared to afford incumbents considerable power but, until Marcos in 1969, none was able to gain reelection. With

increasing mass mobilization in the 1960s, the political system faced growing demands.

With martial law, Marcos moved to establish a more centralized patrimonial polity. He reorganized business associations, apparently hoping to give them a corporatist cast.[191] While Marcos opposed those who stood in his way, he could not afford to attack the oligarchy as group. Marcos never was able to increase tax revenue from the powerful and therefore continued to rely on indirect taxes for between 70 and 80 percent of state revenue. While tax rates were high, collection rates were low, forcing continued dependence on regressive indirect and trade taxes.[192]

A succession of Filipino leaders failed to reorient the economy despite apparent opportunities, most notable in the cases of Marcos and Aquino. Was the socioeconomic inheritance – a weak state apparatus and powerful, almost feudal, societal elites – a guarantee that any efforts toward far-reaching reforms would fail? Are institutions, even in the face of a skilled politician with centralized political power, so resistant to change? As noted above, answering this question requires that we know the impossible – what these leaders intended and the relative priority they placed on the variety of goals they pursued. Marcos' advisor Adrian Cristobal contended that Marcos "believed he could have a vision for society . . . and still loot it."[193] Aquino seems to have been more concerned with restoring democracy and political stability than effecting economic changes.

Marcos failed to construct an enduring basis of legitimacy, a set of institutions able to underpin a steady commitment to pro-growth policies, or a workable political coalition ready to sustain those policies. Where Marcos failed, economic forces emanating from Pacific Asia may succeed in fostering the emergence in the 1990s of an alternative political coalition favoring growth through openness. The more difficult issue remaining, however, concerns the Philippine polity's capacity to sustain stability, to extract the necessary level of revenue, and to maintain macroeconomic stability.

CHAPTER SIX

Thailand

Through the early postwar period until the late 1960s, Thai politics remained tightly circumscribed, with top officials of the bureaucracy governing a small and relatively nonintrusive state. Ethnic, geographic, and historical factors enabled these leaders to collect necessary levels of state (and personal) revenue and foreign exchange without launching ambitious state programs or directly mobilizing large segments of Thai society. Strong comparative advantage in rice production allowed officials to garner significant government revenue from the country's leading foreign exchange earner by taxing exports. Steady expansion in land under cultivation produced both revenue and foreign exchange. Exports of commodities grew rapidly and generally without state promotion. As a result, by the 1960s observers were lauding Thailand's "outward-looking" economic growth.[1]

The legacy of conservative fiscal, monetary, and exchange rate policy choices dating back to the nineteenth century exercised a powerful influence on state officials making policy choices in later periods in response to novel external conditions. Nonetheless, by the latter 1960s, inflationary pressures in Thailand increased along with external imbalances. Then, in the mid-1970s, externally induced pressures following the first oil shock and newly mobilized domestic demands for economic redistributive policies began to shift state officials away from their traditional cautious macroeconomic policy orientation. For the first time, political leaders with roots in business began to have strong influence over government policies. During the 1970s and early 1980s, a significant clash emerged among officials and political leaders concerning the country's development strategy. While one group sought to boost economic growth and address equity concerns by expanding state promotion of industry and providing macroeconomic stimulus, the other wanted to restore stable prices and external balances as means toward the same goals. This conflict between policy approaches reached its peak in the early 1980s. By 1986, however, those favoring cautious state economic policies and enhanced economic openness clearly were dominant. Their views prevailed thanks to negative demonstration effects (the desire to avoid the Philippines' debt problems), the prominence Prime Minister Prem Tinsulanonda (1980–88) accorded to the liberal camp among the government technocrats, the impact of earlier reluctant macro-economic policy measures (most importantly, the 1984 devaluation of the baht), and the shifting global and regional trade and investment currents that favored Thai export-oriented manufacturing in the late 1980s. By this period, Thais were drawn less to a Northeast Asian model of "Thailand, Inc." than to a more traditional Thai policy of economic openness that built on local comparative advantage in agriculture and services as well as manufacturing.

In the discussion below, we provide a sketch of Thailand's social organization, politics and state institutions, and relations between business groups and state officials. This gives the background to the subsequent attempt to explain policy choice in Thailand.

Political regime

Social organization

During the nineteenth century, the traditional Thai ruling nobility drew the immigrant Chinese merchant community into a profitable but subservient relationship. By facilitating the growth of trade and providing the state with necessary revenue, the Chinese helped to make it possible for traditional social institutions to survive more or less intact through modest economic growth and international economic openness. Most economic expansion came in agriculture, particularly increased rice production and exports, and without major public investments in infrastructure, agricultural extension, or research.

The monarchy overturned a system of "slave" labor in the late nineteenth century, thereby increasing the size of the labor force available to produce rice for export, and boosting the acreage of newly cleared land under cultivation using traditional agricultural methods.[2] Rice exports grew twenty-five-fold from 1874 to 1930 as the Chinese took on the financial and commercial functions critical to rice cultivation, milling, distribution, and export.[3] They dominated the private sector and provided the bulk of state revenue. As a politically weak minority, however, they did not constitute a direct threat to the political power of the Thai ruling elite.

Once the country had integrated into the world economy in the nineteenth century, life changed relatively little for the vast majority of Thais living in villages until the second half of the twentieth century. While they were increasingly brought into a national community, traditional local institutions maintained their integrity. Economic survival in Thailand did not require major social dislocations until well into the twentieth century.

As a result, the expansion of a market economy and economic growth brought little social upheaval or political instability in their wake. Thailand's political independence and the resulting absence of an anticolonial, nationalist struggle, left the mass of Thais politically unmobilized. The Thai military, for its part, despite its dominant political role after 1932, was slow to assume clear ideological positions.[4] Not until the late 1960s did Thailand begin to witness mass mobilization for political action or a bourgeois-led movement for democratic reforms and institutions promoting capital accumulation. By that time economic and social forces were sufficiently powerful to challenge Thailand's "bureaucratic polity,"[5] a court politics in which civil and military officials had replaced traditional aristocrats as the top-level leaders.

Politics and the bases of state power

Thai state officials under the monarchy secured Thailand's independence through the colonial era, but did not undertake developmental roles (Thailand was then known as Siam). The state made only modest investments in irrigation[6] (a factor helping to explain the apparent lack of per capita income growth between 1850 and 1950).[7] It did, however, invest more in transport, including railroads and, with US aid in the 1950s and 1960s, roads. Officials followed conservative fiscal and monetary policies and maintained the stability of the baht.

This modest developmental record was partly a result of the constraints imposed by colonial powers as they tried to influence Thai affairs beginning in the nineteenth century. Colonial powers had used threats to the security of their investments, such as those resulting from financial insolvency, as a pretext for establishing colonial rule elsewhere, including in what is now Malaysia. To fend off such dangers, Thai officials, with the assistance of British advisors, worked to maintain a sound currency. Another factor limiting the emergence of a significant developmental impulse among Thai elites was that few Thais were mobilized to make demands of state officials.

After the overthrow of the absolute monarchy in 1932, officials grew more active in trying to stimulate economic growth. They promoted a variety of state enterprises. For the most part, they placed ethnic Thais in these new jobs and closed off certain occupations to foreigners. The state enterprises, however, proved more important as sources of revenue for competing political factions than as agents of economic growth. Not until the late 1950s when the state began to limit its competition with private Sino-Thai capital did Thailand experience significant industrial growth.

Field Marshal Sarit Thanarat launched the rationalization of the Thai state and import-substituting industrialization in the late 1950s and early 1960s. By shifting resources away from the state enterprise sector, Sarit undercut his political opponents who relied on state firms for the funds they needed to foster political followings. Sarit encouraged private Thai and foreign investment. Thereafter, officials used fiscal policies, including tariff protection, to promote industrialization.

Political power remained concentrated in the hands of a small group of officials. The military emerged increasingly as the dominant political institution in Thailand. Competing factions within the military and civil service, however, led to frequent changes in leadership of the government. By the late 1960s, a significant middle class had emerged in Bangkok and the swelling numbers of university students began to assume active political roles. When they took to the streets in 1973, student demonstrators unwittingly leveraged divisions within the military leadership and brought down the military government. They ushered in a brief and unstable period of parliamentary government. Although the military had reestablished its political dominance by 1976, its power relative to parliament, political parties, and business interests using those institutions continued to ebb.

With steady expansion in political participation and the mobilization of social groups, the number of interests able to influence state policies also grew. Inevitably, this threatened traditional Thai conservative macroeconomic policies. During the 1970s, pressures from farmer and student groups, and intensifying rural insurgencies, ensured that reducing rural poverty became a salient political goal. To address that end, financial officials, for the first time, began regulating the distribution of private commercial bank credit, in this instance directing it to the countryside. Public finances, meanwhile, had to cope with considerable expansion in military expenditures at a time when communism was on the rise in most of Thailand's neighbors and in some rural Thai districts as well.

The gradual worsening of inflation beginning in the late 1960s and external and budget imbalances produced increasing concern among Thai economic officials. The external shocks of the 1970s made the implementation of adjustment policies difficult. The growing number of social groups able to influence policy also hindered concerted state action. Nonetheless, over the early 1980s, officials began to grapple with growing macroeconomic imbalances. Under Prime Minister Prem Tinsulanonda in the 1980s, even as political parties increased their control over various line ministries, macroeconomic policymaking continued to fall under the sway of technocrats in the Bank of Thailand, the Bureau of the Budget, the Ministry of Finance, and the National Economic and Social Development Board. Increasingly, two distinct patterns of Thai economic policymaking emerged: sectoral policymaking under the direction of political party leaders and macroeconomic policymaking under technocratic guidance. With the strengthening of political parties and parliament, redistributive politics assumed greater importance. The key political parties had their bases in rural provinces where the majority of voters resided. Increasingly, members of parliament from rural areas worked in Bangkok to secure benefits for their constituents (generally rural business interests) in the provinces. Macroeconomic policymaking, however, remained relatively insulated from political pressures.

Following Prem's retirement in 1988, Chatichai Choonhavan became the first member of parliament to serve as prime minister since 1976. This appeared to mark the triumph of political parties and parliament over the bureaucracy, particularly the military. Three years later, however, amid well-founded charges of pervasive government corruption, the military overthrew the Chatichai government and installed as prime minister Anand Panyarachun, a former bureaucrat and a leading businessman. When the military, in violation of earlier pledges, tried to place one of its own in the premiership following a strong performance in elections in 1992, Bangkok residents staged large demonstrations opposing the move. The military response was bloody and the king eventually had to intervene to settle the conflict. The military, as a result, lost some of its political influence.

Field Marshal Sarit had begun to raise the profile of the monarchy in the 1950s as a means of augmenting the legitimacy of his own rule. By the 1970s, the king was able to play a key role in stabilizing the country during that decade's turbulent politics. His political role thereafter continued to expand, as was evident in his ability to end the bloodshed in 1992.

Chuan Leekpai of the Democrat Party became prime minister following elections in late 1992 and, in the wake of 1995 elections, Banharn Silpa-archa of the Chart Thai (Thai Nation) Party assumed the premiership. The latter's ascendance, in particular, appeared to signal (once again) the increasing control over the state exercised by political parties and the rising influence over parties wielded by provincial business figures.[8]

Linkages between business and the state

Under the absolute monarchy and the bureaucratic polity lasting into the 1960s, the Chinese immigrants who controlled the private sector were politically too weak to mount a challenge to the political dominance of the state officials. A considerable degree of cooperation between elite Thais and leading Chinese eventually emerged and survived the overthrow of the absolute monarchy, bouts of economic nationalism, and anti-Chinese *étatisme*. This accommodation assumed new, more institutionalized forms in the 1950s. Thai officials continued to be the dominant players in these relations. They needed the Chinese, however, to manage state firms and to funnel funds to support different political factions.

State officials in the 1940s and 1950s operated what were in essence protection rackets *vis-à-vis* Chinese businesses. This pattern of relations, however, already had begun to change by the time of the democratic interlude of the mid-1970s. During that period, political parties, in many cases dominated by business figures, grew increasingly important. Over the late 1970s and early 1980s, individual business figures such as Boonchu Rojanasathien, Ob Vasuratana, and Pramarn Adireksarn for the first time gained prominent ministerial portfolios. The rise of business power continued through the 1980s. Indeed, by the late 1980s, conditions had changed so markedly that many observers in Thailand grew concerned about the brain drain out of the public and into the private sector. (This movement was a product of the latter's higher salaries and the diminished status gap between the two.)

In the 1980s, Prime Minister Prem, Deputy Prime Minister Boonchu Rojanasathien, and some leading technocrats worked hard to institutionalize new bases for state–business communication and cooperation. The Prem government helped to establish Joint Public – Private Consultative Committees at the national and provincial levels.[9] Leading state officials hoped to use these new fora to socialize business leaders and make of them responsible citizens. For their part, business leaders expected to benefit from regular access to high-level officials.[10] The influence of these business groups, and of other longer-established business associations such as the Board of Trade and the Federation of Thai Industries,[11] waxed and waned depending on the government in power. In general, business associations had relatively greater influence under military-backed technocratic governments. When political parties were in power, their leaders enjoyed alternative channels of access to state resources that they could use to benefit select business interests and, as a result, business associations' roles declined. The associations, while greater in number and prominence in the 1980s and 1990s than in the past, remained weak and of limited usefulness to national leaders in need of coherent advocacy groups able to back particular economic policies. While some business groups were important in encouraging greater outward orientation in the country's trade policies in the 1970s, the impact of their roles lay more in the provision of information to officials than in mobilizing political support for those policies.

Leading Thai business firms are often parts of family-based business groups. In this respect, the Thai private sector resembles Chinese business organization elsewhere in the region. While these business groups have their roots in a variety of particular sectors, most critically in finance, they have operations that extend across different activities. Families with roots in the financial industry, for example, play major roles in industry; commercial interests are tied to financial ones; and, within industry, single business groups produce a broad variety of goods. When Thailand's petrochemical industry began to expand rapidly in the late 1980s, for example, among the major players were a cement manufacturer (Siam Cement, which diversified into a wide variety of manufacturing activities), family members of Thailand's largest financial institution (the Sophonpanich of the Bangkok Bank,) an agricultural group (Charoen Pokphand also diversified into various businesses in Thailand and China), and a textile conglomerate (Saha Union).

Having briefly sketched in the context within which Thai economic policy-makers operate, we now offer a more detailed discussion of postwar conditions in Thailand before turning to a review of our four events. Our concern in the sections that follow is to explain Thailand's relatively persistent adherence to open economic policies. As this discussion will make clear, not all powerful Thai groups have shared a commitment to open economic policies, and state policies have fluctuated, albeit within comparatively narrow bounds, over the last fifty years.

Postwar developments

Thailand was a major beneficiary of US economic and military aid beginning in the 1950s, military spending in the 1960s, and Japanese aid thereafter. Thailand also received considerable assistance, both economic and technical, from international financial institutions. However, Thailand probably did not benefit to an exceptional degree from the general openness of the world economy that was a central characteristic of the postwar era of US hegemony. The Thai ratio of exports to GDP rose only slowly between 1961 and 1985, moving from about 19 percent to 24 percent.[12] Capital inflows to Thailand during this period were modest in size and most incoming direct investment was oriented toward production for the local market. Foreign capital inflows did not exceed 11 percent of gross fixed capital formation during any single year in the postwar period. Foreign capital, however, did provide a yearly average of 35 percent of private non-financial investment from 1967 to 1973.[13]

The United States began to provide Thailand with significant levels of economic, military, and technical assistance in the 1950s. As the United States grew more concerned about the conflict in Vietnam in the early 1960s, Thailand's importance to Washington increased. By the middle of the decade the United States was providing high levels of assistance. In addition, US military spending associated with major US air and naval bases in Thailand, as well as spending by US troops based or vacationing in Thailand, provided considerable economic stimulus. From 1950 to 1975, US military aid amounted to over half of total Thai defense expenditures; between 1966 and 1971 US military aid along with World Bank loans provided some one-third of public capital spending.[14] Increasing US military spending in Thailand after 1965 helped boost the construction sector through the 1960s.[15] Foreign loans allowed Thai officials to expand public investment without engaging in inflationary spending or external borrowing.

Throughout this period, Thailand was not heavily dependent on trade. As a share of total production, trade's role was modest (36 percent of GDP between 1965 and 1969, rising to 38 percent over the subsequent five years).[16] Thailand's economy remained largely agricultural. In 1965, only 4 percent of Thai exports were manufactured goods.[17] Hence, Thailand was not a prinicipal beneficiary of open international markets. Perhaps the most significant result of Thailand's exposure to economic markets during the 1960s was the diversification of agricultural production (partly a product of the tax on rice exports that depressed farmers' incomes and encouraged them to grow other crops). Also linked to Thailand's growing commodity exports was the development of a variety of relatively sophisticated distribution and financial institutions that spread throughout the country and moved the goods raised by decentralized peasant producers down to Bangkok and on to foreign markets.

It is important not to overstate the degree of continuity during the postwar years, however. In fact, Thai officials' economic policy framework shifted sharply during the late 1950s. The Thai economy had required a full decade to recover from the economic shocks and policy shifts associated with the Pacific War and the period of Japanese influence over Thai economic policies (1941–45). Exports took some time to recover and, as a result, Thai officials imposed a variety of economic controls, including state management of the rice trade, and adopted a multiple exchange rate system that remained in force until 1955. Thai officials also, as in the 1930s, discriminated actively against the Chinese and promoted state enterprises that could serve as sources of revenue for competing Thai political groups.

The collapse of one such enterprise in 1957, the National Economic Development Corporation (NEDCOL), helped bring about a shift in state policies. NEDCOL had rapidly grown into one of Thailand's largest companies. It had stakes in various manufacturing operations (sugar, jute, marble products, and paper.)[18] The firm was highly leveraged, raised many of its loans abroad, and had secured state guarantees of its foreign debt. When the firm went bankrupt, it threatened Thailand's creditworthiness. As a result, government officials decided to honor the debts and, as Robert Muscat notes, effectively committed the public investment budget for the next several years.[19] At least among many technocrats, this experience helped to strengthen the conviction that they had to limit the state's direct role in the economy. Sarit embraced this principle when he assumed power (though he used the state as an instrument of his own phenomenal enrichment – over $3 billion in 1994 dollars),[20] and the number of state enterprises fell from thirty-seven in the mid-1950s to fourteen by the end of that decade.[21]

When Thailand shifted toward an import-substituting industrialization strategy in the late 1950s, authorities provided private capital, both Thai and foreign, with reassurances against nationalization or the establishment of competing public enterprises. Officials also offered a variety of tax and other investment inducements, largely through the newly created Board of Investment, including protection against imports. By 1964, effective rates of tariff protection in Thailand were fairly high, ranging from 22 to 65 percent for a variety of consumer goods.[22] Tariff escalation was designed to foster the emergence of assembly in consumer goods industries. Officials raised tariffs in 1964 and again in 1970, initially seeking enhanced revenue but subsequently aiming to protect local firms.[23] Board of Investment policies subsidized the use of capital at the expense of labor.[24] While economic growth picked up, export growth was often below the rate of production expansion, increasing by an average of just under 7 percent a year from 1965 to 1973.[25] Over the 1960s, the average rate of export expansion in Thailand was only slightly higher than the mean for all developing countries (6.8 percent against 6.5) and well below that for global trade (9.5 percent).[26] This modest rate of trade growth was particularly striking as Thailand's terms of trade began to improve in the 1960s, following over a decade of decline.[27]

In the late 1950s and early 1960s, Sarit worked with technocrats in the government and with foreign advisors, particularly from the United States and the World Bank, to reorganize public administration. A central concern among the technocrats was the rationalization of economic policymaking. As part of this process, economists in the macroeconomic policymaking agencies – the central bank, Ministry of Finance, Budget Bureau, Fiscal Policy Office, and National Economic Development Board – eventually gained greater control over the ministries regulating commerce, agriculture, and industry.[28] These ministers lost some of their freedom to treat their respective jurisdictions as private fiefs – patrimonies the rewards from which they allocated among their clients. This important development stemmed from the government reorganization noted above, and the influence of a handful of prominent technocrats who were intent on restraining politicians' efforts to meddle with public finances. Still more critical was Sarit's great political power. That power afforded him the opportunity to delegate to technocrats broad discretionary authority over macroeconomic policies.

Technocrats managed to reprivatize the rice trade and end the multiple exchange rate system in the mid-1950s. Thereafter, they extended their control over public finances, imposed a ban on public guarantees of private sector debt, and rapidly reduced the central bank's role in financing public debt.[29] Remarkably, not only did public sector deficits remain small until they expanded modestly in the latter 1960s, but price stability was so great that in several years mild deflation set in.[30]

Economic growth began to slip slightly after 1968, partly because of lower US military spending in the region and Thai officials' efforts to curb a growing trade deficit that hovered around 4 percent of GDP from 1968 to 1970.[31] Government deficits continued to expand until 1971 despite a rise during the 1960s in tax revenue as a percentage of GDP (and a sharp diminution in the share of trade taxes in total government revenue).[32] Much of the increasing public expenditure was for security-related goals.[33]

As noted above, by the 1960s, observers were praising Thailand's "outward-looking" economic policies. The Thai economy, however, was not strikingly open to imports. While officials refrained from frequent recourse to import controls, tariff levels were quite high (although tariff changes in 1972 reduced slightly the bias against exports and increased the use of import rebates as part of an export promotion strategy).[34] Nonetheless, officials consistently sustained stable macroeconomic management, with the exception of the wartime and early postwar years. The baht maintained its 1955 dollar parity until 1981. Inflation was generally low and economic growth consistent. In addition, while the economy was not heavily engaged in trade, most prices clearly were subject to international signals and structural changes in the economy suggested a considerable degree of flexibility. Indeed, observers long hailed the Thais' abilities to reallocate productive resources and to diversify exports.[35] These capacities emerged most clearly when the economy began to face a series of external shocks in the 1970s.

Hence, in the years prior to the first external event discussed below, Thai officials had committed themselves to maintaining macroeconomic stability and a modest degree of international economic openness. Several factors help us to explain the choices Thai leaders made during the 1960s. As noted above, Sarit's political interests were served by a shift away from a strategy that emphasized a direct state role in production. In addition, Sarit was able to attract support from the United States and the World Bank, both of which urged greater reliance on the private sector. Further, the NEDCOL disaster of the 1950s demonstrated the wisdom, in the Thai context, of a policy of state restraint and effectively made continuation of a policy emphasizing the state's direct role in production far more difficult.

State officials had to contend with neither revenue nor foreign exchange shortages during most of this period (although the current account deficit began to widen in the late 1960s as US military spending began to decline). In the early 1960s, trade taxes (evenly divided between import and export taxes) had accounted for over half of government revenue. Trade remained a major source of government revenue (about one-third by the late 1960s) so that raising import taxes to promote local industry probably met with support from Ministry of Finance officials charged with balancing fiscal budgets. (Initially, Ministry of Finance officials had opposed the move toward an import-substituting development strategy in the 1950s out of a concern for the negative consequences on trade tax yields.)[36] Worries about collecting adequate revenue increased over the 1960s despite still moderate levels of state spending. Central government spending in 1967 made up 15 percent of GDP, rising to 18 percent by 1972.[37] Much of this increase came in response to growing security concerns.[38] At the same time, external imbalances also grew. In response to these trends, and the saturation of some domestic markets, state officials began to try to promote exports.[39] Ministry of Finance moves to increase tariffs in order to augment revenues, however, often worked at cross-purposes with modest export promotion efforts.

The Thai private sector, for its part, apparently favored openness to foreign capital. The privileges Thai state authorities accorded foreign firms also appied to local capitalists. And where foreign partners were involved, local Chinese faced less threat of nationalization or harassment by state officials.[40]

Challenge and response

In this section, as in the three preceding chapters, we examine policymakers' responses to four different sets of international incentives associated with the four events. In discussing each of these and the associated policy responses, we begin by detailing the impact external changes had on the Thai economy. We then describe and attempt to account for the policy responses. Our explanations draw on the hypotheses we introduced in chapter 1.

First oil shock, global recession, easy credit, 1974–75

Impact The shock of the first oil price increases was offset in part by high prices for Thailand's commodity exports. Indeed, overall, Thailand's terms of trade were favorable during the mid-1970s.[41] Economic growth in 1973–75 was higher than in the 1970–72 period along with faster export expansion. Exports grew at an impressive average annual rate of over 30 percent from 1970 to 1976.[42] Nonetheless, changes in Thailand's trade following the oil price increases had a significant negative effect on its trade balance.[43] On the one hand, higher commodity prices helped to push up export earnings from rice, rubber, maize, and tapioca. On the other hand, imports expanded more rapidly and Thailand's current account jumped from modest deficits in 1973 and 1974 (0.7 and 0.8 percent of GDP respectively) to 4.4 percent of GDP in 1975.[44]

Foreign investment dropped precipitously in 1975,[45] and stayed at a low level for several years. This was not an immediate cause for concern, however, at least not in its impact on the country's balance of payments. It was only after the second oil price increases at the end of the decade that officials became seriously alarmed over external imbalances and growing external indebtedness. Official transfers did not increase during these years and Thai borrowing offshore began to expand.[46] Both state enterprises and private corporations expanded their foreign borrowing significantly during the 1974–76 period compared with the early 1970s.[47]

In sum, the first oil shock had negative effects on Thailand's external economic balances. This impact was particularly worrying because it coincided with the higher rates of inflation evident since the late 1960s. On balance, however, and viewed in isolation, the oil price increases had only relatively mild negative effects on the Thai economy.

Policy record Following the oil shock, Thai officials moved quickly to take measures to correct the country's worsening macroeconomic conditions. Policy adjustments included curbs on public spending (achieving a public sector surplus in 1974) and restraining monetary growth. These moves, however, were responses not only to changing external conditions but also to rising inflationary pressures evident before the sharp oil price rise. In any case, these steps were generally cautious and limited in nature. More important in reducing the inflationary pressures that had emerged in the late 1960s were falling commodity prices, poor harvests, and surplus capacity that dampened domestic investment.[48] Thai officials' rapid response, in short, was to conditions predating the external shock, was limited in nature, and, to the extent that it was effective, depended on serendipitous developments independent of the policy response. Nonetheless, these limited policy adjustments helped to moderate the severity of subsequent economic conditions and to preclude the need for later sharp policy changes of the kind evident in many developing countries in the 1980s.[49]

The policy response sketched above was an effort to restore fiscal and external balances. Officials did not respond to the first oil price hike by trying to open the economy. To dampen inflationary pressures, however, officials did lower tariffs temporarily in 1974.[50] Tariffs continued to favor import-competing firms[51] and effective trade protection increased in the mid-1970s along with tariff escalation (a growing gap between tariffs levied against finished consumer goods and those levied on capital and intermediate goods).[52]

After the oil price increases, Thai macroeconomic discipline began to come under increasing challenge. During this period of democratic politics (the military government had collapsed late in 1973), political pressures grew for more expansionary fiscal policies and for directing resources toward rural areas of Thailand. In an unusual development in Thailand, real interest rates were negative from 1973 to 1975.[53] Controls on direct foreign investment grew more restrictive and state officials adopted, for the first time, significant programs of mandated bank credit (aiming at agricultural borrowers). Officials kept oil prices well below world prices. These trends in Thai economic policies attracted the attention of the International Monetary Fund which extended its first Standby Loan to Thailand in 1976. In short, Thai officials made few moves to effect long-term adjustments to higher energy costs or to restore macroeconomic stability beyond those measures that were prompted by the imbalances of the late 1960s.

Explaining policy choices The policy response to the first oil price increase was limited. Brief adoption of tighter fiscal policies, as noted above, resulted from inflationary concerns predating the price rises. Deflationary impacts before the price rises were largely results of fortuitous international and domestic market developments, but probably limited the extent of economic overheating following the oil price rises in the mid-1970s. Other policy adjustments came in response to altered domestic political conditions and had the effect of reducing the economy's openness.

The first oil price rise came at a time when Thai politics were undergoing their first significant changes in fifteen years. As political parties became important vehicles for seizing control over ministerial resources, politicians became more entrepreneurial in their efforts to enlarge their electoral coalitions. During these years, the numbers of business leaders in parliament and holding ministerial portfolios increased sharply. Popular mobilization among farmers, students, and workers rose dramatically. The number of labor disputes exploded late in 1973 and stayed at a relatively high level until military rule returned in 1977.[54] These changes had the effect of challenging the independence of those state agencies responsible for economic planning, budgeting, and managing monetary policy. Populist attacks on the economic and political power of private banks took on greater fervor[55] at the same time as the Minister of Finance pushed expansionary policies and seemed to undermine the independence of the central bank. Nonetheless, despite growing uncertainties prompted by communist victories in Vietnam, Cambodia, and Laos, and resulting pressures to boost security spending, central government expenditures as a share of GDP actually decreased between 1972 and 1977, while revenues rose.[56]

Circumstances in Thailand at the time of the first oil price shocks were not propitious for a response in the direction of more open economic policies. Officials faced revenue shortfalls and were dependent on import taxes for a significant share of taxation. The political changes associated with the collapse of military rule resulted in a temporary and partial eclipse of technocratic influence over economic policymaking, including fiscal and monetary policies. Any amorphous political coalitions with programmatic concerns that were emerging during this period would have been unlikely to champion open economic policies. Few Thai industries yet had the ability to compete internationally. And demonstration effects, if any, were likely pushing away from open economic strategies. After all, governments in most of the more successful developing economies, even in East Asia, were expanding their roles during these years.

The single exception to this conclusion that few forces were pushing for greater economic openness concerns the role of business. Business power was increasing, but we do not find any evidence of strengthened business pressure to increase trade protection during this period. Rather, the exhaustion of import-substituting opportunities and the existence by the late 1960s of surplus manufacturing capacity in many sectors, led some firms to look increasingly to export opportunities. That policy nonetheless grew more protectionist resulted primarily from the budgetary concerns of Ministry of Finance officials. (It is important to recognize, in addition, that by combining import-substituting policies with export promotion measures, Thai officials in the 1970s and 1980s were able to meet many business concerns for easier access to foreign markets without opening up the Thai economy.)

Second oil shock and debt crisis, 1979–83

Impact Higher interest rates and declining terms of trade following the second round of oil price increases slowed both Thai economic growth and export expansion between 1979 and 1983.[57] Thailand's terms of trade fell 22 percent from 1979 to 1985 and exports hardly grew at all between 1980 and 1986.[58] Oil imports increased as a share of GDP from 3.5 percent in 1978 to 5.7 percent in 1980.[59] International reserves continued to slip downward and foreign debt as a share of GNP rose sharply.[60]

Yet, Thailand also benefited from significant increases in access to foreign resources that helped to offset these effects. After a large increase in 1978 (including IMF Standby Arrangements concluded in July 1978), higher levels of official development assistance continued through the period of higher oil prices. The average size of resource inflows between 1977 and 1982 was 3.8 percent of GNP. Between 1979 and 1981, the average was closer to 7 percent. Government and public enterprise borrowing abroad increased rapidly.[61] While foreign investment in Thailand increased from the lows of 1975–79, it remained at 1 percent or less of GDP.[62] The current account deficit stood at over 7 percent of GDP between 1979 and 1981.[63] Between 1979 and 1985, it stood at a very high 6 percent or more of GDP in five of those six years.[64] These were the most severe external imbalances Thai officials had faced since the years immediately after World War II. Facing tough economic conditions and with emerging overseas opportunities, particularly in the Middle East, more Thais began to seek work abroad and to remit a part of their earnings.[65] Exports of manufactures as a share of merchandise exports, meanwhile, began to move rapidly upward after 1981.[66]

Policy record As noted above, Thai officials made only limited policy adjustments to the first oil price increases. They also were slow to adjust to the second round of price hikes. Domestic energy price subsidies continued. In 1980, military officers drove Prime Minister Kriangsak Chomanan from office following a sudden increase in energy levies (later rescinded) and the selection of a technocrat-led cabinet.[67] Officials continued to follow expansionary policies with the result that in 1978 the rate of GDP growth was close to 12 percent.[68] Public sector deficits, which had averaged close to 3.2 percent of GDP between 1970 and 1977, moved above 5 percent in the following two years before reaching 8 percent in 1980.[69] Government revenue continued to grow as a share of GDP until 1983 when it stood at close to 16 percent.[70] Foreign borrowing by both the central government and state enterprises helped to fuel rapid growth in Thailand's external debt. Debt service rose from an average of 11 percent in 1973–75 to 19 percent in 1982–84.[71] Trade and current account deficits induced borrowings from the International Monetary Fund in1981 and 1985, and World Bank structural adjustment loans in the early 1980s.

Thailand's Fifth Development Plan (1981–86) envisioned major elements of structural adjustment.[72] Among the measures Thai officials, in coordination with advisors in the World Bank, hoped to implement were energy price increases and the ending of all related subsidies, cuts in trade taxes and other trade controls, reductions in foreign exchange controls, privatization of state firms, and an emphasis on export-oriented industries.[73] The departure in 1981 from the ruling coalition of Boonchu Rojanasathien, Thailand's economic czar, might have facilitated economic adjustment. Boonchu, a political party leader formerly with the Bangkok Bank, had used his political standing to launch rural spending programs. He envisioned using state direction to stimulate economic growth in agricultural areas of Thailand and to foster closer economic co-operation between business firms and state officials. With his departure, the voices of more cautious technocrats became more influential.

In fact, state authorities did implement important policy adjustments during these years. Economic growth between 1978 and 1981 averaged about 7 percent. As inflation began to grow, Bank of Thailand officials tightened monetary policy in 1980.[74] They were able to reduce inflation quickly, from 20 percent in 1980 to 5 percent the following year. Officials liberalized restrictions on agricultural commodity exports, devalued the baht in 1981, instituted a system of rebates on export taxes as part of an export promotion policy, raised some energy prices and state enterprise levies, and increased state revenue. In designing these policy changes, Thai officials worked more closely with World Bank officials than at any time since the late 1950s when they first adopted a private-sector led import-substituting development strategy.[75] Officials also moved to promote exports through small adjustments in tariffs. More significant were changes in Board of Investment and other policies that counteracted the ongoing anti-export tariff bias.[76] With investment and imports falling, the current account deficit contracted to 3.2 percent of GDP by 1982. Total external debt continued to grow, however, from 23 percent of GDP in 1979 to 35 percent in 1982.[77] As a result, the cabinet adopted an annual ceiling on public sector foreign borrowing. Offsetting a drop in private investment during the two oil crises, public investment increased considerably, from 3.7 to 9.2 percent of GDP, before moderating after 1981.[78] Meanwhile, the contraction of trade resulting from lower levels of investment diminished state revenue collection and increased the size of the government deficit.[79] Import taxes' share of total government revenue had fallen by the mid-1970s to some 24 percent from 31 percent at the start of the decade.[80]

During these years, Thai policy responses were not limited to economic measures, but included institutional adjustments as well. For example, the cabinet created the Council of Economic Ministers, a smaller subgroup of economic ministers designed to enhance coordination and control over economic policies. In addition, under Prime Minister Prem, technocrats were able to increase their control over macroeconomic policymaking. This proved important in enabling the adoption of adjustment measures. Despite the absence of any policy shift toward economic openness during the 1970s, Thailand's trade had expanded rapidly so that by 1980 it accounted for about 46 percent of GDP, from 28 percent in 1970. Exports had increased from 13 percent of GDP in 1967 to 19 percent in 1979 and 24 percent in 1983–84.[81] Manufactured goods had increased their share of those exports to 30 percent by 1983 from 22 percent in 1978.[82] However, for the 1981–85 period, trade's contribution to Thai economic growth was far lower than during any other period in the 1970s or 1980s.[83]

Nonetheless, the Thai economy apparently remained comparatively open. Robert Muscat reviewed a number of comparative studies of economic openness in developing countries and noted that all of them concurred in finding in Thailand relatively low levels of price distortion (high levels of economic openness). By the end of the 1970s, however, such distortions clearly were growing and helped prompt officials' efforts to reverse the direction of policy.[84] In 1982, officials made a major effort to restructure tariffs. The results, however, were disappointing.[85] Exports as a share of GDP fell between 1974 and 1983.[86] And total trade as a share of GDP fell from 1980 to 1985.[87] A decade of policy drift had produced a perceptible closing of the economy.

Little *et al.* characterize the Thai official response to the second oil shock as appropriate, although possibly too cautious.[88] More positively still, Muscat suggests that Thailand may have implemented the most gradual and successful structural adjustment program among developing countries in the 1980s.[89] Indeed, by 1983 the country's external position was much what it had been in 1979.[90] Nonetheless, it had yet to undertake necessary external adjustments. Thai trade, for its part, remained highly protected[91] and the baht appreciated after 1981 as a result of its link to the dollar and helped to slow expansion in Thailand's trade.[92] Pasuk Phongpaichit, for her part, suggests that government policies had little to do with any successful adjustment on the part of the Thai economy.[93]

Explaining policy choices As during the first event, Thai officials did not respond to the second oil shock by pushing the economy dramatically in the direction of greater economic openness. Based on concerns about revenue losses during a period of chronic fiscal deficits, Ministry of Finance officials were chary of sharp tariff reductions. Trade taxes continued to account for about one-quarter of government revenue, still divided about evenly between import and export taxes.[94]

Ongoing political instability impeded any concerted response to deteriorating external conditions. When Prime Minister Kriangsak abruptly (and ineptly) announced higher energy prices early in 1980, broad opposition thwarted his efforts and helped pave the way for his overthrow. Later efforts to raise energy prices under Prime Minister Prem's more stable cabinets were more successful. Prem, however, also faced incessant political difficulties, including attempted coups in 1981 and 1984 and regular challenges in parliament. He benefited, nonetheless, from the king's support and divisions within the military, and, ultimately, remained in office for eight years. Hence, Prem managed to return technocrats to their accustomed dominance of macroeconomic policymaking.

Thailand began mid-century as a highly open economy and gradually over time became less so, at least by certain measures, including impediments to trade and capital flows. Indeed, by the late 1970s, in part in response to the instabilities induced by the oil price increases, Thais were for the first time moving tentatively in the direction of a coherent economic strategy that departed from traditional macroeconomic policies. Deputy Prime Minister Boonchu was closely associated with a view that saw a larger state role as holding the promise of enhanced industrial deepening and greater investment that would reduce rural poverty and trade imbalances by strengthening Thailand's secondary import-substituting industries. Certain elements of this approach, particularly the adoption of secondary import-substitution policies, implied further departures from open economic policies. Boonchu's advocacy of "Thailand, Inc." can be viewed as an example of demonstration effects, in this case pushing in the direction of more expansionary and interventionist policies.

State spending grew rapidly in response to the second oil price increases, from 17.2 percent of GDP in 1977 to 21.7 percent in 1982, with almost none of the increase accounted for by larger capital outlays and only a small part of the boost met by enhanced revenues. Part of the growth in spending was for defense, which increased to 5 percent of GDP in the late 1970s (from 3.5 percent in 1972).[95] Spending to service the growing interest charges on foreign debts also accounted for a significant share of the increase.[96]

By the late 1970s, concerns about income inequalities in Thailand had grown more pronounced. Heightened worries reflected the impact not only of rural insurgencies, but also the gradual expansion in the power of parliament and rural-based political parties after 1978, and particularly after 1981. While political parties certainly did not present clear and comprehensive policy alternatives, the electoral concerns of party leaders dictated the wisdom of trying to direct resources to rural areas. These developments tended to make more difficult the imposition of deflationary macroeconomic policies. The impact of these political developments on the openness of Thai economic policies, however, was more ambiguous.

By the late 1970s, business interests were playing more important roles in shaping government policies. Under Deputy Prime Minister Boonchu and, subsequently, National Economic and Social Development Board Secretary General Snoh Unakul, increasingly institutionalized contacts between government officials and business associations emerged. This development helped to ensure that government officials were better informed about developments in different sectors of the economy. Business leaders also channeled their growing influence through the increasingly powerful political parties in parliament. Strengthened business influence, however, had little discernible impact on the direction of economic policies. An important exception to this generalization concerned the roles played by business associations in the late 1970s in identifying obstacles to the implementation of export-promoting policies. Ob Vasurat, president of the Thai Chamber of Commerce, also urged the prime minister to create a top-level committee to plan an export strategy for Thailand.[97]

In response to exhausted opportunities in the domestic market by the early 1970s, some private firms became more intent on expanding their exports. Textile producers, for example, began to look with increasing interest at export markets. Business firms also developed greater stakes in having access to foreign sources of capital. With direct foreign investment inflows slowing and the collapse of the local equities market in 1979, private foreign borrowing grew rapidly. As a result, Thai firms' stakes in international flows of capital and goods were growing more pronounced.

As noted above, economic instability and growing income inequality gave rise by the late 1970s to sharper debates among government officials concerning the desirability of various development strategies. The reassertion of authoritarian government in 1976, deteriorating economic performance by the early 1980s, and, also in the early 1980s, a committed drive on the part of the country's leading technocrats to avoid a Philippines-like debt quagmire, undermined the coalition in support of relatively expansionary policies. Prime Minister Prem's ability to sustain his rule backed by shifting coalitions of parties and military factions provided the political space within which technocrats had greater freedom of maneuver. In addition, with private sector political power increasing and public sector resources sharply constrained, a perceived commonality of interests between the public and private sectors continued to emerge. The lack of adequate financing confirmed elites in their view of the superior wisdom of a private sector-led development strategy. The growing strength of private manufacturing interests helped technocratic policymaking agencies increase their influence over the policy process. All these developments eventually worked together to pave the way for a more determined shift toward more open economic policies.

Commodity shock, 1984–86

Impact Thailand's terms of trade began to decline after 1973 and reached a major trough by 1982. They remained very low until 1985 despite the beneficial impact of lower energy prices, and did not recover significantly during the remainder of the 1980s.[98] Public borrowing abroad continued to grow rapidly. It breached the $1 billion mark for the first time in 1983, but was near $5 billion by 1986. During those same years, however, foreign borrowing by government enterprises expanded more slowly, from 4 to 6 billion dollars, after more rapid increases in the late 1970s and early 1980s. Private borrowing, after rising rapidly from 1976 to 1978, and again in 1981, remained fairly stable thereafter until the late 1980s when economic growth was increasing significantly.[99] For the period 1984–86, Thailand's average annual inward resource transfers came to less than half of 1 percent of GNP.[100] The average annual inward resource transfer for the 1983–88 period was 0.9 percent of GNP against 3.8 percent for the 1977–82 period.[101]

Thailand's 1985 growth rate (3.4 percent) was the lowest recorded since the 1950s. On the other hand, after three consecutive years of decline, world trade began to expand again in 1984 and Thai exports grew by 16 percent that year, after two years of decline (they fell again in 1986).[102] Over a longer period, the Thai economy recorded almost no growth in trade measured as a share of GDP from the mid-1970s to the mid-1980s.[103] During the early 1980s, inflation was low (2.4 percent from 1982 to 1984) and current account deficits, still high at about 5 percent of GDP, fell from the levels of 1979–81. Trade expansion was sluggish. Budget deficits were under 4 percent of GDP with both expenditures and revenue expansion down to about 10 percent annually.[104]

Policy record Despite the difficulties of low export prices, falls in world trade, and limited direct foreign investment inflows, the principal problems facing the Thai economy during the mid-1980s resulted not so much from new shocks as the cumulative impact of earlier ones and the ensuing policy responses. Not only was the Thai economy continuing to run large current account deficits, but the years of slow growth in 1981 and 1982, when exports were receding, began to exacerbate dangerous weaknesses in the financial sector as a whole. When, in addition to dismal terms of trade, the country hit a financial sector crisis in 1983, the result was a painful (by Thai standards) economic retrenchment. In 1986, the level of domestic investment reached its lowest ebb since 1972.[105] Debt service peaked in 1986 at 25 percent of export earnings.[106]

In terms of adjustment, Thai officials in 1984 took what may have been the single most important policy step since abandoning the multiple exchange rate system in 1955. They devalued the baht and subsequently tied it to a basket of currencies. Given the still strong weighting of the depreciating dollar, this allowed the baht to continue to depreciate through the 1980s. Indeed, the baht depreciated almost as much in trade-weighted terms between 1985 and 1988 as it had between 1982 and 1985 (with the devaluation).[107]

More unusual was the decision in 1983 by Bank of Thailand officials to impose quantitative ceilings on increases in commercial bank lending as a means of cooling down the economy. This was the first time the central bank had resorted to such quantitative measures on lending. The move excited fierce opposition from bankers, their clients, and parliamentary champions of both. The bank eventually repealed the restrictions and the finance minister fired the central bank governor.

To boost economic growth and reduce external imbalances, Thai officials were growing increasingly concerned to stimulate exports. Thailand's tariff structure, however, continued to frustrate the implementation of a coherent export-led industrialization policy regime. Officials made modest changes to tariff rates in 1984, but substantial reductions had to wait another six years.[108] A new minister of industry after the 1983 elections dropped earlier tariff reform initiatives. This was partly due to sharp disagreements on proposed tariff policy changes among and within various industrial sectors.[109] Tariffs actually rose in 1985 as Ministry of Finance officials sought increased revenues. By this point, Thai nominal tariffs were the highest among Pacific Basin countries.[110] Average tariff levels in 1984–87 were higher than they had been in 1980–83.[111] The principal result of the tariff reforms was an increase in revenue yields.[112] High tariff levels, however, were partially offset by a variety of import tariff rebates designed to facilitate exports.

During the mid-1980s, Thai officials curbed the growth of government spending and, between 1982 and 1987, spending as a share of GDP shrank from 22 to 19 percent. Approximately one-third of that contraction came from a reduction in military spending. More significant still were declines in capital expenditures. Revenue, meanwhile, increased by 2.7 percent of GDP, helping to shrink significantly the government deficit (which, however, was still high at 5 percent of GDP in 1986).[113] Gross domestic investment as a share of GDP dropped to 22 percent by 1986.[114] These contractionary measures were particularly difficult to achieve because officials were committed to an expensive series of ports, industrial parks, roads, rail links, and public enterprises along the Eastern Seaboard, southeast of Bangkok. Tight fiscal policies and the significant slowing in economic growth, however, helped to shrink the current account deficit and, in 1986, Thailand recorded a small surplus, its first since 1978.[115] Price stability continued. After reaching 20 percent in 1980, inflation remained below 5 percent between 1982 and 1988.[116]

In sum, the direction of Thai economic policies had reached a turning point by the time of the third event. Beginning with a relatively open economy before the first oil price rises, policy gradually drifted toward a more closed posture. Some moves to arrest that trend were evident following the second round of oil price increases. And by the mid-1980s, officials committed to significant policy adjustments clearly had gained the upper hand in internal power struggles. They were able to implement important policy measures facilitating economic adjustment, the devaluation of the baht in 1984 being the most important. Nonetheless, countertrends toward a more closed economy, such as the tariff increases in 1985, remained. Overall, the pace of adjustment in Thailand was measured.[117]

Explaining policy choices The difficult economic conditions of the early to mid-1980s, in part results of changes in global prices, helped to generate a consensus among Thais concerning the need for a development strategy featuring a leading role for the private sector. This consensus represented more than simply making a virtue of necessity, given the state's financial constraints. It also reflected an appreciation of the private sector's capacities and a deeper ongoing pro-capitalist shift in attitudes toward business and the ethnic Chinese. Private investment also came to play an increasingly dominant role, although low levels of public investment, in infrastructure in particular, were to have serious negative consequences once economic growth began to pick up.

The emerging elite consensus in favor of a private-sector led development strategy offered promising grounds for forging an effective political coalition in support of open economic policies. The task of translating a distribution of sentiments into effective organization remained largely undone, however. Widespread elite preference for relatively liberal policies suggested, nonetheless, that any government would likely push policies in a similar direction, toward a greater role for the private sector, including enhanced economic openness. Events following the fourth external event offered support for this assumption.

Under the direction of Prime Minister Prem and Snoh Unakul of the National Economic and Social Development Board, technocratic influence over macroeconomic policy increased in the 1980s relative to the late 1970s. Officials in the Bank of Thailand, the Ministry of Finance, the National Economic and Social Development Board, the Budget Bureau, and the Fiscal Policy Office played more important roles. Within the cabinet, the Council of Economic Ministers assured greater coordination of economic policies and vetting of public investment decisions. The National Economic and Social Development Board played similar roles. Prem balanced off leaders of the military and political parties and used his enhanced room for political maneuver to delegate policymaking authority to technocrats.

The rising power of political parties over the 1980s generally did not challenge the increasingly well institutionalized insulation of macroeconomic policymaking. There were some notable exceptions, however, including the 1984 devaluation of the baht and the 1983 decision to use quantitative controls in limiting commercial bank credit expansion. The first move triggered an unusually public protest by the country's leading military figure acting, at least in part, on behalf of private importing interests and their financial backers. On learning of the devaluation, he cut short his travel abroad, returned to Bangkok, and on prime-time television demanded the move be reversed.[118] The adoption of quantitative controls contributed to the eventual sacking of the governor of the Bank of Thailand by the minister of finance. Despite these notable exceptions, party politicians by and large looked to secure advantages for their supporters from the line agencies they controlled and accepted technocrat direction of macroeconomic policies.

During the mid-1980s, technocrats were on the economic defensive even though they were more politically insulated. As in Indonesia in the mid-1960s and again in the early 1980s, the very severity of Thailand's economic problems enhanced the authority of economic officials able to address them and to broker assistance from foreign sources. Thai officials, however, had little opportunity to promote a reform agenda before the end of the 1980s. Earlier in the decade they faced a series of economic crises, particularly in the financial sector. From April 1983 through 1986, the Ministry of Finance rescued thirty-two finance companies and three banks comprising a quarter of total financial institution assets in Thailand. Fifteen other finance companies collapsed and the Bank of Thailand revoked their licenses.[119]

As was true during past events, moves to liberalize the trade regime continued to face opposition from Ministry of Finance officials concerned about public sector deficits. Corporatist arrangements linking business and state officials, meanwhile, do not seem to have contributed signficantly toward adoption of open economic policies. The principal demonstration effect during this period was the negative one exercised by the heavily indebted (and politically convulsed) Philippines. In fact, Thai officials often pointed to the Philippines in support of their arguments for getting Thailand's public finances under control.

To recapitulate these various trends, Thai elites in both government and the private sector were converging in the mid-1980s in their advocacy of a development strategy giving a larger role to markets and private economic actors. Political conditions enhanced the influence of technocrats wanting to implement policies effecting a shift toward such a strategy. A number of factors, however, limited the extent of policy changes. Critical among these were ongoing revenue shortfalls and dependence on import taxes, the fallout from the financial system collapse, and the ability of particular private interests to work the increasingly open political system to protect their interests. The most important policy measures in response to declining commodity prices and trade flows were the steps that devalued the baht beginning in late 1984. These ensured that, even without further major policy adjustments, the Thai economy was well positioned to reap the benefits of external economic changes later in the decade.

International finance changes course, 1987–

Impact The realignment of the dollar and the yen, and subsequently of the Korean won and Taiwanese yuan, along with continuing unmet demand for consumption in the United States, spurred a major ongoing restructuring of manufacturing in East Asia. Factor costs (land and labor) also shifted and drove firms from high-cost economies in Northeast Asia to cheaper ones in Southeast Asia. Oil prices, meanwhile, also remained low. Thailand's economic retrenchment in the mid-1980s, private firms' recoveries from tight financial strictures, and, in particular, the devaluations of the baht in the 1980s left Thailand well poised to exploit the opportunities that emerged as a result of these forces.

Direct foreign investment in Thailand rose sharply in the late 1980s, from $164 million in 1985 to some $2.5 billion in 1990.[120] By that year, foreign direct investment amounted to 2.3 percent of GDP, more than three times the average for all low- and medium-income countries.[121] In the early 1990s, direct foreign investment accounted for 6 percent of fixed capital formation in Thailand.[122] Between 1988 and 1992, Thailand ranked sixth among all developing countries in cumulative capital inflows (near $10 billion). Foreign investment in Thailand in 1993 reached $7 billion, including $2.7 billion in Japanese direct investment.[123] Thailand was the third largest recipient of Japanese manufacturing direct investment abroad (about 5 percent of the total) between 1988 and 1991, and by the early 1990s, Japanese firms were employing some 7 percent of the Thai labor force in manufacturing. Thailand remained a major recipient of Japanese official development assistance, over half a million dollars in 1993.[124]

Thai merchandise trade continued to expand, averaging 64 percent of GDP between 1985 and 1990.[125] As a share of GNP, trade had stood at 30 percent in 1970, increased to 47 percent by 1980, and reached 70 percent in the mid-1990s.[126] After 1987, Thailand's terms of trade also began to improve.[127] Exports grew at an annual rate of well over 10 percent in the early 1990s,[128] including particularly strong trade growth with East Asian economies. Thai trade with Singapore nearly doubled between 1991 and 1993. Imports of capital goods from Japan grew by 500 percent between 1987 and 1993. Imports of Japanese electrical machinery and parts grew even more rapidly.[129] Exports of machinery, meanwhile, jumped from $625 million in 1985 to $11 billion in 1993.[130] And the economy enjoyed its largest boom ever, recording real GDP growth rates of 9.5 percent in 1987, 13.3 percent in 1988, 12.2 percent in 1989, and 11.6 percent in 1990 before settling back into high single digit figures. During that boom, inflation never reached as high as 6 percent.[131]

Policy record In addition to the devaluation of the baht in 1984, Thai policymakers had taken a number of significant steps in the early and mid-1980s that helped to stabilize the economy, reduce export disincentives, and promote capital inflows. More fundamental reforms, however, came in the latter part of the 1980s and early 1990s. These changes in the direction of economic openness included key fiscal and monetary policies.

In 1985, the Thai government budget deficit stood at over 5 percent of GNP. Two years later, it remained over 2 percent of GNP. Thereafter, however, the deficit moved into surplus, reaching well over 6 percent of GNP in 1991.[132] This turnaround resulted in part from measures to increase revenue (including higher tariffs), but largely from very rapid economic growth. Subsequently, in 1992, officials implemented a long-planned value-added tax. This replaced a business (turnover) tax that not only was inefficient, but also had been used to protect local producers and had tended to discourage the creation of small-scale manufacturers of parts and components. The adoption of the new tax finally ended the Ministry of Finance's long-standing concerns to preserve import tariffs in order to secure necessary revenue. The new tax was perhaps the most notable of many cases of significant policy reform in the late 1980s and early 1990s, when rapid economic growth gave to policymakers greater leeway than they had enjoyed for over twenty years.

In the late 1980s, officials launched the first of a long series of major financial policy changes by beginning to deregulate interest rates. They later moved to reduce segmentation within the financial industry, to promote offshore banking, and to expose local financial institutions to increased competition, including that from foreign firms. In 1990, Thai officials declared that Thailand would adopt the International Monetary Fund's Article VIII status, removing controls on capital account flows.

Policies designed to boost investment and trade advanced into the 1990s. Officials created an Import-Export Bank and a Securities and Exchange Commission to regulate the local equities markets. In 1989, officials eased regulations barring foreign ownership of land. In 1995, they approved full foreign ownership of utilities and infrastructure concessions.[133] In 1990, officials ended Board of Investment surcharges on imports and removed some import bans and export taxes. That same year, Prime Minister Anand slashed tariffs on most kinds of machinery from the range 30–35 percent to 5 percent. The weighted average tariff, which stood at 11.4 percent in 1990, was down from 13 percent in 1986 (but up from 9.7 percent in 1982).[134]

In fact, tariffs for all goods, particularly manufactures, increased in 1984–87 over the 1980–83 period, and rose again during 1988–90. While they fell slightly for all goods in 1991–93, they continued to rise for manufactures.[135] The continuing anti-export bias probably contributed to worsening income inequality in Thailand.[136] Clearly, neither trade policies in particular nor economic adjustment measures in general played major roles in producing the economic boom of the late 1980s. The most significant reforms followed rather than preceded the boom.[137] Non-tariff barriers, never significant impediments to Thai trade flows,[138] came down during the 1984–93 period. Offsetting tariff disincentives, officials expanded exporters' access to duty rebates and other tax breaks, while the number of bonded warehouses and export processing zones increased. In 1989, eighty-nine factories had bonded warehouse status and four export processing zones were in operation.[139] Reflecting ongoing resource reallocation consistent with Thailand's comparative advantage, labor-intensive exports as a share of total exports increased by 70 percent during those same years (this increase, however, was the smallest recorded among the ASEAN Four).[140]

Explaining policy choices The crucial policy initiatives of this period focused on financial and fiscal reforms. Rapid economic growth paved the way for economic reform. A further factor allowing policy change was the long gestation of the reform agenda. For about a decade, officials had been considering a variety of policy shifts but the long sequence of macroeconomic and financial crises had precluded earlier action.

The Anand government, backed by the military, hastened implementation of policies that moved the Thai economy toward greater openness. Technocrats led the new government and many of them had no significant political ambitions. With political insulation provided by the military that had put them in power, these technocrats enjoyed unusual levels of freedom to pursue their policy preferences.

Strikingly, however, regime shifts appeared to have little impact on the overall direction of policy in the late 1980s and early 1990s (though no other government was able to push through as many measures as the first of the Anand governments). Hence, when the Chatichai government, dominated by political parties, assumed power in 1988 and again when Thailand returned to parliamentary government after the 1992 elections, the basic direction of reforms continued more or less unchanged.

The consistency of policy goals under different regime types and governments testifies to the extent to which elite Thais had reached a broad consensus on a desirable development strategy. Demonstration effects exercised by other successful East Asian economies may have played a role in fostering this consensus. The result, however, was that under both generals and technocrats, on the one hand, and party politicians, on the other, the broad commitment to more open economic policies continued.

The single most important factor facilitating a commitment to an open trade strategy was the removal of the revenue constraint with the string of fiscal surpluses in the late 1980s and implementation of the value-added tax in 1992. As noted above, tariff reduction proceeded fairly slowly initially. However, participation in several multilateral economic institutions (ASEAN Free Trade Area, Asia-Pacific Economic Cooperation forum, and the World Trade Organization, particularly the General Agreement on Trade in Services) ensured ongoing commitment to tariff reductions and other measures designed to open up the Thai economy. In sum, favorable economic conditions, a strengthening consensus on the gains to be realized from expanding exports, the disappearance of revenue constraints, the favorable stimulus that resulted in part from the boom in direct foreign investment, and varying degrees of political insulation provided the conditions necessary for a decisive shift toward greater economic openness.

Conclusion

Reviewing the explanatory power of our hypotheses, we find that revenue shortages help to explain the reluctance of Thai state officials to move toward more open economic policies. Tariff changes in the early and mid-1980s did little more than enhance revenues.[141] Revenue remained a significant obstacle until the late 1980s. A string of budget surpluses and institution of a value-added tax in 1992 effectively removed the revenue constraint.

Thai officials never enjoyed the luxury of a foreign exchange windfall. We might argue, however, that the ease of earning foreign exchange into the 1960s, given exportable commodities (in particular, Thailand's comparative advantage in rice production), reduced the pressures that might otherwise have existed to actively stimulate exports (or curb imports). In any case, consistent with hypothesis H1b, the relatively mild, but persistent, current account deficits of the 1970s and 1980s under an import-substituting development strategy eventually pushed Thai officials to move toward a more open economic model. Officials effected this shift only gradually, however, beginning with export promotion policies in the early 1970s and continuing by various means through the mid-1990s.

While state officials worked to foster forms of corporatist linkage with business interests in the 1980s, we found little evidence that the nature of these links significantly influenced state policymaking. One important exception, as noted above, was the role business associations played in the late 1970s and early 1980s in streamlining export and export promotion mechanisms in Thailand. We also observed that squabbling among industrial interests induced the minister of industry in 1983 to throw up his hands and abandon efforts to formulate policy adjustments. Corporatist arrangements, conceivably, might have facilitated private interests' efforts to achieve cooperative outcomes. Corporatist arrangements were more marked under Prime Minister Prem than under his successors. And at least one observer suggests that talks within the Joint Public – Private Consultative Committee reduced opposition to very limited trade reforms.[142] The weakening of these arrangements, however, did not appear to influence the direction of economic policy choices.

A surprising finding with regard to the fourth event was the limited degree to which regime type influenced policy responses to that event. However, while regime type may not have proved critical, it does appear that a minimum level of political stability was important in allowing leaders to initiate policy shifts. This was less critical in the 1990s in the context of fiscal surpluses and rapid economic growth. It was more significant, however, in the late 1950s when Sarit launched a major policy reorientation and in the mid-1980s when Prem, more cautiously, oversaw policy shifts toward greater openness (and, in particular, toward external equilibrium).

The evidence on the impact of external models is ambiguous. Officials pointed to external models both as negative examples (the Philippines) and positive ones (Japan, Singapore, South Korea, and Taiwan). Even when referring to this latter group of countries, however, some officials were interested in these states' *dirigisme*, while others were more impressed with their dynamic export sectors. By the late 1980s, however, most Thais converged in emphasizing the latter aspects of the East Asian model.

A supportive political coalition facilitated moves toward greater economic openness. This coalition, however, was not a broad, formal one. While a broad *implicit* coalition, a consensus, favoring export-oriented policies emerged in the mid-1980s, this was not a formal, political coalition. Narrower, informal coalitions were important, particularly those among state technocrats and military leaders who provided the former with policymaking autonomy.

Political disjunctures do not appear to have played as important a role in shaping foreign economic policies as did the insulation that technocrats occasionally enjoyed under military-backed governments. When party influence increased in the late 1980s, politicians challenged this autonomy. Finance Minister Pramual, in particular, tried to exert his authority over financial policymaking. One encouraging development for advocates of open economic policies was officials' ability to sustain economic reform under Prime Ministers Prem, Chatichai, Anand, Chuan, and Banharn, from 1980 into the mid-1990s, backed by a variety of coalitional and institutional arrangements.

Thai technocrats long dominated macroeconomic policymaking. Their influence over other areas of economic policy, however, was far more limited. Over the 1990s, we find some evidence that officials from the Ministry of Finance were extending their influence into other areas, including industrial policies[143] (this was less clear, however, after Banharn assumed the premiership in 1995). Finance officials were charged with tariff reform and therefore found themselves attempting to forge agreement among the often clashing interests of Thai firms in different industrial sectors or of upstream and downstream firms within the same sector. Any reinforcement of such a trend putting Thailand's most prestigious civil servants at the service of goals other than macroeconomic stability would hold the potential of undermining the long-standing Thai commitment to open economic policies.

In the 1960s, Silcock argued that the Thai political economy could be described as liberalism by default.[144] Prime Minister Anand argued, before assuming office, that Thai policies should be understood as "*laissez-faire* by accident."[145] The record reviewed above clearly is not one of unblemished commitment to open economic policies. Nonetheless, the Thai economy remained efficient and prices never diverged too far from world prices. Indeed, it is something of a puzzle why both empirical and more impressionistic surveys of the Thai economy so consistently conclude that it is open and market-guided, yet public policies, such as those on tariffs, lend less support for such a view. This apparent inconsistency between policies and prices suggests the possible importance of actors and variables inadequately studied here. In particular, private firms, business groups, and market institutions may help to account for the economy's efficiency, flexibility, and sustained outward orientation, at times in the face of policies that would seem to have discouraged those achievements and orientations. Another possible interpretation, of course, is that formal Thai policies (for example on tariffs) and their actual implementation diverged considerably.

CHAPTER SEVEN

Conclusion

We have traced the policy responses of four Southeast Asian developing countries to four different sets of external events, allowing us, therefore, to examine sixteen cases of policy response. The four countries had diverse economic and political conditions at the time they faced the first of these external events. Moreover, the external impacts did not affect the four countries in the same ways. In particular, higher oil prices affected the four economies in very different fashion. The combination of diverse initial conditions, common external influences, and different external effects provided us with comparative bases for assessing the intervening impact of our specified domestic economic, institutional, and political variables. In particular, we now are in a position to gauge the influence of those variables on economic openness.

Our independent variables explaining degrees of openness include ones relating to state resources and capacities, domestic institutional arrangements, political disjunctures, and political coalitions. We also looked at the impacts on openness of those institutions linking business interests to policymaking officials and of foreign development models. So as to isolate those domestic factors that most influence policymakers' responses to changing external economic constraints, we limited the number and range of independent variables from which we developed our hypotheses. Our choice of four broadly similar economies in a single region had a similar effect. It reduced the range of possible variables that might be responsible for divergent policy responses across the four economies we studied. While the four events were significant for each of the economies, in the case of energy prices, the impact varied widely between Indonesia, at one extreme and the Philippines and Thailand, at the other, with Malaysia somewhere in between.

The degree of similarity of patterns of response across the four countries to the four external events and within each country across those events suggests both problems and strengths in our research design. On the one hand, when

157

neighboring countries respond similarly to the same external event, this suggests that common regional or international factors may be overwhelmingly important in shaping national policy responses and may be eclipsing national differences. If the character of the external shock is the predominant influence on the policy response, this indicates the critical importance of external effects, but it also obscures those ways in which domestic political variables may condition the impacts of less profound events. This is what we saw, for example, among the ASEAN Four over the 1980s, as they each adjusted, at different rates and at different times, to both foreign exchange losses and external opportunities, by making their economies more open to international flows of goods, services, and capital.

The power of external forces in the late 1980s produced broadly similar outcomes among the ASEAN Four in terms of the direction of policy response – a move toward openness. Indeed, this has been true of almost all economies since the early 1980s when Ronald Reagan became president of the United States, Mexico's default triggered the debt crisis, and the pace and size of international financial flows was expanding. Nonetheless, the ASEAN Four differed considerably in terms of the specific elements, timing, and extent of their policy responses. To the extent that differences persisted in the face of these powerful common impacts, our research design allowed us to focus on those domestic factors that account for variation in response to these exogenous forces. We have tried to assess the degree to which our domestic political and institutional hypotheses help to account for those differences (we review our efforts below). If, in practice, these hypotheses serve to help explain the differences, they also should help us in understanding the differences between the ASEAN Four as a group and other developing countries.

A degree of similarity of response within each country to the four events also indicates to us the wisdom of deciding not to treat the cases as entirely independent of each other. We made that decision in recognition of the impact of political, institutional, and policy legacies. We noted in chapter 1 that prior decisions shape the institutional and political context confronting policymakers at any subsequent time when they select among policy options. As a result, decisions in response to one event are not entirely independent of those in response to prior events. Countries have development trajectories, and if we viewed sets of decisions as independent, we would tend to ignore these.

In general, we can divide the four countries in this study into two groups: the politically stable, energy-rich (Indonesia and Malaysia) and the unstable, energy-poor (the Philippines and Thailand). The former group made its most notable policy changes in response to the third set of external events (the collapse of oil and other commodity prices and stagnation in international trade, 1984–86). In both countries, officials altered policies in a context of relative crisis, particularly foreign exchange shortages. (These crises, however, were mild and, in particular, brief, when compared with those in many developing countries. We return to this point later in the chapter.) The Philippines and Thailand initiated fundamental policy reorientations later than the former two countries, following the redeployment within East Asia of export manufacturing facilities from Northeast to Southeast Asia. In these latter cases, officials changed policies in response to crises (in the case of the Philippines), but for the most part could do so only after the onset of more favorable economic, and hence political, conditions. We summarize these histories below.

This chapter has two parts. The first is a cross-country comparison of the impact of each event and a description and explanation of the economic policy response. Event by event, we summarize how and why policymakers in the ASEAN Four responded to external economic developments. There follows an assessment of the five broad sets of potential explanatory variables introduced in chapter 1. We suggest which have proven most useful in explaining the policy choices observed in association with the four external events. In the chapter's second section, we indicate where competing sources may be better suited to explaining policy choices, relate that discussion to the comparative political economy literature, and suggest how this study contributes to a broader understanding of the politics of economic development.

Events

For each external event, we here compare how country policy responses differed and why. We begin with the question of how the event was felt in each of our four countries. That is, to understand variation in the responses of four countries, with broadly similar economies in close geographic proximity to one another, to common external economic stimuli, we need first an appreciation of how the common external event was felt in the domestic economy of each country. Domestic conditions – such as resource endowment and prevailing economic conditions – shaped the impacts of the external events at the domestic level.

Then we compare the character and timing of the policy responses across our countries and assess the extent to which such policy responses left each economy more open or more closed to the international economy. Last, we assess the variables most important to explaining the policy choices of decision-makers in each country, and compare these findings across all four countries.

First oil shock, 1974–75

Impact   As oil and gas producers, Indonesia and Malaysia felt the first oil price rise initially as a windfall revenue gain for their respective treasuries. Although by no means in the league of the Gulf states, Indonesia's oil exports were substantial, while Malaysia was more or less self-sufficient in energy. The impact of the shock on the Indonesian economy was generally positive, while that on Malaysia's economy mixed good and bad effects.

The oil price rise caused dramatic improvement in Indonesia's terms of trade and in the value of the country's exports, leading to large balance-of-payments current account surpluses and substantial increases in government revenues. The oil shock in Malaysia led to a significant gain in government revenues from energy, but the higher cost of most imports that followed the oil price rise led to a decline in the terms of trade and a deficit in the current account.

The impact of the first oil shock on the Philippines and Thailand was also mixed. While the oil price increase aggravated already serious balance-of-payments problems in the Philippines, this was partially offset by higher prices for commodity exports and by increased flows of foreign aid. GDP growth dipped from 8.8 percent to 3.4 percent, but had picked up again by 1976.

In Thailand, the shock of the first oil price rise was also offset somewhat by high prices for other commodities, so that the terms of trade remained favorable. When trade deficits increased, these were offset by inward capital flows, eventually including higher aid flows. The main adverse impact of the event on Thailand was not on growth, which slowed but momentarily (to 4.8 percent), but on prices, since higher prices for both imports and exports stimulated inflation.

Policy record Indonesian economic policy responded directly to what were generally felt as positive effects of the first oil price rise. The response rendered the economy less open to flows of goods and services and of capital than had been the case before the external event. Policymakers diminished Indonesia's reliance on foreign savings by reducing the foreign debt. They directed the government's windfall revenue gains into productive investment in rural areas and agricultural infrastructure, rather than into current consumption. But this had undesirable short-term effects in that it bid up the relative price of nontradable goods, thereby discouraging the production of tradables. Meanwhile the revenue windfall from the oil boom encouraged bureaucratic red tape and corruption that obstructed both imports and exports. The net result was that the economy in 1975 was less welcoming to foreign goods and less capable of exporting Indonesian goods (other than oil) than had been the case in 1973. Only in 1978 were the adverse effects of these policy changes on trade partially redressed with the devaluation of the rupiah.

Malaysian economic policy changed in the wake of the oil price rise, but largely in response to domestic political developments. Policymakers were most concerned at this time with achieving the redistributive targets of the New Economic Policy (NEP, 1970–90), the government's response to the disastrous Malay–Chinese urban ethnic riots of 1969. To this end, officials greatly expanded the role of public enterprises, using them as proxies for the less advantaged Malay community. When domestic investment from the minority Chinese business community flagged, officials increased foreign borrowing to finance a state-led effort at income redistribution (facilitated to some extent by the government's windfall oil revenues and by the easy availability of international credit resulting from the OPEC countries' recycling of petrodollars). Government policies also offered greater incentives to foreign investors to try to substitute for lower levels of domestic private investment.

Officials in the Philippines after the oil price rise borrowed recycled petrodollars from banks abroad and employed expansionary fiscal and monetary policies to maintain previous levels of domestic economic activity. Thus, as was the case in many developing countries, the government put off adjusting the economy to the first oil shock. Instead it borrowed and used government spending to pump-prime the economy. Officials had adopted tariff increases and a tax on exports in 1973, and policy became increasingly less open to foreign goods (but more open to foreign investment capital) throughout the 1970s.

There was little direct policy response to the first oil shock in Thailand during the years 1974–75. Policymakers did reduce government spending and restrain the growth of the money supply, but these changes had been on the table much earlier and were responses to inflationary pressures that officials already recognized as a problem before the event. During the democratic interlude (1974–76), policy changes increased restrictions on foreign investment, boosted tariffs on foreign goods, and imposed government controls on some of the lending practices of private banks. Overall, however, Thai policy adjusted little to higher energy costs, and those policy changes that were evident did not represent a dramatic shift either towards greater openness or towards closing the economy.

Explaining policy choices Indonesia's policy response to the first oil price rise left the economy less open to flows of goods, services, and capital than before. This shift in policies, however, resulted from various adjustments that were shaped by a range of factors: the nature of the governing political coalition and, in particular, the relative power of the technocrats within that coalition; the historical experience of previous economic disjunctures; the personal preferences of the leader; and the effect of the impulse on the relative size and sources of government revenues.

The governing political coalition included both technocrats and economic nationalists, but the technocrats, though smaller in number, held sway over macroeconomic policy because of their success in rescuing Indonesia from near economic collapse in 1966. From this formative historical experience emerged the New Order regime. Their prominent role in ensuring the economic survival of the New Order gave the technocrats' advice special weight with the president in the years that followed. This was especially true in the wake of the near collapse of the Pertamina empire in the 1970s. This influence helps explain why

Indonesia did not follow the Nigerian pattern, of squandering on consumption the government revenue windfall from oil. Instead, officials drew down foreign debt and invested in infrastructure and resource-based industry. The direction of the policy change reflected the conservatism and long-term orientation of the technocrats. However, the dominance of the technocrats did not result in a policy response in the direction of greater openness, contrary to our prediction in chapter 1 (hypothesis H2).

The other aspect of the political coalition that helps explain the Indonesian policy response to the first external event is the declining influence of the technocrats over microeconomic policy. In particular, the technocrats could not influence bureaucratic practices in line agencies of the government, dominated by economic nationalists, that dealt directly with imports and exports. So, at the same time as the technocrats succeeded in developing a careful macroeconomic response to the flood of oil revenues from the price rise, these same revenues freed officials in the line agencies from the discipline of budget constraints and scarce foreign exchange. Red tape and corruption siphoned off the potential gains from trade and resulted in higher levels of effective protection than official tariffs and quotas would indicate. These practices amounted to a reduction in the openness of the economy to cross-border flows of investment capital, and of goods and services. In short, the ascendance of the technocrats in macroeconomic policy and the increasing bureaucratic obstruction in the line agencies led to policy responses that, for different reasons, had the same effect, lessening economic openness.

Our findings for this first event in the case of Indonesia support the idea that an external event resulting in windfalls in state revenues and foreign exchange earnings encourages a policy response that is less open (hypothesis H1c). However, we see here that the different components of the policy response suggest the existence of more than one mechanism by which windfalls can influence policy (even though the different mechanisms yielded policy changes which shared the same general effect on openness).

The principal factor motivating domestic economic policy change in Malaysia around the time of the first oil shock was the desire of leaders of the dominant party, UMNO, to effect the redistributive agenda laid out in the New Economic Policy (1970–90). The external event indirectly sustained this policy agenda by providing increased revenue and enabling higher official borrowing abroad. The domestic policy agenda, however, predated the event, and therefore was not a response to it.

In the Philippines, policy did not respond to the first oil shock. By the mid-1970s, the economy received little consistent or coherent attention from Marcos. One could argue that the oil shock upset Marcos' plans to promote economic reforms following his declaration of martial law in 1972. However, there is little evidence to sustain such an interpretation. Marcos marshaled whatever power he could muster to undermine his political opponents. Consequently, the concentration of power increasingly became an end in itself and was not linked to any coherent economic strategy.

Economic policy in Thailand in 1974–75, to the extent it changed at all, did so in response to preexisting economic imbalances or to domestic political developments. With the collapse of military rule (1973–76), populist attacks on foreign multinationals and local banks precipitated policy changes restrictive of each. Obstacles to foreign imports stemmed both from desires to protect local producers and officials' concerns to enhance revenue collection. Political instability, rising security concerns, and a rapid increase in demands on state resources made unlikely a coherent economic response, whether in the direction of a more open or more closed economy.

Policy did not respond to the external event in Malaysia, the Philippines, or Thailand. In the Philippines, Marcos was preoccupied with solidifying his political power. In Malaysia and Thailand, policy changes were responses to prior domestic concerns (though Thailand's inflation in the late 1960s resulted in large part from external factors). Only in Indonesia did the first event stimulate a policy response, but one that included diverse elements and that tended to reduce the economy's openness. In this respect, the policy response was consistent with our hypothesis H1c.

Second oil shock and debt crisis, 1979–83

Impact Our second external event had a mixed impact on the Indonesian economy because it encompassed two related developments, separated in time by 2–3 years, that yielded opposite effects. Initially, the second oil shock represented a further windfall gain for Indonesia, with the terms of trade improving and export revenues increasing. By 1982, however, the 1979 oil price rise had precipitated a downturn in the markets of the developed world which in turn depressed demand for Indonesia's non-oil exports. The increased export revenues from oil had meanwhile caused appreciation in the real value of the rupiah, with the result that Indonesia's non-oil exports were more costly and hence less competitive in foreign markets. Then the price of oil dropped sharply. Together, these aspects of our second event were felt as a negative shock to Indonesia's balance of payments and to government revenues. This pattern of gains and losses from the second external event was repeated in the case of Malaysia, although the negative impact of falling oil prices in 1982 was less pronounced in the more diversified Malaysian economy.

The Philippines faced severe adjustment costs as a result of the second round of oil price increases, which lost the economy between 6 and 10 percentage points in GNP growth. By the late 1970s, the Philippine foreign debt was considerable (a consequence of the "strategy" of not adjusting to the first oil shock) and the rising international interest rates and strengthening dollar that followed in the early 1980s posed an added burden for the balance of payments.

For Thailand, the second oil price rise had a relatively modest impact. Its effects were counteracted by higher levels of foreign official development assistance and by higher remittances from Thais working abroad. The trade deficit that emerged following the first round of oil price increases grew steadily worse with the second round, necessitating greater borrowing abroad, including from the IMF. The economy continued to grow at a healthy rate of about 7 percent a year, reigniting inflationary pressures.

Policy record Just as the second external event had two distinct impacts on the Indonesian economy, so official policy had two different aspects. There was effectively no domestic economic policy response to the 1979 oil price rise. Officials stayed the course established in 1974, and the 1978 devaluation helped make this approach sustainable. However, by 1982 the adverse impacts of the developed markets' downturn, the sharp fall in the oil price, and the inflated value of the Indonesian rupiah caused by oil revenues, all led to deterioration in domestic economic conditions and precipitated a policy response. This response, in March 1983, involved more quantitative restrictions on imports and reduced government spending (officials opted for import quotas in large part as a response to domestic political pressures and as part of the effort to foster heavy industries). The effect was to make policy less open to cross-border flows of goods and services. At the same time, to boost exports, officials devalued the rupiah, countering its real appreciation since 1978.

The main Malaysian policy initiative following the second oil price rise was the heavy industries policy (1980). This policy amounted to second-stage (capital-intensive), import-substituting industrialization, and was accompanied by restrictions on imports that rendered the economy less open to cross-border flows of goods. It was motivated by the desire of government leaders to meet the economic aspirations of Malays by placing Malay civil servants in high management positions in the new, publicly run enterprises. Plans for the initiative predated 1979. It was not a response to the oil price rise, although the large revenue gains from oil hastened its realization.

The most obvious feature of the policy record in the Philippines around the time of the second oil shock was public sector mismanagement of the economy. Although clearly no longer tenable, officials employed, with ever more vigor, the non-strategy of borrowing abroad to cover the economic imbalances caused by the rising cost of oil. Government expenditures exceeded revenues and insolvent industrial and financial firms, both public and private, became the burden of state entities by the end of this period. Despite the urgency of macroeconomic reform, the Philippines failed to achieve significant growth in exports, to reduce fiscal deficits, or to shrink the shortfall of domestic savings.

The one area in which adjustment was apparent in the Philippines was import policy. Following the second oil price increase, officials significantly reduced both import tariffs and quantitative restrictions on imports. These measures, however, were insufficient for the Philippines, in the throes of the political turmoil that following the August 1983 assassination of Benigno Aquino, to escape the tentacles of the international debt crisis. By October 1983, with IMF support withdrawn in the face of mismanagement, the government was unable to meet its commitments and declared a moratorium on debt repayments to private foreign banks and imposed import controls. Attempting to contract the economy, officials triggered a sharp recession.

In Thailand, policymakers gently advanced a set of economic adjustments to the second oil price increases. These included some tax increases, slight rises in energy fees, devaluation of the baht, fiscal restraint, and a limit on public sector foreign borrowing. By 1983, however, Thai officials had yet to significantly increase the economy's openness and World Bank officials were growing more concerned over the slow pace of policy reform. Policymakers tried to launch significant tariff reforms in 1982, but failed to effect significant changes. Limited adjustment measures only gradually slowed the deterioration in the country's external imbalances. At the same time, officials remained committed to major (though scaled down) public spending programs along the Eastern Seaboard that promised to exacerbate external indebtedness.

The end result was that Thailand after the first two external events, while still relatively open by world standards, had become steadily less so. Initiatives to adjust to the oil shocks failed in cases such as energy pricing and tariff reform. At the same time, it is important to realize that Thai officials had never allowed economic imbalances to reach the levels evident in the Philippines. Thus, while the policy reponses were muted, the problems facing the Thai economy were relatively less acute as well.

Explaining policy choices While policy in Indonesia did not change in response to the 1979 oil price rise – and therefore explaining any change there is moot – it did change in 1983, as non-oil exports sank, the exchange rate appreciated, and oil went down in price. With falling oil and non-oil exports, the proportion of government revenues drawn from export levies fell, as indeed did the sum total of government revenues. Such a change encouraged fiscal conservatism on the part of technocrats, but it also encouraged measures to match declining exports with constriction of imports, as advocated by economic nationalists. Thus, while technocrats remained in the ascendant in some policy areas, and indeed led the response to the 1982–83 oil price fall, this did not result in policy change in the direction of greater openness (our hypothesis H2 is contradicted).

Malaysia's principal economic policy change around the time of the second oil shock was adoption of the heavy industries policy, designed to build capital-intensive, import-substituting industries. But this policy change had its origins before the oil price rise and cannot be said to have been a response to it. However, the windfall revenue gains to the government from the oil price rise did facilitate the new policy. They represented spare resources that decision-makers had available to undertake state-led industrialization.

In the Philippines, Marcos and his cronies were plundering the state and economic policy was in disarray. While officials did adopt some tariff reforms under pressure from international financial institutions, the dominant political coalition favored protection of domestic industry and was able to deflect moves to devalue the peso or develop an export-oriented policy. So long as external funds were available from the United States and from international agencies, and so long as Marcos could use technocrats to hoodwink lenders into thinking conditions were better than they were, he could avoid any significant correction. When the IMF refused any longer to be misled, and foreign sources of loans dried up, the only response left was a rapid contraction and inevitable recession.

The beginnings of a policy response in Thailand toward a more open economy reflected the enhanced influence of technocrats in the policymaking process after 1980 as compared with the 1970s when political parties and the military had played more direct roles. The absence of corporatist bargaining institutions may have been important as well. This is suggested by the frustration experienced by the new industry minister in 1983 in the face of sharply conflicting trade policy demands from different manufacturing sectors and sub-sectors. This cacophony of demands resulted from a lack of mechanisms within the private sector for forging agreements among competing interests, and resulted in the minister's abandonment of the trade liberalization initiative.

Officials in the ASEAN Four responded to the second round of oil price increases more than they had to the first price rises. Nonetheless, the policy responses were neither significant nor clearly in the direction of increased economic openness. As with the first event, Malaysian policy did not respond to higher oil prices in the second event. Ample state revenue and access to foreign exchange facilitated the policy shift toward heavy industries, but officials had identified that policy goal prior to the event. By contrast, toward the end of the period, Indonesian officials responded to decreasing non-oil exports and falling oil prices by curbing fiscal spending and imposing import restrictions. Facing still graver external imbalances, officials in Manila responded to pressure from international financial institutions by lowering tariff and other trade barriers. In Thailand, technocrats used their enhanced policy influence to broach, cautiously, policy reforms opening the economy.

Commodity shock, 1984–86

Impact The worst part of the commodity shock and stagnant world trade situation to hit Indonesia was the collapse in the price of oil in the first part of 1986. This, combined with low prices for many of Indonesia's other commodity exports, represented a severe adverse shock for the economy. Declining terms of trade and export revenues produced growing balance-of-payments current account deficits and fewer taxes for the government.

The impact of the commodity shock and trade fall-off in Malaysia was just as severe, representing the most serious economic setback since independence in 1957. There, it was the slump in world prices for major commodities, such as rubber, tin, and palm oil, that led to external deficits, lower government budget revenue collection, and drops in production. The state-run, import-substituting, heavy industries projects became even more heavily indebted.

The collapse of the Philippine economy in the mid-1980s had more to do with officials' failure to deal successfully with a wide range of economic imbalances over more than a decade than with the specifics of the commodity shock or the contraction in global trade. The government failed to meet agreed budget targets and both the IMF and the United States hardened their stand on further loans. Without access to those loans, officials had little choice but to retrench. These influences converged with financial and political crises, thereby exacerbating capital flight.

For Thailand, the third external event was the straw that finally broke the camel's back. Declining terms of trade and the slump in world commerce coincided with a financial crisis in Thailand. While the economic consequences were less severe in Thailand (growth remained solidly positive), these conditions were the worst Thais had seen since the 1950s.

Policy record Indonesia's policy response to the third external event was by far the most dramatic of any observed in the ASEAN Four. It entailed a liberalization of the entire trade regime that began in 1986 and continued into the 1990s, and a substantial devaluation of the rupiah. Officials reduced import quotas and tariff levels, exempted exporters from tariffs on imported equipment, and removed most export licensing requirements. They also reformed the financial sector and further opened the economy to foreign investment. The response clearly made the Indonesian economy more open.

The commodity shock also represented a watershed for policy in Malaysia. For a decade and a half, policy increasingly had been inward oriented, and the state's role in the economy had increased steadily. Beginning in 1986, Malaysian policymakers reversed course, cutting back on state involvement in the economy, reducing the load of regulations intended to help redistribute income to the Malays, and emphasizing exports over import substitution. The economy became much more open to capital and trade flows.

When foreign loans dried up, policymakers in the Philippines adopted draconian economic measures that curbed inflation but caused investment and growth to plummet. These included higher tariffs (to cope with external imbalances), tougher exchange rate controls, a devaluation and a moratorium on debt repayments. The economy grew less open to trade. The informal market in foreign exchange added to the severity of the difficulties confronting government officials. Then, in late 1985, Marcos inflated the economy in the period leading up to elections, creating a surge of inflation and capital flight. In 1986, under President Aquino, officials began to implement a sharp policy reorientation, cutting both import tariffs and controls.

Policymakers in Thailand responded to the commodity shock with significant exchange rate reform and tariff changes that increased revenue but not the economy's openness. Together with earlier policy adjustments, these moves made the Thai economy healthier, even if no more open. Significant measures to restore fiscal and external balances, or to open the economy to international flows of capital and goods as yet were not forthcoming.

Explaining policy choices The character and severity of the domestic economic crisis in Indonesia presented decision-makers with relatively few policy options. Plummeting demand in the domestic economy undercut the economic nationalists' arguments in favor of import-substituting industries and more restrictions on imports. The perception of crisis led President Soeharto once again, as two decades before, to grant the technocrats relatively more authority over economic policy. Technocrats drew on their track record of successful husbandry of the economy through difficult times and the support of Soeharto, as well as that of a growing public outside the state who stood to benefit from greater openness.

For Malaysia, budgetary and external deficits, along with recession, rendered the existing policy course no longer viable. In response, policymakers took an about-face, reducing the state's role in the economy and orienting it more towards exports. Shortages of foreign exchange and government revenues theatened the "expanding pie" upon which Malaysian redistributive policy depended. Government spending to promote Malay enterprise appeared less tenable. Officials turned, therefore, to opening the economy and promoting exports.

Broad socioeconomic changes also encouraged this response. A new class of Malay entrepreneurs could prosper in a privatized and export-oriented economy. Furthermore, as a result of the support of this class, Malay political dominance no longer depended upon financial resources from UMNO's partner, the Chinese MCA party. Changes in the character of the elite coalition that ruled Malaysia encouraged a response to the commodity shock that reduced the state's direct economic role and its previous emphasis on import substitution. Policy became, on average, more welcoming to foreign investment and more encouraging to exports than was the case before the commodity shock.

In the Philippines, Marcos' officials were unable to respond preemptively to the negative effects of slumping world trade. They simply relied on foreign loans and deferred economic adjustment until they were left with no choice. As Marcos' political support dwindled in the wake of the assassination of Benigno

Aquino in 1983, he was caught between policies aimed at cementing the support of his cronies and those reforms necessary to sustain external funding. When the former took priority over the latter, the IMF in 1985 withdrew the external support on which so much depended. The resulting economic conditions hurt the business elite which then allied with the church, millions of Filipinos, parts of the army and Corazon Aquino to unseat Marcos in 1986.

Thailand's policy response to the mid-1980s commodity shock reflected politics during the middle years of Prem's rule. Prem lent his skills to providing political and policy stability in the face of challenges from leaders of the military and of the political parties. These leaders enjoyed access to the spoils afforded by control of government line agencies. At the same time, Prem provided cover for a relatively cohesive group of technocrats that controlled macroeconomic policymaking. They were able to control fiscal and monetary policies and the rate of growth in the external debt, and devalue the baht. They had less success with trade policy. The greatest obstacle to a more open trade regime remained the continuing concern of finance ministry officials to avoid diminishing revenue yields from import taxes.

The third event was the first of the four we studied to yield pronounced policy changes toward greater economic openness. Indonesian officials moved decisively toward a more open economy. Officials devalued the rupiah, promoted exports, and solicited more foreign direct investment. In Malaysia, a similar, if less dramatic, policy shift was also evident. In Thailand, the policy response was more muted. Technocrats curbed macroeconomic imbalances and devalued the baht, but did not significantly increase (if at all) the economy's openness. Finally, Philippine officials had their hands full coping with an expanding set of crises. In response, they devalued the peso, but also increased import tariffs and exchange controls (although the Aquino government began to remove these in 1986).

International finance changes course, 1987–

Impact The redirection of capital flows from Northeast Asia associated with our last event was felt in both Indonesia and Malaysia as a windfall gain of new, export-oriented, investment capital and subsequently as an explosion of manufactured exports. In Malaysia, real GDP growth averaged over 8 percent a year from 1988 into the mid-1990s.

In contrast to its ASEAN Four neighbors, the Philippines initially was poorly placed to exploit the opportunities that emerged as international financial flows changed course and headed for Southeast Asia while oil prices remained low. Net long-term capital inflows to the Philippines actually fell in 1987. But by 1989, capital inflows from Hong Kong and Taiwan were increasing rapidly and the economy had expanded between 5 and 6 percent annually between 1987 and 1989. After a brief lull, economic growth resumed in the 1990s.

The beneficial effects of these external changes flowing to Thailand's economy were even more pronounced. Between 1988 and 1992, Thailand ranked among those developing countries with the highest rate of cumulative inflow of investment capital. Much of this capital was trade oriented, increasing subsequent export growth (particularly of manufactures) to very high levels. In what amounted to the fastest and longest expansion in Thailand's history, overall economic growth eclipsed that of most countries, including Thailand's ASEAN neighbors.

Policy record Indonesian economic policy did not so much respond to the inflow of investment capital from East Asia as continue a policy course laid down in response to the commodity shock of the mid-1980s. The trade, investment, financial, and exchange rate liberalization initiated in 1986 (1983, in the case of some financial sector reforms) was sustained as the reform program unfolded over four years, continuing thereafter at a less hectic pace. This program markedly increased the openness of the Indonesian economy to inflows of foreign capital and to flows of both imports and exports.

Malaysian officials responded to this external event in similar fashion, with policy changes aimed at attracting more foreign investors. Officials eased restrictions on foreign ownership, eliminated ethnic hiring requirements, controlled labor unions, lowered tax rates, reduced tariffs, and increased export incentives.

In the Philippines under Aquino, officials introduced tax reforms, dismantled monopolies, adopted a new investment code, and undertook trade liberalization. Under Ramos, they adopted more liberal foreign investment rules and promoted privatization and trade liberalization. All of these measures made policy more open to foreign flows of capital, goods, and services.

Likewise, blessed with a virtual tidal wave of foreign investment, policymakers in Thailand responded decisively to reduce market distortions. The budget deficit disappeared, officials ended the business tax, and phased out controls on interest rates. The two governments under technocrat Prime Minister Anand accelerated the process, introducing major tariff reductions and financial reforms, including the deregulation of capital flows. Tariff and other trade barriers finally began to diminish in the 1990s. The cumulative impact of these changes not only strengthened market forces, but also opened the economy further.

Explaining policy choices The policy changes evident in Indonesia since 1987 in the direction of greater economic openness reflect a policy response to the economic crisis of the mid-1980s. That economic liberalization has been as pervasive and has continued as long as it has owes much to the continued political ascendancy of the technocrats in the late New Order regime of President

Soeharto. But the inflow of foreign capital associated with our last event has ensured that the technocrats have reaped the political benefits of the high-flying economy. In this sense the capital inflow has sustained a policy path laid down earlier in response to very different economic conditions.

The story is remarkably similar in Malaysia, where the policy choices made in the mid-1980s, in response to the commodity shock and the reeling domestic economy, have shaped the more recent policy initiatives. This path-dependence is most apparent in the trend away from the redistributive agenda that dominated policy in the 1970s, and in the downplaying of the direct state role in the economy, especially with respect to the heavy industries.

In contrast to the Indonesian and Malaysian cases, in both the Philippines and Thailand, in response to rapidly improving economic conditions triggered largely by external forces, officials launched the most critical economic reforms seen in those economies since independence (in the case of the Philippines), or the late 1950s (in the Thai case). The Philippine government under Aquino, however, was constrained in promoting its reform agenda by political instability and its inability to manage the money supply or government finances. Attempts to bring domestic prices (for example, for gasoline) into line with international prices precipitated concerted popular opposition and labor strikes. Congress and the courts proved obstacles to both Aquino and Ramos in their efforts to improve government revenue collections. Thus, while officials sought policy change in the direction of greater dependence on market forces and openness to attract more foreign investment, these efforts were often only partially successful because of the populist character of Filipino politics in the post-Marcos years, and the return of the oligarchical families to pork-barrel politics. On the trade front, however, the Aquino and Ramos governments were more successful, pushing through dramatic reductions in tariffs and import controls in the face of major political opposition. Ramos appeared to benefit from an increasingly vocal coalition in support of open economic policies. The Ramos government, however, enjoyed far greater success in increasing the openness of the economy than it did in raising the revenue necessary to support state expenditures. The latter weakness remained a significant Achilles' heel for Philippine public policy.

Many of the reforms adopted by Thai policymakers after 1987 had long been contemplated (as responses to the economic effects of earlier events). However, short-term crises, for example banking failures of the mid-1980s, precluded these responses until the beneficial economic effects of the fourth event were apparent. With budget surpluses and growing export earnings following inflows of foreign capital, policymakers at last could implement the structural changes deemed necessary for longer-term macroeconomic stability.

While there were political changes in Thailand – particularly the military ouster of Chatichai and the placing in power of Anand, whose no-nonsense, technocratic style was widely respected – these do not appear to have been the

most powerful influences on policy choices. A broad consensus on policy preferences had emerged in Thailand by the mid-1980s. Once propitious external
circumstances arrived, policy change proceeded under both relatively
authoritarian and relatively democratic governments.

Thus, associated with our fourth event were policy changes in the direction
of greater economic openness that showed remarkable similarities. The sources
of these policy responses, however, differed. In Indonesia and Malaysia, officials' responses to the fourth event appeared as a deepening of policy courses
laid down in the mid-1980s. In the Philippines and Thailand, by contrast, the
inflow of capital associated with the fourth event provided the conditions necessary for policymakers finally to adopt long-sought reforms. The outcomes
were the same. In all four countries, policies became more international in their
orientation, with greater openness to flows of capital as well as of goods and
services.

We have here compared the policy responses to our four external events
across the four countries. Now we turn to an evaluation of the variables which
we introduced in chapter 1 as possible explanations for variation in the character of domestic policy responses to external events, both within countries over
time, and across different countries at the same time.

Variables

Economic policy change, whether in the direction of greater openness or
closedness, in response to altered external conditions, might be shaped by a
variety of different factors. We concentrated on five broad hypotheses (chapter
1 elaborates on these hypotheses and provides their justifications). First, we suggested that the health of an economy's external balances, and the levels and
sources of state revenue, might predispose state officials to respond in predictable ways to changing external conditions. A second idea we entertained was
that the degree of technocrats' influence in macroeconomic policymaking
might affect the extent and character of policy change. The third and fourth
possibilities we explored concerned the character of political coalitions and of
institutions that link society (especially business interests) and the state. Finally,
we considered the likelihood that elites might be influenced by the development
strategies employed in other countries. These possible explanations, of course,
are neither mutually exclusive nor by any means exhaustive. We excluded other
hypotheses, such as those that attend to the make-up of formal political coalitions, or that focus on the degree of authoritarianism of any particular regime,
or that emphasize states' positions in the international state system,[1] because the
values of the variables did not vary sufficiently either across our four countries
at a particular time or within each country over different points in time to be
considered plausible explanatory variables for policy change. We also ignored
externally linked variables, such as rising import penetration or industries'

dependence on export markets because of our decision to focus on the domestic determinants of policy responses to external events.

Our first variable concerns state revenues and current account balances. We suggested that, as the proportion of state revenues from import taxes goes down, policymakers are more likely to respond to an external event with policies that make the economy more open (hypothesis H1a). Thailand provided the strongest support for this hypothesis, though we also found some supporting evidence in the Philippines. Import tariffs played less important roles in the other countries. Concerning revenues, the Malaysian government's strong revenue base offered support for the "orthodox paradox" – that the success of liberal, hands-off development strategies is predicated on high levels of competence among state administrators and of capacity on the part of state institutions. The Malaysian government's strong extractive capacities, a legacy of developments in the 1950s before its independence, suggests the advantages for an open economic strategy, specifically of a strong tax base (not dependent on import tariffs), and more generally of capable administration.

We also hypothesized that when shortages in foreign exchange result from an external event and where there is a history of failure of import-substituting policies, then policy is likely to change in the direction of efforts to generate increasing amounts of foreign exchange from exports (hypothesis H1b). Unlike (related) business-cycle explanations of trade policies that explain higher levels of protection as responses to slower economic growth, we anticipated lower protection (or at least greater export promotion) with the loss of foreign exchange.[2] This expectation was not sustained in the case of Indonesia where the supply of foreign exchange contracted in 1982 when oil prices fell, the memory of the import restrictions of the 1960s was still alive, and yet policy changed in March 1983 in the direction of a less open trade regime (and fiscal conservatism). The same thing happened in the Philippines later that year. We interpret these developments, however, as short-term policy moves designed to avert foreign exchange crises. Indeed, Indonesian officials eventually responded in 1983 and, especially, in 1986 and 1988 to persistent foreign exchange shortages by moving in the direction of economic openness. In the case of the Philippines, trade liberalization measures preceded and followed the October 1983 adoption of exchange controls designed to cope with a major foreign exchange crisis. Shifts toward greater openness in the face of large and persistent external deficits were evident in Malaysia and, to a lesser degree, Thailand in the mid-1980s. Hence, we find fairly strong support for hypothesis H1b.

The last of our hypotheses with respect to the first variable, H1c, was that external events that resulted in state revenue or foreign exchange windfalls likely would lead to policy responses favoring a less open economy. We based this hypothesis on the expectation that officials no longer would be constrained from pursuing ambitious policy and political goals via interventionist policies or from responding favorably to either business or labor pressures for protection from imports. We find some support for this hypothesis. Hence, this hypothesis reflects an assumption that such desires and demands generally exist, at least in latent form, but often are constrained by economic limits. Indonesian policy changes after the first oil shock support this idea. And evidence from the policy responses of Malaysia in the late 1970s seems to support the hypothesis as well, as Malaysia pursued ambitious domestic policy goals while it enjoyed sub-stantial foreign exchange cushions. We could also interpret the Philippines case until the mid-1980s as consistent with this hypothesis, though it seems question-able whether regular access to US and other aid constituted a windfall (either in its magnitude or in the sense of increasing suddenly).

In sum, we find reasonably strong support for our first set of hypotheses that concern the constraints exercised by varying levels of access to foreign exchange and the sources of government revenue. We grouped these three hypotheses together because of their common logics and because, in the short term, offi-cials are likely to view these variables as exogenous factors not subject to manipulation. In the longer term, of course, policymakers can shape these factors as we saw most dramatically in Thailand when officials achieved a change in the state's long-standing dependence on import tariff revenues with the 1992 adoption of a value-added tax.

The evidence for the influence of policy delegation to technocrats (hypothe-sis H2), particularly those charged with macroeconomic policies, on economic openness is not conclusive. We suggested at the outset that the greater is tech-nocrats' influence over policy, the more likely is a policy response favoring open-ness (hypothesis H2). While this is supported in the case of Indonesia in the wake of the third event, the commodity shock, when technocrats were able to launch a liberalization drive, it is not supported for Indonesia in either of the previous two events. Policy responses led by technocrats in both cases reduced cross-border flows of capital and goods (we suggested above that the second episode might be explained as a short-term measure designed to restore macro-economic stability before launching reforms, a typical sequence in structural reform episodes). A particularly interesting instance of effective policy delega-tion in Indonesia concerns technocrats' opening up Indonesia's capital account in 1971, before the first event covered in this study. This measure effectively tied the hands of future policymakers, making more difficult any future assault on open economic policies.

In Thailand, technocrat-led policy responses to both the third (falling commodity prices and slumping world trade) and, in particular, fourth (reorientation in global capital flows) events were in the direction of greater openness. The policy dominance of the technocrats during the two Anand governments, however, only accelerated a policy thrust evident under different regimes both before and after the Anand governments.

In Malaysia, it appears that the partial eclipse of technocrats in economic policymaking in the late 1980s had limited influence on the direction of economic policy. Leaders sustained the move toward greater economic openness that began in the mid-1980s even as both UMNO's and Mahathir's political concerns tended to limit technocratic dominance of policymaking. In the case of the Philippines, the problem always was the political difficulty of creating adequate space within which the technocrats could maneuver. Incessant political instability and constant intra-elite competition made it difficult even for Marcos under martial law or Aquino following his fall to delegate policymaking to technocrats. Hence, the Philippines offers little by way of test of the hypothesis.

Our second hypothesis (H2) argues that technocrats approach policymaking with an eye on their economies' long-term needs, in contrast to politicians' needs to weigh heavily the short-term goal of sustaining a supportive political coalition. Hence, where institutional and political arrangements afford technocrats a dominant voice in economic policymaking, we anticipated a greater propensity to respond to external economic changes by moving toward more open economic policies. Despite its apparent logic, the evidence for this argument in this study is surprisingly weak. One possible explanation for this weakness is that technocrats frequently faced severe external imbalances. These conditions (as noted above) highlight the first priority of technocrats, which is to stabilize their economies, resorting to import and capital controls as necessary. In the longer term, however, these same technocrats tend to opt for open economic policies.

We suggest a further possible explanation for the weak observed correlation between policy delegation and open economic policies. In this study, we found that technocratic influence did not always lead to open economic policies. We also found that the loss or reduction of technocrats' influence over economic policies did not necessarily result in policies leading to more closed economies. While institutional arrangements, including those that afford technocrats relative policy autonomy, are critical, an understanding of their impact requires an appreciation of the relevant political context. For example, most observers conclude that the German central bank's strong anti-inflationary record results not only from its legal independence, but also from the strong political support in Germany for anti-inflationary policies.[3] On the one hand, where political support is lacking, institutional autonomy alone is insufficient. On the other hand, where political support is strong (for example, Thailand in the late 1980s and early 1990s), technocratic dominance over macroeconomic policymaking is not a precondition for the expansion of open economic policies. This suggests that institutional design (affording technocrats policy dominance) may be critical to openness responses only at the margins.

Our third variable concerned the "openness" orientation of the governing coalition. Policy responses, we predicted, are likely to be more open when the support coalition that a leader has forged comprises groups which are predominantly outwardly oriented, such as manufacturers selling overseas, or traders and financiers in international business (hypothesis H3a). Only in the Philippines, however, can we identify relatively easily different business or socioeconomic groups with clearly contrasting policy interests. There the dominant coalition opposed open economic policies, at least until the 1990s. In Indonesia and Malaysia, foreign economic policymaking generally was insulated from the pressures of groups outside the state apparatus. In the latter cases, as well as in Thailand, however, coalitions among state officials were important. We find the governing coalitions becoming increasingly outwardly oriented in the late 1980s in Indonesia, Malaysia, and the Philippines (perhaps somewhat earlier in the Thai case), and, as our hypothesis predicts, the policy response to the fourth of our external events favored an increasingly open economy. Thus, policy changed in the direction our hypothesis H3a predicts.

To say, however, that policy reflected the interests of dominant actors is to state the obvious, if it is not indeed tautological. We were interested here in leaders' abilities to generate from previously disparate and politically quiescent interests, effective political coalitions. An example would be the fundamental partisan realignment attempted by President Bill Clinton in 1992–94 in linking the Democratic Party, relatively protectionist since the late 1960s, with open trade policies. Unfortunately, we found only limited evidence of such entrepreneurial leadership attempts in any of the sixteen cases we covered, with the possible exception of Philippine President Ramos in response to the fourth event. Others might discern similar leadership in Marcos in the early 1970s, Soeharto since the 1960s, Mahathir since the 1980s, or Prem in the 1980s.

Along similar lines, we hypothesized that political disjunctures open opportunities for policy shifts, including those toward outward-oriented policies (hypothesis H3b). Political disjunctures, however, were not particularly frequent in our four countries, particularly in Indonesia and Malaysia. Disjunctures did appear to create opportunities for policy changes in the direction of greater openness in the Philippines after Marcos' 1986 ouster, in Malaysia after 1987, and in Thailand after 1991. Conversely, disjunctures in Malaysia in 1969 and Thailand in 1973–74 may have precipitated responses closing their respective economies. The evidence is mixed, suggesting that while political disjunctures indeed provide opportunities for policy change, the direction of that change is determined by other factors.

We find only limited evidence for our hypothesis linking corporatist institutions and open policy responses (hypothesis H4). We advanced this hypothesis, drawing on the comparative political economy literature,[4] because we assumed that such institutions are best suited to the tasks of redistributing the gains and losses associated with open trade policies and, therefore, of winning and maintaining political support for such policies. We assumed that the frequency with which small, open economies adopt corporatist institutions reflects causal influences running in either direction, or in both directions. That is, where political leaders cushion losses from trade by means of corporatist arrangements, voters are prepared to support open trade. Conversely, where trade is open, voters are likely to seek to cushion losses by embracing corporatist institutions.

Turning to our cases, in Thailand, with the economy slumping from the 1984–86 commodities shock, officials adopted more open policies at a time when corporatist institutions were on the rise. Earlier, business associations helped Thai state officials identify and implement export promotion measures. We also found that the weakness of Thai corporatist institutions in the early 1980s frustrated the efforts of Thailand's industry minister to forge a policy consensus among a disparate group of business interests around more open economic policies. Evidence from Thailand in the late 1980s and early 1990s, however, contradicts these instances supporting the hypothesis. During the latter periods, notwithstanding the fact that by this time corporatist institutions had fallen into disuse, more sweeping policy reforms unfolded under various governments. Furthermore, the businesses most active in Thailand's proto-corporatist institutions in the 1980s tended to be relatively export-oriented, rather than import-competing losers in need of compensatory policies. Elsewhere, we observed evidence pointing to the possible emergence of significant business organization in support of economic openness in the Philippines in the late 1980s and early 1990s. This development appeared to strengthen the coalition of forces favoring economic openness. These institutional patterns in the Philippines, however, fell well short of corporatism. In short, evidence relevant to our hypothesis H4 is limited primarily to Thailand (and even there it is ambiguous) and appears not to establish a strong relationship between corporatist institutions and policies favoring openness.

Our final hypothesis (H5) concerns the role of demonstration effects in encouraging more open policy responses. Unfortunately, evidence in support of this hypothesis is weak and indirect. The direction of influence of demonstration effects on economic policy typically covaries with other influences. For example, advice from multilateral financial institutions and broader shifts in dominant global ideologies were often consistent with perceived demonstration effects (encouraging more active and interventionist state policies in the 1970s, and greater openness and retrenchment thereafter). In any case, what emerges from this study is that partisans to some degree use and interpret external models to suit their particular interests. Thai officials harnessed East Asian models in support of both interventionist and free market policies. Prime Minister Mahathir also conjured up an East Asian model to validate policies he was pursuing for distributional as much as for developmental reasons.

We can now summarize our findings in respect of the five sets of hypotheses. We find solid support, where it is relevant, for our hypothesis linking dependence on import taxes with open economy policy responses. The findings concerning the link between foreign exchange shortages and open policies proved somewhat ambiguous as did the inverse hypothesis (linking foreign exchange windfalls with policies closing the economy). Further research may substantiate our hunch that these hypotheses do apply under particular circumstances. That is, foreign exchange shortages are likely to result in more open economic policies, but only after immediate crisis conditions have passed. A foreign exchange windfall, however, may not lead to more closed economic policies, unless powerful political interests are demanding such a policy shift. Hence, we now are able to propose pairing these hypotheses with "conditioning" elements that influence their usefulness.[5]

Where leaders were able and interested in delegating decision-making authority to technocrats, this generally resulted in more open economic policies (though not, largely because of inadvertent changes in the relative prices of tradables and nontradables, in Indonesia in the mid-1970s). But less delegation did not always result in less economic openness (note Thailand in the late 1980s). This suggests to us the particular importance, for open economic policies, of interactions between delegation to technocrats and the strength of political coalitions formed from interests which are served well by open economic policies. Clear instances of leaders attempting to forge such coalitions are, however, hard to find, unless of course, one chooses to interpret every leader's redistributive policies, such as Mahathir's in Malaysia, in a context of economic openness as representing an effort to forge a coalition in favor of openness. Hence we had little opportunity to gauge the utility of the latter hypothesis.

Interaction between political disjunctures and the rise of political coalitions favoring openness may also be important. The cases of Prem in 1980, Anand in 1991, and Ramos in 1992 suggest that, in order for political disjunctures to prove significant in leading to greater economic openness, leaders need not only a fresh start, but also political incentives to use that opportunity to forge an effective support base that favors openness. Political disjunctures considered in isolation were not powerful explanatory variables (though it should be noted that the four countries as a group saw few instances of political disjunctures over the four events covered in this study).

We found little evidence that corporatist arrangements facilitated the adoption of open economic policies. A persuasive argument can be made that either corporatist arrangements or complete insulation of economic policymakers from business pressures facilitates the adoption of open economic policies, while limited, *ad hoc* links between business firms and state officials – as under clientelist arrangements – are more conducive to closed policies.[6] In practice, however, our four states are all to varying degrees characterized by both relatively open economies and clientelist politics. Finally, while we might also expect demonstration effects to be important, external models were employed by leaders in the ASEAN Four for a variety of political purposes. Generalizations about demonstration effects in the abstract are shown here to be problematic. The substance of the external models and the political purposes to which they are put necessarily vary. Thus, embrace of an external referent is shown here to be consistent both with policies favoring greater openness and with those producing a more closed economy.

To recapitulate, we found fairly strong support for our first three groups of hypotheses. We also suggested promising modifications of some of our hypotheses, pointing to interactions among them. Our latter two groups of hypotheses, by contrast, proved less useful.

Competing explanations and analytic approaches

Using the same hypotheses and independent variables we employed in this study, we might have extended our research in four different ways: increasing the number of cases; expanding the range of countries included; redefining our dependent variable; and expanding the ways in which we operationalize our dependent variable. Among the cases we might add to our research are the four countries' responses to an additional external event such as the deep integration agenda. As part of the Uruguay Round of trade talks and the inclusion of services within the World Trade Organization's jurisdiction, developing-country financial services, in particular, have received more attention from US and other rich-country trade negotiators. Growing capital flows increase the incentives for developing countries to adjust their regulatory environments in order to be able to draw on those flows. Those incentives also make them more susceptible to external pressures for more open economic policies. The external pressures for more open markets for services associated with the concluding years of the Uruguay Round could serve as an interesting fifth external event. Unfortunately, chronologically this event would largely overlap with our fourth event, complicating the task of identifying the sources of policy shifts. For this reason, we dropped initial plans to include this external impact as the study's fifth external event.

Expanding the range of countries included in this study might add to the value of our findings and shed additional light on the value of our hypotheses. A large-n study, in particular, could perhaps enable us to recognize tendencies that are too weak to appear clearly in a study of only four countries across four events. With greater diversity among the cases, however, we would introduce many more potential sources of variation in the impact of external events. We were able to limit that variation, to some degree, by looking only at states within a single region. (We lost some of that control, however, in opting to include both oil-importing and oil-exporting economies.) While a large-n study promises significant rewards, it was beyond our means for the purposes of the present research.

A third way of extending this study would be to reformulate our dependent variable. We operationalized our dependent variable, economic openness, primarily in terms of openness to international flows of goods. An alternative would be to give more attention to trade in services, and to flows of capital and labor. International flows of capital, both financial and investment, are increasingly important to the global political economy. Likewise, international labor flows have not received the scholarly attention they deserve (the impact through foreign remittances of labor flows on the economies of Indonesia, Thailand, and, in particular, the Philippines was very significant). Here again we anticipate significant returns for those able to invest the resources necessary to expand this study's scope.

Finally, we might have extended this analysis by operationalizing economic openness not simply in terms of state policies, or the extent to which the gate is raised or lowered at the border. We could look, for example, at the behavior of firms and networks of firms within and across borders. This line of research might prove particularly valuable in East Asia, where scholars have coined terms such as "network state,"[7] "guerrilla capitalism,"[8] "Chinese capitalism,"[9] "mobile exporters,"[10] and "commodity chains,"[11] to name a few. While such an approach also offers potential rewards, it also poses great difficulties in operationalizing the relevant variables.

Alternative formulations of our research design are not limited to the four changes just discussed. We could have elected to focus on different independent variables, yielding a different set of working hypotheses. Indeed, given the mostly unremarkable performance of our chosen hypotheses, the reader may be inclined to question our explanatory framework and its choice of independent variables. After all, we excluded from consideration of the impact on policy choice the role of crises (we have, however, incorporated foreign exchange crises), of policymaking autonomy and capacity, of ethnicity, and of stable macroeconomic policies. We consider these competing explanations in turn below and, in the process, revisit broader themes of the comparative political economy literature introduced in chapter 1. We begin with the role of economic crises in order to highlight some of the anomalies we uncovered and to consider ways of accounting for them.

Economic crises

Many scholars have argued that crisis is a necessary condition for significant policy change.[12] Our cases lend support to this shared understanding that policymakers often will act in particular ways when their choices are circumscribed sharply. (In this case, this expectation is reflected in our hypothesis H1b, which predicts moves toward open economic policies in response to sustained foreign exchange crises.) In reviewing our cases, however, we are struck by two findings. First, with the Philippines an exception, the ASEAN Four states responded very rapidly to crises; so rapidly, indeed, that we might almost argue that there were no crises. Crisis, of course, is in the eye of the beholder. However, neither Indonesia, Malaysia, nor Thailand experienced prolonged foreign exchange shortages of the kind found in many other developing countries (including the

Philippines). Policy adjustment, then, did not require prolonged or periodic foreign exchange crises as a precondition, except in the Philippines. Second, and this point applies particularly to the late 1980s and into the 1990s,[13] significant economic reform continued long after the perception of (potential) crisis had passed and economic conditions had turned favorable. To refer to the late 1980s or early 1990s as a time of crisis in Indonesia, Malaysia, or Thailand would truly be an exaggeration. So, in contrast to the expectations of those who emphasize crisis as a necessary precipitating condition for significant policy change, ASEAN Four policymakers (with the Philippines the frequent exception) showed themselves capable of reorienting policy in the direction of greater openness before crises circumscribed policy choices (or, in an alternative formulation, after buoyant growth expanded policy choices). Moreover, officials continued to introduce important innovations in policies affecting economic openness long after even the threat of crisis receded. This finding may be explained in a number of ways.

An understanding of the role of crises is of major importance because: crises are central to so many explanations for economic policy change; the role of crises highlights distinctive features of the ASEAN Four; and such understanding leads us to consider other possible significant factors accounting for the adoption of open economic policies.

We suggest seven possible explanations for continuing moves toward economic openness in the absence of crisis. First, in the cases of economic measures adopted after 1986 in Indonesia, Malaysia, and Thailand, something as simple as inertia may have been at work. Once these states were on a particular policy course, changes of policy direction (away from openness) were unlikely in the absence of crisis. This would suggest that continuation of policy direction – deepening liberalization, for example – would not require the spur of economic crisis. In our cases, we observed that where a significant political watershed resulted in a particular policy course, officials often sustained this course largely unchanged through several subsequent changes in external conditions. Examples include the policies established in Indonesia in 1967–68 and 1986, in Malaysia in the 1950s, 1970 and 1987, and in Thailand in the late 1950s and again, after the commodity price shock, in the mid-1980s. Conceivably, the policy changes President Ramos implemented in the early 1990s might be seen in the same light.

A second possible explanation for policy change in the absence of crisis concerns the power of ideas and the hegemony enjoyed by liberal economic thinking by the mid-1980s. With policymakers, scholars, government authorities, and officials of international financial institutions around the world converging in their policy prescriptions, crises may no longer be necessary to instigate the adoption of market policies. In this respect, the current period would resemble Charles Kindleberger's understanding of the moves in Europe toward open trade policies in the nineteenth century.[14] A third, and related, alternative, also considered in our model, involves the operation of demonstration effects. The ASEAN Four, according to this view, opened their economies in order to stay in the East Asian "flying geese" formation composed of open economic exemplars.

A fourth factor could be the ability of the United States and the other leading economies, in part through the international financial institutions, to implement the new deep integration agenda discussed above.[15] An important part of this explanation rests on the politics of two-level games[16] that enable advocates of liberalization measures to employ foreign pressure in support of their policy preferences, even in the face of domestic opposition. A partly related factor could be the rising levels of economic interdependence between economies and within particular economic sectors.

We derive a fifth potential explanation of policy change in the absence of crisis from Peter Katzenstein's analysis of the politics of plenty. Under certain auspicious circumstances, the lure of future, uncertain gains can exercise a powerful influence on policymaking.[17] Where economic good times raise in policymakers' minds the likelihood of achieving economic gains and reduce the salience of concerns over relative gains and losses, they may be more prone to pursue economic cooperation and policies leading to greater economic openness and interdependence. In essence, this argument concerning the opportunity costs of a relatively autarkic development strategy is a variation of the children's story about the greater ability of a beneficent and warm breeze to induce the removal of a protective coat than that of a malevolent and violent storm that only leads the wearer of the coat to cling to it more tenaciously.

We are particularly interested in two further potential explanations for economic liberalization that occurs without the catalytic influence of a crisis. The first concerns the structural power of international capital (establishing the set of choices from which policymakers find themselves selecting). The ASEAN Four depend heavily on foreign capital, management, marketing, and technology to drive expansion in their manufactured exports. With supplies of manufacturing investment finite, they compete with one another as well as other countries to attract that investment. Hence, they bid against one another to attract foreign firms and, in the process, progressively open up their economies.

This familiar argument is a source of encouragement to some and of concern to others. For example, many analysts worry, even in the context of competition between states within the United States, about a "race to the bottom" that sees competition for private investment resulting in neglect of necessary public investments as officials dispense incentives and forego revenue in order to lure investment. In a different context, however, Japanese officials found encouraging the competition among Asian developing countries for investment capital. They argued that this competition produced a dynamic of self-sustaining economic opening even in the absence of international bargaining and pressures associated with two-level games. They suggested, in the context of the Asia Pacific Economic Cooperation forum, that negotiated economic opening was unnecessary, as voluntary (competitive, or structurally induced) liberalization in the early 1990s was rapid and could be expected to continue.[18]

Finally, we note a related argument that draws on Rogowski's work, introduced in chapter 1, concerning the impact of relative factor scarcities. Owners of relatively scarce factors enjoy the benefits of the high prices those factors command. They are apt, therefore, to oppose economic openness that would tend to increase the supply of that factor and drive down its price. As factors face more adverse economic conditions, the opportunity costs of active lobbying decline and they are prone to invest more in getting political support, and less in improving their economic performance.[19] The 1980s and 1990s clearly were an era in which capital became increasingly mobile internationally. This suggests that the relative scarcity of capital in developing countries declined. Accordingly, all else equal, we would expect capitalists in capital-scarce (developing) countries to become (after the fact) less fervent in their opposition to economic opening. Our study lends support for such a conclusion. In all four countries, at least some business groups became important voices urging increased economic openness in the late 1980s and the 1990s.

As with the five sets of hypotheses we introduced in chapter 1 and subjected to examination in chapters 3 through 6, the seven potential explanations for policy openness in the absence of crisis outlined above are not mutually exclusive, with one another or with our five original groups of hypotheses.

We did not, for two reasons, include any of the variables introduced above (with the exception of demonstration effects) in our analytic framework. First, most of them are concerned with external factors while our interest here lies in the domestic forces that account for divergent responses to external regional or global influences. Second, in practical terms, most of these variables (including demonstration effects, as noted above) are exceedingly hard to measure or operationalize (see the discussion in chapter 1 of the difficulties attending an analysis in the ASEAN Four of the effects of relative factor costs). The evaluation of the comparative merits of these seven explanations represents an agenda for future research.

Explanations for the adoption of open economic policies despite the relative absence of economic crises are only part of the picture. We now turn to consider other potential competing explanations for open economic policies in the ASEAN Four, beginning with regime type.

Policymaking autonomy and capacity

It is possible that the ASEAN Four have pursued relatively open economic policies largely because of the comparatively high degree of policymaking insulation from political pressures (in part a reflection of regime type) in those countries. This explanation would have the virtue of helping us to account for the divergence we observe between the Philippines and the other three countries. Only in the Philippines did we see significant levels of broad social organization, in the forms of both *ad hoc* popular protest and more enduring institutions such as labor groups, that worked to limit officials' policymaking autonomy. The political mobilization of popular forces and, in particular, the opposition of powerful, entrenched interests, long worked against Philippine government efforts to open up economic policies. If policymaking autonomy has been critical to the adoption of open economic policies, reductions in that autonomy could signal more closed policy orientations (all else, including the distribution of societal preferences, equal). Hence, there are grounds to expect that pursuit of open economic policies will become increasingly difficult in the ASEAN Four as their politics become more participatory and redistributive pressures grow in strength. This might result if the losers (even if only in the short or medium terms) from enhanced economic openness increase their capacity to influence policy decisions to a greater degree than do the winners. At some point, of course, fuller political participation could include consumers benefiting from openness and this might blunt the influence of the losers. In the shorter term, however, expanding participation may well enhance the opportunities for powerful business groups hurt by open economic policies to oppose them. We return to this issue later in this chapter.

We argued in chapter 1 that the ASEAN Four are distinct from the Northeast Asian states in part because state officials in ASEAN enjoy less policy autonomy – they are more likely to have to accommodate the demands of particular social groups in order to maintain regime stability – and less capacity, i.e., the ability to implement chosen policy measures. This point runs against the suggestion made above that policymaking autonomy in the ASEAN Four (and elsewhere) may help to explain the pursuit of open economic policies. That is, if autonomy in the ASEAN Four is low relative to the NIEs, why is openness comparatively high (as we argued in chapter 1)? Here we suggest a modification of the argument that officials in the ASEAN Four enjoy significantly less policy autonomy than those in the NIEs. While the level of state competence in the ASEAN Four is, we believe, below that found in Northeast Asian states, autonomy and capacity, like power, need to be understood in relative terms; that is, they should be assessed against the degree of effective political organization and influence of groups making demands of state officials. Because societal actors in the ASEAN Four are generally weak compared to their counterparts in Northeast Asia, state officials in the former should be seen as enjoying considerable relative capacity. (This raises the question of whether the Philippines appears as an outlier among the ASEAN Four because of the weakness of the state, or because of the strength of society – and the further question as to whether or not we can make such a distinction meaningful.)

Evidence of the relative autonomy of state officials in the ASEAN Four comes from leaders' abilities quickly to reorient economic policies when neces-sary. With the Philippines again as an exception (and, to a lesser degree, Thailand), it is clear that state leaders have been able rapidly not only to learn from policy mistakes, but also to apply that knowledge. In Indonesia, Malaysia, and (to a lesser degree) Thailand, policy adjustments in the direction of greater economic openness have followed shortly after the emergence of fairly incontrovertible evidence that previous policies have failed to produce desired economic outcomes. In the Philippines, because societal actors organize them-selves more effectively, the political risks involved in moving quickly toward greater economic openness generally were too great for leaders to accept.

This discussion of the impact of policymaking autonomy is intended simply to clarify our understanding of the differences between the ASEAN Four and the East Asian NIEs, as well as those among the ASEAN Four themselves. We do not propose here an additional hypothesis for inclusion in future research. Our second hypothesis (H2) attempted to capture the critical impact of policy delegation that can result with policymaking autonomy.

Impact of ethnicity

Another issue that some readers may feel we have given short shrift in our explanations of the adoption of open economic policies concerns ethnicity. As in many countries, the politics of ethnicity are central, to greater or lesser degrees, to the political economies of the ASEAN Four. Can the role of ethnic-ity in the ASEAN Four help us to understand politicians' proclivity to adopt open economic policies? In Malaysia, in order to raise the economic status of Malays relative to the Chinese, officials discriminated against local (Chinese) capital while courting foreign capital. In Thailand, officials' lack of commit-ment to the local Sino-Thai business class in the late 1950s may have led to their welcoming of foreign capital with open arms. For their part, local Thai capital-ists welcomed foreign firms as a means of buying protection from arbitrary offi-cial actions operating against their interests. When business power in Thailand increased in the mid-1970s, openness to foreign capital declined. These cases suggest an important and neglected relationship between the intimacy of gov-ernment–business ties and the extent of openness to foreign capital. (Our suggestion that corporatist institutions facilitate open economic policies [H4] is only tangentially related to this point.)

In both Malaysia and Thailand, the ethnic gulf between business and government leaders seems to have induced a greater openness to foreign capital than we might otherwise have expected. As that gulf closed in Thailand, open-ness declined. (At least for a time: the gulf later closed much further still, indeed all but disappeared, while openness increased significantly.) The case of the Philippines, however, raises questions about the centrality of ethnicity. In the Philippines, we observe a similar pattern to that in Malaysia and Thailand.

Marcos opened the country up to foreign investment at a time when his relations with local business groups were at their nadir, in the early 1970s. Marcos' opponents, however, were not concentrated among the Filipino Chinese. Rather, they were members of competing elite families (whose frequent mestizo origins had no political significance). We might then conclude that cooperative links between business and government elites, independent of ethnic identities, tend to induce a closed posture *vis-à-vis* foreign capital, while antagonistic relationships produce greater openness (American trade negotiators with long familiarity with Japan would find this point unexceptionable). Ethnicity, at least in the Indonesian, Malaysian, and Thai cases, helps to explain the aloof nature of state–business ties (though this is no longer true in Thailand and is less true in Malaysia, although personalistic ties long were evident in each of the countries). In the Philippines, where the Chinese were less dominant in the business world, the divide between state and business was less clear. Here we see a link with the issue of policymaking autonomy. Ethnic factors, at least in some of our cases, seem to have enhanced state officials' autonomy.[20] This suggests again the possibility that over time officials in the ASEAN Four will find it increasingly difficult to sustain commitments to open trade policies.

The complexity of even this brief discussion of ethnicity suggests reasons for our decision not to employ a hypothesis linking ethnicity with the degree of trade openness. We offer these comments, however, in the hope that others might prove more successful in formulating convincing and testable hypotheses. In addition, the possible (though assuredly complex) link between ethnicity and policymaking autonomy may have an important influence on ASEAN officials' future abilities to pursue open trade strategies, as the salience of ethnic identities in the region declines.

Organization of societal groups and asset diversity

We now turn to a consideration of the potential for the political organization of societal groups and of factor scarcities to explain foreign economic policy choices in developing countries in response to external economic events. Societal interests in the ASEAN Four in general were poorly organized politically. Business, the most powerful group in all four countries, exercised its influence more through clientage networks and particularist channels than through well-institutionalized political parties or corporatist arrangements.

The Philippines emerged again as an outlier, however. In the Philippines, in part because they were less clearly ethnically Chinese and in part because of the greater concentration of ownership (in the case of agriculture), business and agricultural interests were better able to influence broad state economic policies than in the other three. Based on relative factor abundance, we would expect industrial interests (though not necessarily agricultural ones) to oppose economic openness – as indeed they did. Furthermore, only in the Philippines was the agricultural sector dominated by plantation production (29 percent of agricultural land)[21] rather than scattered small plots. Consistently with what we would expect based on relative factor scarcities, the agricultural sector in the Philippines generally opposed, albeit largely unsuccessfully, closed economic policies. While labor-intensive agriculture elsewhere might also stand to gain from open economic policies, they would face greater collective action problems that would tend to militate against effective political organization. In the Philippines, by contrast, political organization on behalf of openness would be relatively easy. Hence, we would expect to find in the Philippines, all else equal, relatively open economic policies. In this expectation, however, we would be mistaken.

We may be able to account for this anomalous finding in the case of the Philippines by considering the effects of asset diversity. We suggested in chapter 1 that asset diversity would tend to dampen the motivation to lobby on behalf of any particular policy orientation. Chinese business groups in the ASEAN Four, in owning land, industrial, financial, and commercial assets, tended to have interests that ran across different factors. Hence, as owners of factors enjoying both comparative advantages and disadvantages, we would expect their commitment to a particular set of foreign economic policies to have been only moderate. In the Philippines, where Chinese business groups were least dominant and, perhaps, asset diversity less pronounced, the intensity of commitment to particular (closed) economic policies was especially strong. While we find this reasoning intriguing, we lack the data that would be necessary to test the implied hypotheses (that Chinese business dominance is associated with greater asset diversity and that greater asset diversity is linked to weaker policy preferences). Accordingly, we determined not to include these hypotheses in this study. Along with some of the other arguments reviewed above, however, these hypotheses do suggest possible ways of accounting for the Philippines anomaly.

Macroeconomic stability or economic openness?

In chapter 1 we argued that one reason why we chose to emphasize economic openness in this study was its correlation with economic growth. We note here, however, the possibility that macroeconomic stability, rather than economic openness, played the dominant role in producing strong economic growth in the ASEAN Four. In general, again with the exception of the Philippines during the Marcos era, macroeconomic policymaking in the ASEAN Four was relatively conservative. Fiscal deficits were not large, monetary growth was moderate, and exchange rates were not significantly overvalued for long periods of time. The weakness of societal groups may well help to account for this strong macroeconomic policy performance. Officials could pursue stable macroeconomic policies because societal groups with alternative policy preferences were too weak to make those preferences prevail. By and large, officials were also quite cautious in implementing macroeconomic policies. Thailand and Indonesia, for example, tended to respond conservatively in the face of external shocks, moving relatively slowly to adjust fiscal and monetary policies. This was particularly true in Thailand where the absence of crises obviated the need for sudden policy changes.

The pursuit of relatively consistent and predictable macroeconomic policies provided an important foundation for future growth and attracted (foreign) investment, even in the face of political instability. In many respects policy consistency and economic stability may have been as important in creating a good climate for business investment as were policies committed to the price mechanism, including economic openness. Hence, stable macroeconomic environments may have played important roles in ensuring that open economic policies produced the desired result – strong economic expansion. Yoshihara suggests, furthermore, that Thailand's more stable macroeconomic climate accounts for its low incidence of import controls relative to the Philippines. Macroeconomic instability, as much as the desire to protect local firms, accounted for extensive import controls in the Philippines. Indeed, he notes, it was in the relative absence of such controls and not in tariff levels (these were comparable) that Thailand's trade regime differentiated itself from the Philippine one.[22] (This argument has important limitations. Consistency and predictability, after all, could not assure that any given levels of investments would result in matching increases in production.)[23]

Macroeconomic stability, like the other variables discussed above, can be seen as an independent variable influencing trade openness.[24] We did not include this variable in this study largely because we failed to recognize its apparent importance, despite its prominent role in the literature on trade. While some observers of the ASEAN Four might be tempted to argue that the same independent variables are responsible for variations in macroeconomic policies and trade openness, the Thai case (with consistent macroeconomic policies and decreasingly open trade policies) not only suggests otherwise, but also makes clear that a priority on the former can result in more closed trade policies than would otherwise be the case (as officials emphasize the need for state revenue over concerns for trade openness).

The Philippine anomaly

In sketching these potential competing explanations for the adoption of open economic policies, we have suggested several factors that may help to account for the Philippines' persistent status as an oddball among the ASEAN Four. In terms of economic performance (the share of manufactured production in GDP hardly increased between 1972 and 1988)[25] and economic policies – lower levels of economic openness – the Philippines regularly appeared as an exception to general patterns we observed in the other three countries. Unlike in

Indonesia, Malaysia, and Thailand, Philippine leaders tended to be so slow in responding to macroeconomic instability that crises recurred, and this may help to account for the lower levels of economic openness there. Filipino leaders regularly had to cope with foreign exchange crises that put a premium on short-term foreign exchange savings, hence the widespread resort to various import controls. Macroeconomic instability in turn, seemed to result in large part from Filipino officials' inability to extract from society necessary levels of revenue, and discouraged investment. The strength of societal groups in the Philippines, particularly business interests both in agriculture and in industry, in turn, accounted for the state's persistent revenue shortfalls. And, finally, the political power of those societal groups may have been linked to their relatively great concentration (in agriculture), their comparatively great dominance by ethnic Filipinos (rather than ethnic Filipino-Chinese), and, perhaps, their lower levels of asset diversity (which, we suggested, also could be linked to their ethnicity and would tend to make them more committed partisans in favor of particular foreign economic policies). Furthermore, the power of societal groups ensured that for Filipino leaders, the risks of prompt policy adjustments that inevitably would have impinged on at least some powerful groups' interests, were relatively great.

The steady divergence in Philippine policy responses points to the importance of domestic factors in shaping policy choices. The four external events had broadly similar effects on the Philippine economy as on the other three (particularly Thailand). To the extent that we can account for the Philippine anomaly by pointing to specific domestic economic and political institutions, we interpret this as an endorsement of our research design. However powerful the global or regional forces at work, national factors exercised critical influences in mediating those international effects.

Conclusion

We have now reviewed the performance of our five groups of hypotheses and entertained, more briefly, competing explanations, as well as considering seven different possible ways of accounting for the adoption of open economic policies in the absence of economic crisis. With the dust settled, where do we now stand? Before turning to answer this question, we first briefly review the concerns that initially led us to raise these questions.

The globalization of markets and the reach of firms, the emergence of a single international market in financial capital, and the collapse of competing ideologies have left liberal capitalism dominant at the close of the twentieth century. Despite these homogenizing trends, however, national economies continue to diverge strikingly in their performances and organization, and in the policies that regulate them. In the 1970s, scholars observing the broad range of rich-country responses to the oil price rises, worked to develop analytical tools with which they could explain these patterns. What characteristics of national economies and politics, they asked, could account for divergent responses to common stimuli? In this study, we adopted a similar line of inquiry, asking what domestic economic and political factors condition the local impact of external economic forces in the ASEAN Four?

A long-running debate among scholars concerns the relative influence on states' foreign policies of domestic and international variables. This dialogue, in turn, is a subset of broader social science and philosophical debates about the causal primacy of units (parts) and systems (wholes) of which they are a part. Most scholars agree that the constraining effects on units of the structure of the whole system are greater in some issue areas than others. These constraints probably are less tight in the area of trade policies than in alliance formations, for example. Looking at trade has allowed us to explore this interaction between the domestic institutions and politics of the ASEAN Four, on the one hand, and externally originating influences, on the other.[26]

Despite the fertile theoretical ground we tilled, several of the hypotheses we employed in the hope of explaining choices of trade policies proved of disappointing explanatory utility, in some cases because they involved hard-to-operationalize variables. Perhaps the most useful hypotheses were those relating to levels of revenue and of foreign exchange, and to the extent of policy delegation. These findings are consistent with the existing comparative political economy literature and offered few surprises. We were, however, able to suggest some interesting ways in which our independent variables interacted so that our hypotheses could be paired with conditioning ones that stipulated the circumstances under which they were most likely to prove useful.

We discovered that dependence on import tariff revenues worked against the adoption of open trade strategies in the Philippines and, in particular, Thailand, as our hypothesis had expected. It appears, however, that this relationship can be more complex than we had anticipated. In the Thai case, it operated about as anticipated. In the case of the Philippines, however, macroeconomic instability emerged as an important intervening variable. Officials were unable to tax at high enough levels to avoid persistent and large fiscal deficits. These deficits dragged down national savings rates and helped to produce regular external imbalances. The ensuing foreign exchange crises then induced resort to import controls. By different paths, but in neither case entirely motivated by protectionist concerns, Philippine and Thai officials adopted policies that resulted in more closed economies than would otherwise have been the case.

Our cases, and the discussion in this chapter, also suggested the critical importance not only of economic openness, but also of macroeconomic stability in yielding economic growth. We suggested above the importance of the following simplified causal relationships: the ethnic Chinese identity of business leaders left them politically weaker than would otherwise have been the case were ethnicity not a factor; that political weakness resulted in greater policy-making autonomy for state officials and helped to account for stable patterns of macroeconomic policies. Leaving aside ethnicity, we can apply this kind of argument to popular groups as well. The political weakness of popular groups, in part a function of the decentralized character of the dominant mode of (rice) production, afforded state officials policymaking autonomy. Furthermore, and not surprisingly (because of capital's structural power and because of collective action challenges), the weakness of popular groups is far more pronounced than that of capital. While catering to the needs of the former would often have required departures from conservative macroeconomic policies, officials gener-ally could meet the needs of the latter simply by providing particularist benefits – economic rents such as licenses, monopolies, state contracts, and so on – without deviating from broadly conservative macroeconomic policies.

Three other findings are worth repeating at this point. First, the social dis-tance between state and societal elites, often a function of ethnicity, seems to have helped to account for officials' relative openness to foreign capital. This is particularly significant, as openness to and dependence on foreign capital are among the most distinctive characteristics of the ASEAN Four and serve most clearly to distinguish them from the East Asian NIEs.

Second, regime type (the extent of authoritarian rule) had surprisingly little impact on foreign economic policymaking. In the Philippines, the one (long) experience of authoritarian rule was not generally associated with an opening of the economy (though Marcos was able to open the economy to foreign invest-ment capital). Significant opening of the economy came after Marcos' fall, under Presidents Aquino and Ramos. In Thailand, measures opening the economy began in the late 1980s under both democratic and military-backed technocratic regimes (though the pace was most furious under the first Anand government).

The third observation also relates to these two countries. In contrast to Indonesia and Malaysia, many of the most fundamental and enduring liberal-izing measures in the Philippines and Thailand came not in response to crisis conditions, but only when both economies were faring comparatively better than they had in the recent past. In these two countries we saw only indirect support for the notion that crises are preconditions for policy reforms. Rather, we found more evidence consistent with the notion that the availability of slack resources enables policymakers to pursue economic reforms (including enhanced openness) that entail (at least short-term) costs for some domestic groups of political significance.

Having tried to explain past trade policy choices in the ASEAN Four, what can we now say about future prospects for their trade policies? Do the commit-ments they made as ASEAN members in 1992 to establish an ASEAN Free Trade Area ensure continuing moves toward more open trade regimes? As we noted above, and in chapter 1, the ASEAN Four present a distinctive development pattern marked by high levels of dependence on foreign capital, a legacy of their open economic policies. If the policymaking autonomy that produced macroeconomic stability and economic openness has been central to their successes, should we expect continued autonomy, stability, and openness?

However important policymaking autonomy may have been to open economic policies in the ASEAN Four in the past, its centrality may decline in the future. Several factors identified above (in the discussion of policy reform in the absence of crises) may result in further moves toward economic openness even in the absence of policymaking autonomy. We noted, for example, that rising interdependence could create groups with interests vested in ongoing trade and capital flows. We also pointed to the asset diversity of dominant business groups in Indonesia, Malaysia, and Thailand, and, perhaps, increasingly in the Philippines. We linked this asset diversity to Chinese patterns of business organization. In addition, Chinese business groups have diverse interests across not only sectors, but also borders. These transnational ties are likely to create powerful interests wedded to open economic strategies. Furthermore, the ASEAN Four's manufacturing industries' links to foreign firms' global production strategies should reinforce support for open trade policies.

All of these factors suggest to us that, despite the likely weakening of policymaking autonomy and policy delegation to technocrats in the ASEAN Four, societal and state elites are likely to elect to remain seated on the horse they rode in on. That strategy, after all, has served them well by most reasonable comparative measures. While lower levels of policymaking autonomy associated with more pluralist politics may well undermine the stability of macroeconomic policymaking, the commitment to open economic policies is likely to remain in place.

Notes

1 Introduction

1 States that opt for openness are letting international markets force domestic economic adjustments. See Peter J. Katzenstein, *Small States in World Markets*, Princeton: Princeton University Press, 1985.

2 The Association of Southeast Asian Nations which also includes Brunei, Singapore, and Vietnam.

3 Richard Doner and Danny Unger pose this question in "The Politics of Finance in Thai Economic Development," in Stephan Haggard, Chung H. Lee, and Sylvia Maxfield (eds.), *The Politics of Finance in Developing Countries*, Ithaca: Cornell University Press, 1993, pp. 93–122.

4 UNDP, *Human Development Report*, New York: Oxford University Press, 1994, pp. 102–5.

5 World Bank, *World Tables, 1994*, Baltimore: Johns Hopkins University Press, for the World Bank, 1994, table 1, pp. 2–3.

6 *Ibid.*, table 4, pp. 14–15; table 8, pp. 30–1.

7 *Ibid.*, table 15, pp. 58–9.

8 *Ibid.*, table 19, pp. 74–5.

9 World Bank, *World Development Report, 1994*, New York: Oxford University Press, for the World Bank, 1994, table 6, pp. 172–3.

10 *Ibid.*, table 13, pp. 186–7.

11 Implicit in our approach is the assumption that economic policies affect national economic development trajectories. See Jeffrey A. Frieden, *Debt, Development, and Democracy*, Princeton: Princeton University Press, 1991, p. 4.

12 In fact we could include all national economies, advanced as well as developing. Indeed, we draw heavily on ideas that have emerged from the study of rich states. Because rich states enjoy greater economic flexibility (see Albert O. Hirschman, *National Power and the Structure of International Trade*, Berkeley: University of California Press, 1945), because the costs and benefits of economic openness tend to vary between advanced and developing economies, and because, at least in the case of the United States, advanced economies can more easily resist pressures emanating from the system within which they are embedded, we have elected to restrict our analysis to developing countries. Note, however, that Peter J. Katzenstein (see Katzenstein, *Small States*) deals with the trade policy responses of advanced states

193

that also, unlike the United States, are without significant choice in making trade policies. As in the cases of the ASEAN Four, they are "rule-takers" and "change-takers" rather than agents making these rules and changes.

13 This formulation contrasts with that of D. Michael Shafer in response to the question of what determines which states, under what conditions, will be able to do how much to further development and improve the position of their economies in the international division of labor. See D. Michael Shafer, *Winners and Losers*, Ithaca: Cornell University Press, 1994.

14 Our study shares methodological affinities with Peter Gourevitch's study of political economic changes in European countries during recessions. See Peter A. Gourevitch, *Politics in Hard Times: Comparative Responses to International Economic Crises*, Ithaca: Cornell University Press, 1986.

15 See Helen Milner, *Resisting Protectionism: Global Industries and the Politics of International Trade*, Princeton: Princeton University Press, 1988, p. 16.

16 Shafer makes a compelling case for the importance of the leading sector through which an economy is tied to the international economy in influencing state capacity, state–society relations, the flexibility of the economy, and ultimately its performance. See Shafer, *Winners and Losers*, pp. 1–48.

17 Henry Nau, Peter Gourevitch, and Anne O. Krueger all emphasize the importance of path-dependence. See Henry Nau, "Preface," in Henry Nau (ed.), *Domestic Trade Politics and the Uruguay Round*, New York: Columbia University Press, 1989, p. xiii; Gourevitch, *Politics in Hard Times*, p. 217; and Anne O. Krueger, *Political Economy of Policy Reform in Developing Countries*, Cambridge, Mass.: MIT Press, 1993, pp. 9–10.

18 Economic openness and export growth, or export orientation, are not synonymous. Countries can and do pursue rapid export promotion in some sectors while protecting their industries in other sectors as part of an infant industry strategy. For example, Korean export expansion in the 1960s and 1970s was not particularly open given the prevalence of significant impediments to the imports of capital, goods, and services.

19 Note for example the importance of open trade policies in John Williamson, "Washington Consensus," in John Williamson (ed.), *The Political Economy of Policy Reform*, Washington, D.C.: Institute for International Economics, 1994, pp. 1–28.

20 The contents of such reform packages typically include some mix of the following policy changes: adoption of flexible exchange rates, higher real interest rates, export promotion, rationalization of public investment policies, improved revenue collection, lower subsidies for public utilities and publicly owned energy providers, and financial and labor market reforms. See Robert H. Bates and Anne O. Krueger, "Introduction," in Robert H. Bates and Anne O. Krueger (eds.), *Political and Economic Interactions in Economic Policy Reform*, Cambridge, Mass.: Blackwell, 1993, p. 6; and Joan M. Nelson, "Introduction: The Politics of Economic Adjustment in Developing Nations," in Joan M. Nelson (ed.), *Economic Crisis and Policy Choice: The Politics of Adjustment in the Third World*, Princeton: Princeton University Press, 1990, p. 20.

21 David A. Lake, *Power, Protection, and Free Trade: International Sources of United States Commercial Strategy, 1887–1939*, Ithaca: Cornell University Press, 1988, p. 19.

22 *Ibid.*, p. 4.

23 *Ibid.*, p. 9.

24 Milner, *Resisting Protectionism*, p. 3.

25 Lake, *Power, Protection*, pp. 43–4.

26 Steffany Griffith-Jones, "Introduction," in Steffany Griffith-Jones and Charles Harvey (eds.), *World Prices and Development*, Brookfield, Vt.: Gower Publishers, 1985, p. 5.

27 See Ronald Rogowski's discussion of the Stolper–Samuelson theorem in Ronald Rogowski, *Commerce and Coalitions: How Trade Affects Domestic Political Alignments*, Princeton: Princeton University Press, 1989.

28 *Ibid.*, pp. 164–5.

29 Katzenstein, *Small States*; Geoffrey Garrett and Peter Lange, "Performance in a Hostile World: Economic Growth in Capitalist Democracies, 1947–1980," *World Politics* 38 (1986), 517–45; David Cameron, "Social Democracy, Corporatism, and Labor Quiescence: The Representation of Economic Institutions in Advanced Capitalist Society," in John H. Goldthorpe (ed.), *Order and Conflict in Contemporary Capitalism*, New York: Oxford University Press, 1984, pp. 143–78.

30 Gustav Ranis, "Contrasts in the Political Economy of Development Policy Change," in Gary Gereffi and Donald L. Wyman (eds.), *Manufacturing Miracles*, Princeton: Princeton University Press, 1990, p. 228; Stephan Haggard also discusses this argument in Stephan Haggard, *Pathways from the Periphery*, Ithaca: Cornell University Press, 1991, p. 35.

31 Nelson, "Introduction," p. 24.

32 See G. John Ikenberry, "The State and Strategies of International Adjustment," *World Politics* 39 (1986), 53–77.

33 Miles Kahler, "External Influence, Conditionality, and the Politics of Adjustment," in Stephan Haggard and Robert R. Kaufman (eds.), *The Politics of Economic Adjustment*, Princeton: Princeton University Press, 1992, pp. 89–136; Thomas R. Callaghy, "Vision and Politics in the Transformation of the Global Political Economy: Lessons from the Second and Third Worlds," in Robert O. Slater, Barry M. Schutz, and Steven R. Dorr (eds.), *Global Transformation and the Third World*, Boulder: Lynne Rienner Publishers, 1993, p. 164.

34 Krueger, *Political Economy of Policy Reform*, pp. 29–31.

35 See Peter Evans, "The State as Problem and Solution: Predation, Embedded Autonomy, and Structural Change," in Stephan Haggard and Robert R. Kaufman (eds.), *The Politics of Economic Adjustment*, Princeton: Princeton University Press, 1992, p. 148.

36 World Bank, *The East Asian Miracle: Economic Growth and Public Policy*, New York: Oxford University Press, 1993, p. 7.

37 Stephan Haggard, *Developing Nations and the Politics of Global Integration*, Washington, D.C.: Brookings Institution, 1995, pp. 18–19.

38 It is important to note that in the short term we should not expect a close correlation between openness and economic growth. Adjustment policies, for example, may induce openness at the cost of short-term losses in production in order to realize greater long-term efficiency and production gains. Similarly, compensatory macroeconomic policies might forestall slower rates of economic growth, but at the cost of lower long term growth.

39 Nau, "Preface," p. 4. See also Paul Davidson, "Reforming the International Payments System," in Robert A. Blecker (ed.), *U.S. Trade Policy and Global Growth*, Armonk, N.Y.: M. E. Sharpe, 1996, pp. 215–17.

40 James C. Ingram, *Economic Change in Thailand, 1850–1970*, Stanford: Stanford University Press, 1971, pp. 203–19. This record may have resulted from an absence of local savings as these were repatriated to China. The lack of firm property rights for Chinese immigrants probably encouraged them to send their savings back to China. Alternatively, Thailand's anomalous record may be related to the extensive nature of its development as surplus land came under cultivation using similar technologies but a growing labor pool.

41 For one example, see I. M. D. Little, Richard N. Cooper, W. Max Corden, and

Sarath Rajapatirana, *Boom, Crisis, and Adjustment: The Macroeconomic Experience of Developing Countries*, New York: Oxford University Press, for the World Bank, 1993, pp. 118, 274, 402.

42 Table 1.5 arrays, between Egypt and Mexico, thirteen other developing countries that are comparable to the ASEAN Four. We excluded others whose GNP per capita came more or less within the range of the ASEAN Four but which have only recently been constituted as independent countries (e.g., the Slovak Republic and the Kyrgyz Republic) and others for which time series data are difficult to obtain (e.g., Myanmar).

For a smaller reference group that we feel comes even closer to being comparable to the ASEAN Four, we extracted a subset of the M15, the Reference-Group-7. The most appropriate comparative cases are those that approximate the ASEAN Four in terms of both GNP per capita and economic size. A comparison of the tiny $2.4 billion Congolese economy with even the smallest ASEAN Four economy (the Philippines, at $54 billion) seems inappropriate. A comparison of the $444 billion Brazilian economy, or the $344 billion Mexican economy, with the largest ASEAN Four economy (Indonesia, $145 billion) is similarly problematic. As table 1.5 shows, the average R7 economy is significantly wealthier than the average ASEAN Four economy, but is also significantly smaller.

43 We know that relying on simple mathematical averages for the various groups of countries is problematic. It might misrepresent the true trade dependence of comparable groups of countries. One factor that might skew these figures is the size of the economies involved. The M15 countries in table 1.5, for example, include a number of very small economies (e.g. Congo and Costa Rica), outliers which, because of their size, tend to be very reliant on trade. A simple mathematical average of the trade openness figures for all countries in M15 might therefore overstate the extent to which most countries in the group are indeed open to trade.

We have dealt with this problem in two ways. First, we recalculated average figures for trade openness in 1973 and 1993 using economy size (GDP) at the time as weights. With the appropriate weights in place, merchandise trade of the average M15 economy in 1973 drops to 22.7 percent of GDP, but the 1973 figures for the average R7 and ASEAN Four economies remain roughly comparable, at 37.9 percent and 40.7 percent, respectively. Two decades later, the trade openness of the average R7 economy (weighted by GDP) is slightly higher than it was (38.9 percent) while the trade openness of the weighted average M15 economy is 12 percent higher than it was in 1973. But the trade openness of the weighted average ASEAN Four economy is *70 percent* higher than in 1973. By these weighted measures, the ASEAN Four economies are today nearly 80 percent more open to trade than the R7 economies, and nearly three times more open to trade than the larger M15 reference group.

Weighting by GDP, however, is an imperfect remedy. While eliminating the outlier effect of small, highly trade-dependent economies, it introduces another bias. The weighted averages give greatest weight to the largest economies (e.g., Brazil and Mexico), which tend to be less trade-dependent than most comparable countries. Our use of the R7 grouping (M15, less the economies much smaller or larger than those of the ASEAN Four) is our imperfect solution to the problem of trade openness averages being skewed by very large and very small economies.

The most appropriate point of comparison to see how *relatively* open are the ASEAN Four, we believe, is the figure for the GDP-weighted average for trade openness, comparing the ASEAN Four with the R7, in 1973 and 1993. As shown in table 1.5, in 1973, the weighted trade openness figure for the ASEAN Four stood marginally higher, at 40.7, than that for the R7, at 37.9. By 1993, the R7 were no more open (weighted average of merchandise trade as a proportion of GDP of 38.9 percent), while the ASEAN Four were significantly more open to trade (68.9 percent). This sustains our claim that there is an important difference between the economic experience of the ASEAN Four and that of comparable countries in other regions that begs explanation.

44 Frieden, *Debt, Development, and Democracy*.

45 See also Danny Unger, "Big Little Japan," in Robert O. Slater, Barry M. Schutz, and Steven R. Dorr (eds.), *Global Transformation and the Third World*, Boulder: Lynne Rienner Publishers, 1993, pp. 288–90; Danny Unger, "Japan's Capital Exports: Molding East Asia," in Danny Unger and Paul Blackburn (eds.), *Japan's Emerging Global Role*, Boulder: Lynne Rienner Publishers, 1993, pp. 155–70; and Haggard, *Developing Nations*, p. 8.

46 Shafer, *Winners and Losers*, p. xi.

47 It is also true that our empirical and linguistic training predisposed us to concentrate on countries in East Asia.

48 Shafer, *Winners and Losers*, p. 1.

49 Capitalist developmental states exhibit the following features: intervention in financial institutions as a means of influencing economic decisions; restrictions on foreign capital; policymaking autonomy for an economic "pilot agency" within the bureaucracy; the use of both markets and authority in allocating resources; tranquil labor relations achieved through authoritarian control or other means; and a variety of private sector institutions such as general trading companies and business groups. See Chalmers Johnson, "Political Institutions and Economic Performance: The Government–Business Relationship in Japan, South Korea, and Taiwan," in Frederic C. Deyo (ed.), *The Political Economy of the New Asian Industrialism*, Ithaca: Cornell University Press, 1987, pp. 136–64. Tun-jen Cheng and Stephan Haggard argue that Hong Kong shared certain crucial advantages enjoyed by the East Asian capitalist developmental states; see Tun-jen Cheng and Stephan Haggard, *Newly Industrializing Asia in Transition: Policy Reform and American Response*, Berkeley: Institute of International Studies, University of California, 1987.

50 The capitalist developmental states of East Asia themselves vary considerably in the degree to which they approximate that ideal type. The debate surrounding this issue with regard to Japan is extensive. Most observers would conclude that South Korea in the 1970s came closest to such a type while Taiwan diverges from it in many important respects. Scholars differ on whether or not the characteristics of a capitalist developmental state have anything to do with those states' economic growth; on which features hold explanatory power and how they operate; and on which states (and during what periods) are, or were, capitalist developmental states.

51 The literature on economic adjustment is voluminous and presents a long list of explicit and implicit hypotheses linking a variety of factors to different facets of reform.

52 For example, given the weaknesses of formally constituted parties and legislative bodies in the ASEAN Four, we have ignored hypotheses that link particular configurations among these institutions to policy outcomes.

53 Our model encompasses hypotheses that conceive of the state both as a "predator" and as a "guardian." See Robert H. Bates and Anne O. Krueger, "Generalizations Arising from the Country Studies," in Robert H. Bates and Anne O. Krueger (eds.), *Political and Economic Interactions in Economic Policy Reform*, Cambridge, Mass.: Blackwell, 1993, pp. 463–7; Krueger, *Political Economy of Policy Reform*, pp. 61–5.

54 Mancur Olson, *The Rise and Decline of Nations: Economic Growth, Stagflation, and Social Rigidities*, New Haven: Yale University Press, 1982.

55 Michael Mastanduno, David A. Lake, and G. John Ikenberry refer to this as favoring mobilization over extraction. See Michael Mastanduno, David A. Lake and G. John Ikenberry, "Toward a Realist Theory of State Action," *International Studies Quarterly* 33 (1989), 457–74.

56 See Shafer's definition of relative capacity in Shafer, *Winners and Losers*, p. 7.

57 In fact, of course, pressures from international financial institutions and the United States and other creditors also help to explain policy choices.

58 See Nelson, "Introduction," p. 21.

59 Some of these, for example those concerned with the relative power of legislative and executive branches of government, are not of much relevance to our cases, particularly given our focus on foreign exchange management policies and capital and trade regimes.

60 See John Williamson and Stephan Haggard, "The Political Conditions for Economic Reform," in John Williamson (ed.), *The Political Economy of Policy Reform*, Washington, D.C.: Institute for International Economics, 1994, p. 542.

61 John Waterbury, "The Heart of the Matter? Public Enterprise and the Adjustment Process," in Stephan Haggard and Robert Kaufman (eds.), *The Politics of Economic Adjustment*, Princeton: Princeton University Press, 1992, pp. 182–220.

62 Bates and Krueger, "Generalizations," p. 457.

63 Haggard, *Pathways from the Periphery*, p. 9.

64 Frieden, *Debt, Development, and Democracy*, p. 16.

65 Rogowski, *Commerce and Coalitions*.

66 We should note that Rogowski expects labor abundance to yield a rural–urban divide, except where agricultural production is labor-intensive, as in the small farm holdings characteristic of all of our cases, to lesser or greater degrees. The extent to which this proves true, however, will depend on the degree to which those different sectors are organized for political action. Generally, capital faces fewer collective action problems than either labor or landed interests where those are dominated by peasant production.

67 Cheryl Schonhardt-Bailey, "Specific Factors, Capital Markets, Portfolio Diversification, and Free Trade: Domestic Determinants of the Repeal of the Corn Laws," *World Politics* 43 (July 1991) pp. 545–69.

68 Hirschman, *National Power*; Shafer, *Winners and Losers*.

69 See Jeffrey A. Frieden's discussion of the role of asset specificity in shaping firms' propensity to invest in policy change, in Frieden, *Debt, Development, and Democracy*. See also Beth V. Yarbrough and Robert M. Yarbrough, "The New Economics of Organization," *International Organization* 44 (1990), 235–60; and Shafer, *Winners and Losers*, pp. 1–48.

70 Edward J. Lincoln, *Japan's Unequal Trade*, Washington, D.C.: Brookings Institution, 1990. See also Hirschman, *National Power*.

71 Niccolo Machiavelli, *Machiavelli, The Chief Works and Others*, translated by Allen Gilbert, vol. I, Durham, N.C.: Duke University Press, 1958.

72 See Bates and Krueger, "Generalizations," p. 456; Haggard and Kaufman (eds.), *The Politics of Economic Adjustment*, p. 27.

73 This point is consistent with Kenneth Jowitt's argument presented in Kenneth Jowitt, *The New World Disorder*, Berkeley: University of California Press, 1992, and Kenneth Jowitt, "A World Without Leninism," in Robert O. Slater, Barry M. Schutz, and Steven R. Dorr (eds.), *Global Transformation and the Third World*, Boulder: Lynne Rienner Publishers, 1993, pp. 9–27.

2 Southeast Asian economic growth: the international context

1 Richard Stubbs, "Geopolitics and the Political Economy of Southeast Asia," *International Journal* 44 (1989), 519–20.

2 Ronald Rogowski, *Commerce and Coalitions: How Trade Affects Domestic Political Arrangements*, Princeton: Princeton University Press, 1989.

3 Today there is greater consensus than in the past on what such a list of variables would look like. For example, see John Williamson, *The Progress of Policy Reform in Latin America*, Washington, D.C.: Institute of International Economics, 1990, or World Bank, *World Development Report, 1991*, New York: Oxford University Press, 1991. This apparent consensus is undermined, however, by debate between development officials and scholars over the lessons represented by the East Asian miracles. See World Bank, *The East Asian Miracle: Economic Growth and Public Policy*, New York: Oxford University Press, 1993, and Albert Fishlow *et al., Miracle or Design? Lessons From the East Asian Experience*, Washington, D.C.: Overseas Development Council, 1994.

4 Akio Watanabe, "Southeast Asia in U.S.–Japanese Relations," in Akira Iriye and Warren I. Cohen (eds.), *The United States and Japan in the Postwar World*, Lexington: University Press of Kentucky, 1989, p. 86.

5 Bruce Cumings, "The Origins and Development of the Northeast Asian Political Economy: Industrial Sectors, Product Cycles, and Political Consequences," in Frederic C. Deyo (ed.), *The Political Economy of the New Asian Industrialism*, Ithaca: Cornell University Press, 1987, p. 59.

6 Shigeto Tsuru, *Japan's Capitalism: Creative Defeat and Beyond*, New York: Cambridge University Press, 1993, pp. 18–20, 40–2.

7 It is important to note, however, that before the Korean War, the Cold War was primarily a phenomenon of Europe and the Middle East. The possibility of confronting Soviet aggression in the Far East was considered remote. The Joint Strategic Survey Committee in its April 1947 report noted, "The area of primary strategic importance to the United States in the event of ideological warfare is Western Europe." Next in importance was the Middle East, then northwest Africa, Latin America, and finally the Far East. Akira Iriye, "Continuities in U.S.–Japanese Relations, 1941–1949," in Yonosuke Nagai and Akira Iriye (eds.), *The Origins of the Cold War in Asia*, Tokyo: University of Tokyo Press, 1977, p. 400.

8 As part of its Cold War containment policies, the United States opposed Japan's resumption of extensive commercial relations with China. Nonetheless, Japanese traders were able quietly to sustain trade ties on a modest scale.

9 Cumings, "Origins and Development," pp. 61–2.

10 Iriye, "Continuities in U.S.–Japanese Relations," p. 402.

11 Faltering Southeast Asian economies, however, together with the development of synthetic substitutes for rubber, eliminated surpluses in that region's trade with the United States after the war. See Watanabe, "Southeast Asia in U.S.–Japanese Relations," pp. 81–2.

12 William S. Borden, *The Pacific Alliance: United States Foreign Economic Policy and Japanese Trade Recovery, 1947–1955*, Madison: University of Wisconsin Press, 1984, pp. 110–11.

13 The irony of the situation was not lost on the Japanese. As Harold Strauss, former member of the Civil Information and Education Section, Supreme Command Allied Powers (SCAP) wrote: "I have heard more than one Japanese predict that the American army would win for Japan what its own army failed to win." Cited in Borden, *Pacific Alliance*, pp. 135–6.

14 *Ibid.*, p. 128.

15 Watanabe, "Southeast Asia in U.S.–Japanese Relations," pp. 89, 93.

16 Cumings, "Origins and Development," p. 62.

17 Jon Halliday and Gavan McCormack, *Japanese Imperialism Today, "Co-Prosperity in Greater East Asia,"* New York: Monthly Review Press, 1973, p. 14.

18 Chalmers Johnson, *Conspiracy at Matsukawa*, Berkeley: University of California Press, 1972, pp. 23–4.

19 Borden, *Pacific Alliance*, pp. 191–2.

20 Halliday and McCormack, *Japanese Imperialism*, p. 14.

21 Cumings, "Origins and Development," p. 67.

22 Halliday and McCormack, *Japanese Imperialism*, p. 14.

23 Singapore, as the regional entrepôt and largest port for rubber and tin, also benefited, as did smaller producers Thailand and Vietnam, to a lesser extent. Stubbs, "Geopolitics," 521.

24 Amry Vandenbosch and Richard Butwell, *The Changing Face of Southeast Asia*, Lexington: University Press of Kentucky, 1966, pp. 368–9.

25 Malaya withdrew upon independence in 1957. Cambodia also rejected the treaty and Laos withdrew in 1962 with the signing of the Geneva Accords. See Vandenbosch and Butwell, *Changing Face of Southeast Asia*, pp. 372–7.

26 Vandenbosch and Butwell, *Changing Face of Southeast Asia*, pp. 376–8, 382–5, 400–1.

27 Borden, *Pacific Alliance*, pp. 141–2, 191, 196.

28 *Ibid.,* p. 214.

29 Vandenbosch and Butwell, *Changing Face of Southeast Asia*, p. 393.

30 Hasegawa Sukehiro, *Japanese Foreign Aid, Policy and Practice*, New York: Praeger Publishers, 1975, pp. 97–8.

31 Chaiwat Khamchoo, "A Historical Perspective on Japan–Thai Relations," in *Japan and Thailand: Historical Perspective and Future Directions* (Proceedings of the Fourth Japan–Thai Symposium in Bangkok, June 1987), Tokyo: The Japan Center for International Exchange, 1987, p. 22.

32 Khamchoo, "Japan–Thai Relations," p. 25.

33 Frank C. Langdon, "Japanese Policy Toward Southeast Asia," in Mark W. Zacher and R. S. Milne (eds.), *Conflict and Stability in Southeast Asia*, Garden City, N.Y.: Anchor Press, 1974, pp. 339–40.

34 Sukehiro, *Japanese Foreign Aid*, pp. 105–6.

35 Masahide Shibusawa, *Japan and the Asian Pacific Region*, New York: St. Martin's Press, 1984, pp. 101–3.

36 Shibusawa, *Japan and the Asian Pacific Region*, pp. 104–5.

37 Sueo Sudo, "The Road to Becoming a Regional Leader: Japanese Attempts in Southeast Asia, 1975–1980," *Pacific Affairs* 61 (1988), 27–50.

38 Sevinc Carlson, *Indonesia's Oil*, Washington D.C.: Center for Strategic and International Studies, 1976, p. 58.

39 I. M. D. Little, Richard N. Cooper, W. Max Corden, and Sarath Rajapatirana, *Boom, Crisis, and Adjustment: The Macroeconomic Experience of Developing Countries*, New York: Oxford University Press, for the World Bank, 1993, pp. 33, 222.

40 United Nations, *World Economic Survey, 1975*, New York: United Nations Department of Economic and Social Affairs, 1976, p. 43.

41 Far Eastern Economic Review, *Asia Yearbook, 1978*, Hong Kong: Far Eastern Economic Review, 1978, p. 14.

42 World Bank, *World Development Report, 1995*, New York: Oxford University Press, for the World Bank, 1995, table 5, pp. 170–1. World Bank, *World Development Report, 1979*, New York: Oxford University Press, for the World Bank, 1979, table 7, pp. 138–9.

43 United Nations, *World Economic Survey, 1975*, p. 42.

44 Stanley W. Black, "The Impact of Changes in the World Economy on Stabilization Policies in the 1970s," in William R. Cline and Sidney Weintraub (eds.), *Economic Stabilization in Developing Countries*, Washington, D.C.: Brookings Institution, 1981, p. 54.

45 In fact, none of the eighteen developing countries surveyed by Little *et al.*, with the exception of India, made a sustained attempt to adjust to the changed terms of trade. Little *et al.*, *Boom, Crisis*, pp. 33, 54.

46 The easy credit phenomenon (long-term real interest rates were zero or negative in 1974 and 1975) was to turn out to have a much more lasting impact than the oil price rise itself. *Ibid.*, p. 29.

47 Parvez Hasan, "Adjustment to External Shocks," in Lawrence B. Krause and Kim Kihwan (eds.), *Liberalization in the Process of Economic Development*, Berkeley: University of California Press, 1991, pp. 10–12; Steffany Griffith-Jones, "Introduction," in Steffany Griffith-Jones and Charles Harvey (eds.), *Global Prices and Development*, Brookfield, Vt.: Gower Publishers, 1985, p. 6, and William R. Cline and Sidney Weintraub (eds.), *Economic Stabilization*, p. 8, make similar points about the offsetting impacts of capital inflows.

48 Malaysia and Brunei produced and exported oil, but only in relatively small quantities. In 1975, Malaysia's production was 7.7 percent and Brunei's one-third that of Indonesia. Carlson, *Indonesia's Oil*, pp. 56, 66.

49 *Ibid.*, pp. 56–7.

50 During the shortages of 1973–74, some ASEAN countries asked Indonesia to supply them with oil. Indonesia offered a small amount to help ease the shortage, but insisted it could supply no more because of long-term contractual obligations. Moreover, the refineries in these countries were not suitable for refining the low-sulphur Indonesian crude. *Ibid.*, p. 66.

51 United Nations, *Salient Features and Trends in Foreign Direct Investment*, New York: United Nations Centre on Transnational Corporations, 1983, pp. 33, 53.

52 *Monthly Energy Review* (Energy Information Administration, United States Department of Energy), June 1995, p. 111.

53 Joan M. Nelson, "Introduction: The Politics of Economic Adjustment in Developing Nations," in Joan M. Nelson (ed.), *Economic Crisis and Policy Choice: The Politics of Adjustment in the Third World*, Princeton: Princeton University Press, 1990, p. 86.

54 Seiji Naya, "Role of Trade Policies: Competition and Cooperation," in Shinichi Ichimura (ed.), *Challenge of Asian Developing Countries*, Tokyo: Asian Productivity Organization, 1988, p. 171.

55 Nelson, "Introduction," p. 8; Anne O. Krueger, *Political Economy of Policy Reform in Developing Countries*, Cambridge, Mass.: MIT Press, 1993, p. 1 suggests these rates were "unprecedentedly high."

56 Little *et al.*, *Boom, Crisis*, pp. 32, 74.

57 Evelyn M. Go and Jungsoo Lee, "Foreign Capital, Balance of Payments and External Debt in Developing Asia," in Shinichi Ichimura (ed.), *Challenge of Asian Developing Countries: Issues and Analyses*, Tokyo: Asian Productivity Organization, 1988, p. 239.

58 Stephen Krasner, "Oil is the Exception," *Foreign Policy* 14 (1974), 68–83.

59 Susan Sell, "Intellectual Property Protection and Antitrust in the Developing World: Crisis, Coercion, and Choice," *International Organization* 49 (1995), 315–49.

60 Naya, "Role of Trade Policies," in Nelson (ed.), *Economic Crisis*, p. 172; Vijay S. Vyas and William E. James, "Agricultural Development in Asia: Performance, Issues and Policy Options," in Shinichi Ichimura (ed.), *Challenge of Asian Developing Countries: Issues and Analyses*, Tokyo: Asian Productivity Organization, 1988, p. 157.

61 World Bank, *World Tables, 1995*, Baltimore: Johns Hopkins University Press, for the World Bank, 1995, table 18, pp.70–1.

62 The debt-service ratio is the total of debt interest payments and repayments of capital expressed as a proportion of the value of total exports. Shinichi Ichimura, "The Pattern and Prospects of Asian Economic Development," in Shinichi Ichimura (ed.), *Challenge of Asian Developing Countries: Issues and Analyses*, Tokyo: Asian Productivity Organization, 1988, p. 47.

63 Miles Smith-Morris, *The Economist Book of Vital World Statistics*, New York: Times Books, 1990, p. 66.

64 UNCTAD, *UNCTAD Commodity Yearbook, 1990*, New York: United Nations, 1990, p. 372; Smith-Morris, *The Economist Book*, pp. 92, 95, 99; United States Department of Agriculture, *Sugar, Background for 1995 Farm Legislation*, Agricultural Economic Report no. 711, Washington, D.C.: USDA, 1995, p. 14.

65 Anne O. Krueger, *Political Economy of Policy Reform in Developing Countries*, p. 1.

66 Little *et al.*, *Boom, Crisis*, pp. 103, 105.

67 *Ibid.*, p. 103.

68 There is some disagreement as to the year in which the developing world became a net exporter of capital. The GAO reports 1986, while Little *et al.* report 1988. See United States General Accounting Office, "Foreign Assistance: International Resource Flows and Development Assistance to Developing Countries," GAO/NSIAD-91-25FS (Fact Sheet for the Honorable Lee H. Hamilton, Chairman, Joint Economic Committee, US Congress), Washington, D.C., October 1990, 12; Little *et al.*, *Boom, Crisis*, p. 103.

69 Nelson, "Introduction," p. 3.

70 Louis T. Wells, Jr., "Mobile Exporters: New Foreign Investors in East Asia," in Kenneth A. Froot (ed.), *Foreign Direct Investment*, Chicago: University of Chicago Press, 1993, pp. 173–96.

71 From Masahide Shibusawa *et al.*, *Pacific Asia in the 1990s*, New York: Routledge, Chapman & Hall, 1992, p. 52.

72 Wells, Jr., "Mobile Exporters," pp. 173–96.

73 On product cycles, see Raymond Vernon, *Sovereignty at Bay*, New York: Basic Books, 1971.

74 Mitchell Bernard and John Ravenhill, "Beyond Product Cycles and Flying Geese: Regionalization, Hierarchy, and the Industrialization of East Asia," *World Politics* 47 (1995), 171–209.

75 Margee M. Ensign, *Doing Good or Doing Well: Japan's Foreign Aid Program*, New York: Columbia University Press, 1992, p. 3.

76 Stubbs, "Geopolitics," 536.

77 Export-Import Bank of the United States, *Report to the U.S. Congress on Tied Aid and Credit Practices*, Washington, D.C.: Eximbank, 1989, cited in Peter A. Petri, "One Bloc, Two Blocs, or None? Political Economic Forces in Pacific Trade Policy," in Kaoru Okiuzumi, Kent E. Calder, and Gerrit W. Wong (eds.), *The U.S.-Japan Economic Relationship in East and Southeast Asia: A Policy Framework for Asia-Pacific Economic Cooperation*, Washington, D.C.: Center for Strategic and International Studies, 1992, p. 65.

78 Organisation for Economic Co-operation and Development (OECD), *Geographic Distribution of Financial Flows*, OECD, Paris, 1982, 1992; Stubbs, "Geopolitics," 536.

79 Cumings, "Origins and Development," p. 81.

80 Japan External Trade Organization (JETRO), *JETRO White Paper on International Trade (Summary)*, Tokyo: JETRO, 1992, p.17.

81 Stubbs, "Geopolitics," 538.

3 Indonesia

1 Ulf Sundhaussen, "Indonesia: Past and Present Encounters With Democracy," in Larry Diamond, Juan J. Linz, and Seymour Martin Lipset (eds.), *Democracy in Developing Countries*, vol. III, *Asia*, Boulder: Lynne Rienner Publishers, 1988, p. 423.

2 Andrew MacIntyre, "Power, Prosperity and Patrimonialism: Business and Government in Indonesia," in Andrew MacIntyre (ed.), *Business and Government in Industrialising Asia*, Ithaca: Cornell University Press, p. 248.

3 *Ibid.*, p. 244.

4 *Ibid.*, p. 245.

5 *Ibid.*, p. 254.

6 Note how this parallels the Malaysian experience, but contrasts markedly with that of the semifeudal Philippines.

7 MacIntyre, "Power, Prosperity," p. 246.

8 David Joel Steinberg *et al.*, "Social Change and the Emergence of Nationalism: Indonesia," in David Joel Steinberg (ed.), *In Search of Southeast Asia: A Modern History*, New York: Praeger Publishers, 1971, pp. 292–311.

9 See Robert W. Hefner, "Islam, State, and Civil Society: ICMI and the Struggle for the Indonesian Middle Class," *Indonesia* 56 (October 1993), 1–35; and Benedict Anderson, *Imagined Communities: Reflections on the Origin and Spread of Nationalism*, London: Verso, 1991.

10 MacIntyre, "Power, Prosperity," p. 252.

11 *Ibid.* See also Alfred Stepan, *The State and Society*, Princeton: Princeton University Press, 1978.

12 MacIntyre, "Power, Prosperity," pp. 259–60.

13 *Ibid.*, pp. 260–1.

14 The awarding of special privileges to one of Soeharto's sons in importing and producing automobiles in partnership with Kia of South Korea prompted dismay in 1996.

15 Donald K. Crone, "State, Social Elites, and Government Capacity in Southeast Asia," *World Politics* 40 (1988), 252–68.

16 Karl D. Jackson, "Bureaucratic Polity: A Theoretical Framework of the Analysis of Power and Communications in Indonesia," in Karl D. Jackson and Lucian Pye (eds.), *Political Power And Communications in Indonesia*, Berkeley: University of California Press, 1978, pp. 3–22.

17 Stephan Haggard and John Williamson, "The Political Conditions for Economic Reform," in John Williamson (ed.), *The Political Economy of Policy Reform*, Washington, D.C.: Institute for International Economics, 1994, pp. 541–2.

18 This paragraph draws on MacIntyre, "Power, Prosperity," pp. 252–3.

19 *Ibid.*, p. 252.

20 *Ibid.*, p. 253.

21 *Ibid.*, pp. 247–8.

22 Richard Stubbs, "Geopolitics and the Political Economy of Southeast Asia," *International Journal* 44 (Summer 1989), 525.

23 I. M. D. Little, Richard N. Cooper, W. Max Corden, and Sarath Rajapatirana, *Boom, Crisis, and Adjustment: The Macroeconomic Experience of Developing Countries*, New York: Oxford University Press, for the World Bank, 1993, p. 206.

24 These data should be taken as indicative of magnitudes only. The economic chaos and poor economic management of the time precluded precise figures for most macroeconomic measures. *Ibid.*, pp. 205, 282.

25 *Ibid.*, p. 206. This plan was implemented in 1967.

26 *Ibid.*, pp. 206–7.

27 *Ibid.*, p. 208.

28 *Ibid.*, pp. 207–8, 284.

29 This fixed parity with the dollar was maintained until October 1978. *Ibid.*, p. 208.

30 This reduction ended in practice in 1968 and thereafter the average tariff actually rose. *Ibid.*, pp. 207, 222, 284.

31 *Ibid.*, p. 208.

32 *Ibid.*, p. 284.

33 Little *et al.* identify nine such episodes in the eighteen developing countries they study during the period 1965–73. Of these only three yielded significant results. *Ibid.*, pp. 266–7, 270.

34 *Ibid.*, p. 206.

35 *Ibid.*, pp. 386–7.

36 World Bank, *World Tables, 1995,* Baltimore: Johns Hopkins University Press, for the World Bank, 1995, p. 358. The current account balance is before official transfers.

37 Calculated from World Bank, *World Tables, 1995*, p. 356.

38 Little *et al.*, *Boom, Crisis*, p. 30. See also Alan H. Gelb, *Oil Windfalls, Blessing or Curse?*, New York: Oxford University Press, for the World Bank, 1988.

39 World Bank, *World Tables, 1995*, p. 356.

40 Little *et al.*, *Boom, Crisis*, p. 50.

41 Calculated from World Bank, *World Tables, 1995*, pp. 356, 358.

42 Little *et al.*, *Boom, Crisis*, p. 43.

43 Calculated from World Bank, *World Tables, 1995*, p. 356. GDP is at factor cost.

44 Calculated from World Bank, *World Tables, 1995*, p. 356.

45 Little *et al.*, *Boom, Crisis*, p. 39.

46 World Bank, *World Tables, 1995*, p. 358.

47 Little *et al.*, *Boom, Crisis*, p. 225.

48 Douglas S. Paauw, "Frustrated Labour-Intensive Development: The Case of Indonesia," in Eddy Lee (ed.), *Export-Led Industrialisation and Development*, Singapore: International Labor Organization, 1981, p. 159.

49 As the Pertamina crisis revealed, by no means all of the oil windfall made its way to the village farmer. The point here is that, in comparison with other gainers – Nigeria and Mexico, for example – a much smaller proportion of the Indonesian windfall was siphoned off into the informal sector or distributed for consumption. Little *et al.*, *Boom, Crisis*, p. 378.

50 *Ibid.*, p. 378, n. 11.

51 *Ibid.*, p. 378.

52 *Ibid.*, p. 356.

53 *Ibid.*, pp. 51, 225.

54 *Ibid.*, p. 81.

55 *Ibid.*, pp. 233, 356.

56 *Ibid.*, pp. 77, 100, 284–5.

57 *Ibid.*, p. 81.

58 *Ibid.*, p. 94.

59 *Ibid.*, pp. 94, 284–5.

60 *Ibid.*, table 9.5, p. 279.

61 *Ibid.*, p. 233.

62 *Ibid.*, pp. 94–5.

63 UNCTAD, *UNCTAD Commodity Yearbook, 1990*, New York: United Nations, 1990, p. 372.

64 A devaluation may be considered a movement in the direction of either greater eco-

nomic openness or a more closed economy, depending upon whether the official exchange rate over- or under-values the currency (in comparison with the open market, equilibrium price). In most cases, because of domestic inflation and a desire to keep down the local currency cost of imports, official exchange rates overvalue the currency, thus making imports appear relatively less expensive to domestic consumers than they should, given international prices, and making exports appear relatively less profitable for exporters than international prices would indicate. Under these conditions, a devaluation is a policy change toward greater openness because it reduces the differential between domestic and international prices, and brings the domestic incentive structure more in line with that prevailing internationally.

65　Little *et al., Boom, Crisis*, p. 80.

66　*Ibid.*, p. 285.

67　*Ibid.*, pp. 269, 284.

68　Exporters also received subsidized credit and preshipment insurance for exports. Further reductions in quotas and tariffs were adopted in 1988 and 1989. *Ibid.*, p. 285.

69　*Ibid.*, p. 115.

70　*Ibid.*, pp. 116, 233.

71　*Ibid.*, pp. 116, 279, 285.

72　*Ibid.*, pp. 107–28.

73　See M. Hadi Soesastro, "The Political Economy of Deregulation in Indonesia," *Asian Survey* 29 (September 1989), 853–69.

74　*Ibid.*, 860.

75　*Ibid.*, 857–8.

76　R. William Liddle, "Contending With Scarcity," *Asian Survey* 27 (1987), 207.

77　R. William Liddle, "The Politics of Shared Growth: Some Indonesian Cases," *Comparative Politics* 19 (1987), 127–46.

78　The details of the political struggles are but murkily perceived by outsiders and we are unable to provide details. See Soesastro, "Political Economy," 853–69.

79　Maggie Ford, "International Business: Spotlight on Indonesia," *Los Angeles Times* (August 18, 1994 [Home Edition]), D6; "Periodic Economic Roundup" (unclassified), US Embassy, Jakarta, March 1995 (Source: on-line Lexis International News).

80　Taiwan, South Korea and the United States were next, in that order. See "Periodic Economic Roundup."

81　Ford, "International Business," D6.

82　Little *et al., Boom, Crisis*, p. 124.

83　*Ibid.*, p. 124.

84　*Ibid.*, pp. 125, 128.

85　The following section draws on Alasdair Bowie, "Responding to the International Challenge: Shaping Policy in Indonesia and Malaysia," paper to the 47th Annual Meeting of the Association for Asian Studies, Washington, D.C., April 6–9, 1995.

86　Ajay Chhibber, Division Chief, World Bank, address to a conference on "Uncovering Indonesia," Washington, D.C., March 15, 1995.

87　Chhibber, "Uncovering Indonesia."

88　Manuela Saragosa, "Favours Blamed for Putting Indonesia in Second Division," *Financial Times* (September 29, 1994), 6.

89　See Margot Cohen, "Still Hard Labour," *Far Eastern Economic Review* (October 27, 1994), 20.

90　Chhibber, "Uncovering Indonesia."

91　"Periodic Economic Roundup."

92 The Kia automobile case similarly points to the limits of transparency in Indonesia.
93 Manuela Saragosa, "Investors Troubled by Suharto's Erratic Moves," *Financial Times* (March 15, 1996), 6.
94 "20% Surcharge on Propylene Imports," *Jakarta Post* (February 15, 1996), 1.
95 The following section on Chandra Asri is taken from Bowie, "Responding to the International Challenge," 28–35.
96 Chandra Asri's plant, completed in February 1995, involves a 550,000 tonnes per year cracker. "Indonesia: Chandra Asri – Olefin Tariff Causes Controversy," *Asian Chemical News* 1 (March 2, 1995). See also Manuela Saragosa, "Test for Jakarta's Free Trade Support," *Financial Times* (December 13, 1994), 4.
97 "Indonesia: Jakarta Observed – Soeharto's Trade Two-Step Leads To Credibility Twist," *Australian Financial Review* (January 11, 1995), 7.
98 Saragosa, "Test for Jakarta's," 4.
99 "Indonesia: Chandra Asri," 1.
100 Saragosa, "Test for Jakarta's," 4.
101 "Indonesia: Jakarta Observed," 7.
102 Andrew J. MacIntyre, *Business and Politics in Indonesia*, Sydney: Allen & Unwin, 1990.
103 "June 1996 Deregulation," press release of Coordinating Ministry for Economy, Finance and Development Supervision, Government of Indonesia.
104 Tunky Ariwibowo, "Address," Washington, D.C., June 14, 1996.
105 *New York Times* (June 21, 1996), A3.

4 Malaysia

1 Personal income taxes contributed negligibly to state coffers and there were no value-added or consumption taxes (except on luxury items such as liquor and cigarettes).
2 This paragraph draws on Alasdair Bowie, "The Dynamics of Business–Government Relations in Industrialising Malaysia," in Andrew MacIntyre (ed.), *Business and Government in Industrialising Asia*, Ithaca: Cornell University Press, 1994, p. 168. Copyright © Andrew MacIntyre. Used by permission of the publishers, Cornell University Press. Copyright and permission is also acknowledged in respect of notes 56, 75, 104, 110, and 123.
3 Clark Neher, *Southeast Asia in the New International Era*, Boulder: Westview Press, 1991, p. 103.
4 Lim Mah Hui, "Contradictions in the Development of Malay Capital: State, Accumulation and Legitimation," *Journal of Contemporary Asia* 15 (1985), 40; Bruce Gale, *Politics and Public Enterprise in Malaysia*, Singapore: Eastern Universities Press, 1981, p. 18.
5 This paragraph draws on Alasdair Bowie, *Crossing the Industrial Divide*, New York: Columbia University Press, 1991, p. 28. Copyright © Columbia University Press. Used by permission of the publishers, Columbia University Press. Copyright and permission is also acknowledged in respect of notes 7 and 25.
6 Gale, *Politics and Public Enterprise*, p. 17; J. H. Drabble, "Some Thoughts on the Economic Development of Malaya Under British Administration," *Journal of Southeast Asian Studies* 5 (1974), 207, cited in Dean Spinanger, *Industrialization Politics and Regional Economic Development in Malaysia*, Singapore: Oxford University Press, 1986, p. 8, n. 15. This policy was commonplace elsewhere in the British Empire, where it maximized exploitation of raw material wealth, minimized social friction by enforcing a (sometimes artificial) division of labor, and revealed a paternal concern with protecting indigenous cultures from being overwhelmed by more commercially shrewd immigrant communities.

7 This paragraph draws on Bowie, *Crossing the Industrial Divide*, p. 34.

8 J. M. Gullick and Bruce Gale, *Malaysia: Its Political and Economic Development*, Petaling Jaya, Selangor: Pelanduk, 1986, p. 34; Hui, "Contradictions," 39.

9 Ai Yun Hing, "Capitalist Development, Class and Race," in S. Husin Ali (ed.), *Ethnicity, Class and Development in Malaysia*, Kuala Lumpur: Persatuan Sains Sosial Malaysia, 1984, p. 299; Gullick and Gale, *Malaysia*, pp. 4, 23, 34.

10 For a contrary view, see Donald K. Crone, "State, Social Elites, and Government Capacity in Southeast Asia," *World Politics* 40 (1988), 252–68.

11 Malaya became the Federation of Malaysia, encompassing peninsular Malaya, Singapore, Sarawak, and North Borneo (now Sabah) in September 1963. Advocacy by the Singaporean Chinese leader, Lee Kuan Yew, of a "Malaysian Malaysia," in which all communities would be treated equally and the special preferences and rights accorded Malays removed from the Constitution, led eventually to the withdrawal of Singapore in 1965. See Gullick and Gale, *Malaysia*, p. 34; R. S. Milne and Diane K. Mauzy, *Politics and Government in Malaysia*, rev. edn., Vancouver: University of British Columbia Press, 1980, pp. 67–8.

12 The following section on British policy toward Malaya in the 1940s and early 1950s draws upon Richard Stubbs, "Geopolitics and the Political Economy of Southeast Asia," *International Journal* 44 (1989), 522–4.

13 Prices are for Rubber Smoked Sheet (RSS) No. 1. Richard Stubbs, *Hearts and Minds in Guerrilla Warfare: The Malayan Emergency 1948–1960*, Oxford: Oxford University Press, 1989, p. 108.

14 *Ibid.*, p. 108.

15 *Ibid.*, p. 112.

16 Calculations from United Nations, *Economic Bulletin for Asia and the Far East* 6 (February 1956) and 7 (February 1957) cited in Stubbs, *Hearts and Minds*, pp. 522–3.

17 Stubbs, *Hearts and Minds*, p. 17.

18 *Ibid.*, p. 109.

19 *Ibid.*, p. 523.

20 *Ibid.*, pp. 148, 151.

21 *Ibid.*, p. 524.

22 Malaya, Department of Labor, *Monthly Report*, June 1948, and *Annual Report 1959*, cited in Stubbs, *Hearts and Minds*, p. 524.

23 The overall record for the 1950s, taking into account the post-Korean War slump and discouragement to new foreign investment during the 1950s arising from the communist insurgency, was of modest growth in real GNP (in peninsular Malaya) rising at an average annual rate of 2.8 percent between 1947 and 1958. Bhanoji Rao, *Malaysia, Development Pattern and Policy*, Singapore: Singapore University Press, 1980, p. 83.

24 International Bank for Reconstruction and Development, *The Economic Development of Malaya*, Baltimore: Johns Hopkins University Press, for IBRD, 1955, p. 13.

25 This paragraph draws on Bowie, *Crossing the Industrial Divide*, pp. 69–72.

26 Malaysia, *Second Malaysia Plan, 1971–1975*, Kuala Lumpur: Government Printer, 1971, p. 11; Spinanger, *Industrialization Politics*, pp. 42, 48.

27 Malaysia, *Second Malaysia Plan*, p. 13.

28 Milne and Mauzy, *Politics and Government*, p. 237; Hui, "Contradictions," 41–2.

29 Kunio Yoshihara, *The Rise of Ersatz Capitalism in Southeast Asia*, Oxford: Oxford University Press, 1988, p. 60.

30 R. M. Sundrum, "Manpower and Educational Development in East and Southeast Asia: A Summary of Conference Proceedings," *Malaysian Economic Review* 16 (1971), 82. The need to escape commodity dependence was recognized as early as 1950, in the first draft of the colony's first development plan. See Malaya, Federation of,

Report of the Industrial Development Working Party, Kuala Lumpur: Government Printer, 1957, pp. 123–69; Spinanger, *Industrialization Politics*, p. 39.

31 Malaysia, *Second Malaysia Plan*, p. 82.

32 Hing, "Capitalist Development," p. 304; Spinanger, *Industrialization Politics*, pp. 43–4; Dean Spinanger, *Regional Industrialization Policies in a Small Developing Country: A Case Study of West Malaysia*, Kiel, Germany: Institute for World Economics, 1980, p. 27; Diplomatic source dated August 7, 1961.

33 IBRD, *Economic Development of Malaya*.

34 Kwame Sundaram Jomo, *A Question of Class: Capital, the State and Uneven Development in Malaya*, Singapore: Oxford University Press, 1986, pp. 220–1.

35 Diplomatic source dated August 7, 1961. See also Jomo, *A Question of Class*, p. 221.

36 Spinanger, *Industrialization Politics*, pp. 26–7; Hing, "Capitalist Development," p. 304.

37 In practice, difficult application procedures and restrictive conditions for loan eligibility meant that MIDF loan funds usually went to subsidize large, highly capitalized, foreign companies – few local enterprises had the resources or sophistication to apply. See David Lim, *Economic Growth and Development in West Malaysia 1947–1970*, Kuala Lumpur: Oxford University Press, 1973, pp. 261–5, and Jomo, *A Question of Class*, p. 222.

38 P. J. Drake, *Financial Development in Malaya and Singapore*, Canberra: Australian National University Press, 1969, p. 164; Jomo, *A Question of Class*, pp. 223–4; Spinanger, *Industrialization Politics*, pp. 45–6; Diplomatic source dated August 7, 1961.

39 Spinanger, *Industrialization Politics*, pp. 44, 47.

40 Hui, "Contradictions," 42; Spinanger, *Industrialization Politics*, p. 12.

41 Milne and Mauzy, *Politics and Government*, p. 323.

42 Neil John Funston, *Malay Politics in Malaysia: A Study of UMNO and Party Islam*, Kuala Lumpur: Heinemann Educational Books, 1980, p. 13; J. H. Beaglehole, "Malay Participation in Commerce and Industry: The Role of RIDA and MARA," *Journal of Commonwealth Political Studies* 7 (1969), 218; Hui, "Contradictions," 42; Gordon P. Means, *Malaysian Politics*, 2nd edn., London: Hodder & Stoughton, 1976, pp. 195–6.

43 Beaglehole, "Malay Participation," 218.

44 Funston, *Malay Politics in Malaysia*, p. 13.

45 Spinanger, *Industrialization Politics*, p. 42.

46 "Malaysia: What Price Success?," *Southeast Asia Chronicle* 72 (1980), 1–28.

47 J. A. C. Mackie, "Changing Patterns of Chinese Big Business in Southeast Asia," paper presented at the conference on *Industrializing Elites in Southeast Asia*, Sukhothai, Thailand, December 9–12, 1986, pp. 14–15; Spinanger, *Regional Industrialization*, p. 23.

48 Hui, "Contradictions," 41; R. S. Milne, "Malaysia – Beyond the New Economic Policy," *Asian Survey* 26 (1986), 1366.

49 Sevinc Carlson, *Indonesia's Oil*, Washington, D.C.: Center for Strategic and International Studies, 1976, pp. 56, 66.

50 Far Eastern Economic Review, *Asia Yearbook, 1978*, Hong Kong: Far Eastern Economic Review, 1978, p. 14.

51 The terms of trade started to recover in 1976 and finally reached their 1974 level in 1979. World Bank, *World Tables, 1995*, Baltimore: Johns Hopkins University Press, for the World Bank, 1995, pp. 440–3.

52 World Bank, *World Tables, 1995*, table 18, pp. 70–3.

53 Real GNP per capita grew during 1976–77 at an average rate of 6.6 percent. World Bank, *World Tables, 1995*, pp. 30–1. Asian Development Bank, *Key Indicators of*

Developing Asian and Pacific Countries, 1993, Manila: Oxford University Press, 1993, pp. 170–1.

54 World Bank, *World Tables, 1995*, pp. 440–3.

55 Calculated from World Bank, *World Tables, 1995*, pp. 26, 74, 78.

56 This paragraph draws on Bowie, "Dynamics," pp. 167–94.

57 Mavis Puthucheary, *The Politics of Administration: The Malaysian Experience*, New York: Oxford University Press, 1978, p. 107; Milne and Mauzy, *Politics and Government*, p. 336.

58 Malaysia, *Second Malaysia Plan*, p. 180; Malaysia, *Third Malaysia Plan, 1976–1980*, Kuala Lumpur: Government Printer, 1976, p. 323.

59 Puthucheary, *Politics of Administration*, p. 107; Milne and Mauzy, *Politics and Government*, pp. 331, 334, 338.

60 World Bank, *World Tables, 1995*, pp. 440–3.

61 Milne and Mauzy, *Politics and Government*, p. 409; Tai Chee Wong, "Industrial Development, the New Economic Policy in Malaysia, and the International Division of Labor," *ASEAN Economic Bulletin* 7 (1990), 108; Pek Leng Tan, "Women Factory Workers and the Law," in Evelyn Hong (ed.), *Malaysian Women: Problems and Issues*, Penang: Consumers Association of Penang, 1983, pp. 65–6, 68, 73; *Wall Street Journal* (September 22, 1975), 24.

62 See Bowie, *Crossing the Industrial Divide*, pp. 105–7; Milne and Mauzy, *Politics and Government*, p. 348. The Malaysian government owned the resource itself.

63 Milne and Mauzy, *Politics and Government*, pp. 348–9.

64 In 1977, the government amended the ICA to exempt a wider range of businesses from the act's requirements. Milne and Mauzy, *Politics and Government*, p. 409; Wong, "Industrial Development," 108; Tan, "Women Factory Workers," pp. 65–6, 68, 73; *Wall Street Journal* (September 22, 1975), 24.

65 *Asian Wall Street Journal Weekly* (December 24, 1990), 10.

66 David Lim, "East Malaysia in Malaysian Development Planning," *Journal of Southeast Asian Studies* 17 (1986), 160.

67 Malaysia, *Third Malaysia Plan*, p. 31; "Malaysia: What Price Success?"; Milne and Mauzy, *Politics and Government*, p. 406.

68 Milne and Mauzy, *Politics and Government*, p. 335.

69 "Malaysia: What Price Success?"

70 Fatimah, Halim "The Transformation of the Malaysian State," *Journal of Contemporary Asia* 20 (1990), 73.

71 Diplomatic source dated September 28, 1977.

72 Many countries were already indebted as a result of their strategy of responding to the first round of oil price rises by simply borrowing and riding out the crisis. With higher international interest rates in the early 1980s, and private lenders less willing to lend, they were quickly engulfed in a serious debt crisis.

73 World Bank, *World Tables, 1995*, pp. 74–5, 440–3.

74 Calculated from World Bank, *World Tables, 1995*, pp. 26, 74, 78.

75 This paragraph draws on Bowie, "Dynamics," pp. 175–7.

76 Malaysia, Mid-Term Review of the *Fourth Malaysia Plan, 1981–1985*, Kuala Lumpur: Government Printer, 1984.

77 Raphael Pura, "Doubts Over Heavy Industrialization Strategy," in K. S. Jomo (ed.), *The Sun Also Sets*, Petaling Jaya, Selangor: INSAN, 1983, p. 380.

78 Malaysia, Heavy Industries Corporation of Malaysia (HICOM), *Annual Report 1985*, Kuala Lumpur: Government Printer, 1986, p. 10.

79 Malaysia, *Fourth Malaysia Plan, 1981–1985*, Kuala Lumpur, Government Printer, 1981, p. 242.

80 Far Eastern Economic Review, *Asia Yearbook, 1988*, Hong Kong: Far Eastern Economic Review, 1988, p. 182; Malaysia (HICOM), *Annual Report 1985*, p. 16; Dilip Mukerjee, *Lessons From Korea's Industrial Experience*, Kuala Lumpur: Institute of Strategic and International Studies, 1986, p. 82; Halim, "Transformation," 85, n. 30.

81 Malaysia (HICOM), *Annual Report 1985*, p. 18.

82 *Far Eastern Economic Review* (October 26, 1989), 116–18; *Far Eastern Economic Review* (February 9, 1989), 53. These developments paralleled initiatives in the Philippines, where plans were unveiled in late 1979 for eleven large industrial projects, including copper and aluminum smelters and an integrated steel mill as part of a process of industrial deepening there. See chapter 5.

83 Indonesia 7.6, Philippines 6.2, Thailand 7.7. Kiyoshi Kojima and Tsuneo Nakauchi, "Economic Conditions in East and Southeast Asia and Development Perspective," in Shinichi Ichimura (ed.), *Challenge of Asian Developing Countries: Issues and Analyses*, Tokyo: Asian Productivity Organization, 1988, p. 114.

84 The Philippines recorded 6.7 percent. *Ibid.*

85 *Ibid.*

86 Peter G. Warr, "Malaysia's Industrial Enclaves: Benefits and Costs," *Developing Economies* 25 (March 1987), pp. 189–94; Wong, "Industrial Development," 113; Peng Lim Chee, *Industrial Development: An Introduction to the Malaysian Industrial Master Plan*, Petaling Jaya, Selangor: Pelanduk, 1987.

87 Jomo, *A Question of Class*, p. 2.

88 Pura, "Doubts," p. 380.

89 Halim, "Transformation," 74.

90 Lip service paid to the projects' potential to generate exports remained just that until much later, when these industries were on the verge of collapse.

91 Calculated from UNCTAD, *UNCTAD Commodity Yearbook 1993*, New York: United Nations, 1993, p. 404.

92 World Bank, *World Tables, 1995*, pp. 440–3.

93 Calculated from World Bank, *World Tables, 1995*, pp. 27, 75, 79.

94 Calculated from World Bank, *World Tables, 1995*, pp. 3, 31.

95 Calculated from World Bank, *World Tables, 1995*, pp. 440–3.

96 *Asian Wall Street Journal Weekly* (December 28, 1987), 14; *Far Eastern Economic Review* (September 1, 1988), 56.

97 Far Eastern Economic Review, *Asia Yearbook, 1988*, p. 182.

98 Halim, "Transformation," 77.

99 *Ibid.*, 77.

100 *Ibid.*, 73.

101 *Ibid.*, 82 n. 28; K. S. Nathan, "Malaysia in 1988: The Politics of Survival," *Asian Survey* 29 (1989), 136–7; *Far Eastern Economic Review* (May 4, 1989), 81; *Asian Wall Street Journal Weekly* (July 3, 1989), 21.

102 Malaysian Industrial Development Authority, *Malaysia: Investment in the Manufacturing Sector*, Kuala Lumpur: MIDA, 1991, pp. 11–28.

103 *Far Eastern Economic Review* (September 1, 1988), 56.

104 This paragraph draws on Bowie, "Dynamics," pp. 184–6.

105 Halim, "Transformation," 80.

106 *Ibid.*, 78.

107 Wong, "Industrial Development," 110.

108 *Ibid.*, 117, n. 7.

109 K. S. Nathan, "Malaysia in 1989: Communists End Armed Struggle," *Asian Survey* 30 (1990), 215.

110 This paragraph draws on Bowie, "Dynamics," pp. 182–3.

111 World Bank, *World Tables, 1995*, pp. 442–3.
112 Calculated from World Bank, *World Tables, 1995*, pp. 442–3.
113 Calculated from World Bank, *World Tables, 1995*, pp. 442–3.
114 Masahide Shibusawa, *Japan and the Asian Pacific Region*, New York: St. Martin's Press, 1984, p. 10.
115 World Bank, *World Tables, 1995*, p. 443.
116 *The Financial Times* (May 6, 1996), 1.
117 Calculated from World Bank, *World Tables, 1995*, p. 443.
118 *The Star* [Petaling Jaya, Malaysia] (July 31, 1991), bus. 1.
119 *Far Eastern Economic Review* (November 1, 1990), 64.
120 Halim, "Transformation," 75–6.
121 Malaysian Industrial Development Authority, *Malaysia: Investment*, pp. 11–28.
122 Nathan, "Malaysia in 1988," 136–7; *Far Eastern Economic Review* (May 4, 1989), 81; *Asian Wall Street Journal Weekly* (July 3, 1989), 21; *Asian Wall Street Journal Weekly* (December 24, 1990), 4.
123 This paragraph draws on Bowie, "Dynamics," p. 188.

5 The Philippines

1 William Overholt, "The Rise and Fall of Ferdinand Marcos," *Asian Survey* 26 (1986), 1137–63.
2 Gary Hawes, "Marcos, His Cronies, and the Philippines' Failure to Develop," in Ruth McVey (ed.), *Southeast Asian Capitalists*, Ithaca: Cornell University Southeast Asia Program, 1992, p. 145.
3 The Philippines suffered unfavorable shocks every year over the period 1972 to 1991 with the exceptions of 1973, 1983, and 1988. F. Desmond McCarthy, J. Peter Neary, and Giovanni Zanalda, "Measuring the Effect of External Shocks and the Policy Response to Them: Empirical Methodology Applied to the Philippines," Policy Research Working Paper 1271, World Bank, Washington, D.C., March 1994, p. 10.
4 Shinichi Ichimura, "The Pattern and Prospects of Asian Economic Development," in Shinichi Ichimura (ed.), *Challenge of Asian Developing Countries: Issues and Analyses*, Tokyo: Asian Productivity Organization, 1988, p. 48.
5 *Ibid.*, pp. 19–21.
6 Mancur Olson, *The Rise and Decline of Nations: Economic Growth, Stagflation, and Social Rigidities*, New Haven: Yale University Press, 1982, pp. 43–7.
7 Quoted in Paul D. Hutchcroft, "Oligarchs and Cronies in the Philippine State," *World Politics* 43 (1991), 420.
8 Lucian W. Pye, *Asian Power and Politics*, Cambridge, Mass.: The Belknap Press of Harvard University Press, 1985, p. 299.
9 See Hutchcroft, "Oligarchs and Cronies," p. 420.
10 David J. Steinberg *et al.*, "Framework for Nations: Ecomomic Transformation, 1870–1940," in David J. Steinberg (ed.), *In Search of Southeast Asia: A Modern History*, New York: Praeger Publishers, 1971, p. 235.
11 Pye, *Asian Power and Politics*, pp. 124–5.
12 Stephan Haggard, "The Political Economy of the Philippine Debt Crisis," in Joan Nelson (ed.), *Economic Crisis and Policy Choice: The Politics of Adjustment in Developing Countries*, Princeton: Princeton University Press, 1990, pp. 254–5.
13 David G. Timberman, *A Changeless Land: Continuity and Change in the Philippines*, New York: M. E. Sharpe, 1991, pp. 37–8.
14 Karl D. Jackson, "The Philippines: The Search for a Suitable Democratic Solution,

1946–1986," in Larry Diamond, Juan J. Linz, and Seymour Martin Lipset (eds.), *Democracy in Developing Countries*, vol. III, *Asia*, Boulder: Lynne Rienner Publishers, 1988, pp. 242–3.

15 Paul D. Hutchcroft, "Preferential Credit Allocation in the Philippines," in Stephan Haggard, Chung H. Lee, and Sylvia Maxfield (eds.), *The Politics of Finance in Developing Countries*, Ithaca: Cornell University Press, 1993, p. 168.

16 Gary Hawes, *The Philippine State and the Marcos Regime*, Ithaca: Cornell University Press, 1987, p. 27.

17 Pye, *Asian Power and Politics*, p. 121.

18 *Ibid.*

19 Sugar and tobacco still faced quotas until the Underwood–Simmons Tariff Act in 1913 eased them. Hawes, *The Philippine State*, p. 25.

20 David Wurfel, *Filipino Politics, Development and Decay*, Ithaca: Cornell University Press, 1988, pp. 9–10.

21 *Ibid.*, pp. 10–11.

22 Jackson, "The Philippines," pp. 234–5.

23 Wurfel, *Filipino Politics*, pp. 83–4.

24 *Ibid.*, pp. 79–80.

25 See the discussion of the contrasts between the Philippine and Thai states in Kunio Yoshihara, *The Nation and Economic Growth: The Philippines and Thailand*, New York: Oxford University Press, 1994, pp. 240–6.

26 Ichimura, "Pattern and Prospects," p. 29.

27 Wurfel, *Filipino Politics*, p. 60.

28 *Ibid.*, pp. 95–7.

29 Jackson, "The Philippines," p. 238.

30 William Riker, *The Theory of Political Coalitions*, New Haven: Yale University Press, 1962. This point is discussed in Wurfel, *Filipino Politics*, pp. 96–7 and Pye, *Asian Power and Politics*, p. 127.

31 Jeffrey Riedinger, "The Philippines in 1993: Halting Steps Toward Liberalization," *Asian Survey* 34 (1994), 140–2.

32 *Washington Post*, May 26, 1995.

33 Haggard, "Political Economy of the Philippine Debt," pp. 216–19.

34 *Ibid.*, p. 218; Thomas R. Callaghy notes that the executive can pose the greatest threat to technocrats' insulation. See Thomas R. Callaghy, "Vision and Politics in the Transformation of the Global Political Economy: Lessons from the Second and Third Worlds," in Robert O. Slater, Barry M. Schutz, and Steven R. Dorr (eds.), *Global Transformation and the Third World*, Boulder: Lynne Rienner Publishers, 1993, p. 169.

35 Kunio Yoshihara, *The Rise of Ersatz Capitalism in South-East Asia*, Oxford: Oxford University Press, 1988, pp. 59, 92.

36 *Ibid.*, pp. 51–2.

37 Frank H. Golay, *The Philippines: Public Policy and National Economic Development*, Ithaca: Cornell University Press, 1961, pp. vii–viii.

38 Stephan Haggard, "The Philippines: Picking Up After Marcos," in *The Promise of Privatization*, New York: Council on Foreign Relations, 1988, pp. 91–121.

39 Yoshihara, *The Rise of Ersatz*, p. 110.

40 *Ibid.*, p. 71.

41 The US Tydings Rehabilitation Act of 1946 provided $620 million for reconstruction in the Philippines ($400 million of this was earmarked to meet private war damage claims). Golay, *The Philippines*, pp. 65–6.

42 *Ibid.*, p. 137.

43 *Ibid.*, p. 97.

44 *Ibid.*, p. 110.

45 *Ibid.*, pp. 68–81.

46 Hawes, *The Philippine State*, pp. 28–9.

47 The 1947 Military Bases Agreement between the United States and the Philippines allowed the USA to keep over two hundred bases, large and small, and to run them essentially as American enclaves. Wurfel, *Filipino Politics*, p. 14.

48 Richard Stubbs, "Geopolitics and the Political Economy of Southeast Asia," *International Journal* 44 (1989), 530.

49 Timberman, *A Changeless Land*, p. 47.

50 Gustav Ranis and Syed Akhtar Mahmood, *The Political Economy of Development Policy Change*, Cambridge, Mass.: Blackwell, 1992, p. 169.

51 Manuel F. Montes, "The Politics of Liberalization: The Aquino Government's 1990 Tariff Reform Initiative," in David G. Timberman (ed.), *The Politics of Economic Reform in Southeast Asia, The Experiences of Thailand, Indonesia and the Philippines,* Manila: Asian Institute of Management, 1992, p. 91.

52 Golay, *The Philippines*, p. 137.

53 *Ibid.*, pp. 98, 242.

54 Wurfel, *Filipino Politics*, p. 15.

55 Golay, *The Philippines*, pp. 242–5.

56 Hawes, "Marcos, His Cronies," p. 148. There were, of course, Filipino industrialists concerned to gain protection for their enterprises, but balance-of-payments concerns seem to have played the dominant role in the state's adoption of import-substituting industrialization policies.

57 Marcus Noland, *Pacific Basin Developing Countries, Prospects for the Future*, Washington, D.C.: Institute for International Economics, 1990, p. 81.

58 Robert B. Stauffer, "The Philippine Political Economy: (Dependent) State Capitalism in the Corporatist Mode," in Richard Higgott and Richard Robinson (eds.), *Southeast Asia: Essays in the Political Economy of Structural Change*, London: Routledge & Kegan Paul, 1985, pp. 247–8.

59 Wurfel, *Filipino Politics*, p. 16.

60 Seiji Naya, "Role of Trade Policies, Competition and Cooperation," in Shinichi Ichimura (ed.), *Challenge of Asian Developing Countries: Issues and Analyses*, Tokyo: Asian Productivity Organization, 1988, p. 172.

61 Walden Bello, David O'Connor, and Robin Broad, "Export-Oriented Industrialization: The Short-Lived Illusion," in Walden Bello, David Kinley, and Elaine Elinson (eds.), *Development Debacle: The World Bank in the Philippines*, San Francisco: Institute for Food and Development Policy, Philippine Solidarity Network, 1982, p. 132.

62 Ichimura, "Pattern and Prospects," p. 16.

63 Yoshihara, *The Nation and Economic Growth*, pp. 41–2.

64 Yoshihara, *The Rise of Ersatz*, pp. 22–5.

65 Golay, *The Philippines*, pp. 76–7.

66 Hawes, "Marcos, His Cronies," p. 149.

67 Wurfel, *Filipino Politics*, pp. 15–16.

68 Hawes, *The Philippine State*, pp. 37–8.

69 Challenging the old Communist Party with its links to Moscow, a group of intellectuals from the University of the Philippines in 1968 established the Communist Party of the Philippines. The following year this party established its military arm, the New People's Army. Jackson, "The Philippines," pp. 250–1. In 1968 in Mindanao, Muslims established the Muslim Independence Movement and, subsequently, the Moro National Liberation Front.

70 Wurfel, *Filipino Politics*, pp. 17–18.

71 *Ibid.*, pp. 21–2.
72 Golay, *The Philippines*, pp. 70–1.
73 *Ibid.*, p. 77.
74 *Ibid.*, pp. 193–5.
75 *Ibid.*, p. 172.
76 Timberman, *The Changeless Land*, p. 46; Ranis and Mahmood, *The Political Economy of Development Policy Change*, p. 170.
77 Ranis and Mahmood, *The Political Economy of Development Policy Change*, p. 196.
78 Ichimura, "Pattern and Prospects," p. 18.
79 United States General Accounting Office, "Foreign Assistance: International Resource Flows and Development Assistance to Developing Countries," GAO/NSIAD-91–25FS (Fact Sheet for the Honorable Lee H. Hamilton, Chairman, Joint Economic Committee, US Congress), Washington, D.C., October 1990.
80 Kiyoshi Kojima and Tsuneo Nakauchi, "Economic Conditions in East and Southeast Asia and Development Perspective," in Shinichi Ichimura (ed.), *Challenge of Asian Developing Countries: Issues and Analyses*, Tokyo: Asian Productivity Organization, 1988, p. 120.
81 Jun Nishikawa, "ASEAN Countries: Economic Performance and Tasks Ahead," in Shinichi Ichimura (ed.), *Challenge of Asian Developing Countries: Issues and Analyses*, Tokyo: Asian Productivity Organization, 1988, p. 364.
82 Charles W. Lindsey, "In Search of Dynamism: Foreign Investment in the Philippines under Martial Law," *Pacific Affairs* 56 (1993), 490–1.
83 Lindsey, "In Search of Dynamism," 477–94.
84 Parvez Hasan, "Adjustment to External Shocks," in Lawrence B. Krause and Kim Kihwan (eds.), *Liberalization in the Process of Economic Development*, Berkeley: University of California Press, 1991, p. 180.
85 World Bank, *World Tables, 1995*, Baltimore: Johns Hopkins University Press, for the World Bank, 1995, table 18.
86 Wurfel, *Filipino Politics*, p. 191. American development assistance, in the form of AID loans and grants, accelerated during the US withdrawal from Vietnam, from $56 million in 1969–72 to $241 million in 1973–76.
87 World Bank, *World Tables, 1995*, pp. 358–9.
88 Timberman, *The Changeless Land*, pp. 87–8.
89 World Bank, *World Tables, 1995*, table 19.
90 Kojima and Nakauchi, "Economic Conditions," p. 109.
91 Robert S. Dohner and Ponciano Intal, Jr., "Debt Crisis and Adjustment in the Philippines," in Dohner and Intal (eds.), *Developing Country Debt and the World Economy*, Chicago: University of Chicago Press, 1989. However, over the 1970s manufactured exports' share of GDP showed no increase and, given the declining local value-added content of those exports, probably actually declined.
92 Naya, "Role of Trade Policies," p. 180.
93 Asian Development Bank, *Key Indicators of Developing Asian and Pacific Countries*, Manila: Oxford University Press, 1994 and 1995, vols. 24, 25, pp. 260–1/280–1.
94 Noland, *Pacific Basin*, p. 81.
95 Ranis and Mahmood, *The Political Economy of Development Policy Change*, p. 179.
96 McCarthy *et al.*, "Measuring the Effect of External Shocks," pp. 16, 45.
97 Haggard, "The Philippines: Picking Up," p. 93.
98 Noland, *Pacific Basin*, p. 81.
99 Timberman, *A Changeless Land*, p. 107.
100 Wurfel, *Filipino Politics*, pp. 136–7.

101 Bello *et al.*, "Export-Oriented Industrialization," p. 128.
102 Stauffer, "The Philippine Political Economy," p. 250.
103 Hutchcroft, "Preferential Credit Allocation," p. 188.
104 Timberman, *A Changeless Land*, p. 104.
105 Wurfel, *Filipino Politics*, p. 144.
106 *Ibid.*, pp. 152–3.
107 Overholt, "Rise and Fall," 1146–8.
108 Hal Hill, "The Philippine Economy Under Aquino," *Asian Survey* 28 (1988), 280.
109 Hasan, "Adjustment to External Shocks," p. 180; Dohner and Intal, "Debt Crisis and Adjustment," pp. 174–5.
110 World Bank, *World Tables, 1995*, pp. 358–9.
111 *Ibid.*, table 18.
112 *Ibid.*, pp. 358–9; Asian Development Bank, *Key Indicators*, vols. 24, 25, pp. 260–1/280–1.
113 *Ibid.*, pp. 534–5.
114 Bello *et al.*, "Export-Oriented Industrialization," pp. 139–52.
115 For the Philippines, 4.6 3.5 in Malaysia and Thailand, and 2.7 in Indonesia. Dohner and Intal, "Debt Crisis and Adjustment," pp. 171, 176.
116 Haggard, "The Philippines: Picking Up," pp. 91–121.
117 Haggard, "Political Economy of the Philippine Debt," pp. 215–55.
118 Haggard, "The Philippines: Picking Up," pp. 91–121.
119 Naya, "Role of Trade," p. 172.
120 Noland, *Pacific Basin*, p. 82.
121 Naya, "Role of Trade," p. 178.
122 Yoshihara, *The Nation and Economic Growth*, p. 180.
123 Noland, *Pacific Basin*, pp. 85–6; Montes, "The Politics of Liberalization," p. 93.
124 Hawes, "Marcos, His Cronies," p. 156.
125 The government negotiated a new agreement early in 1983 as well as a second structural adjustment loan of $300 million (with another $300 million coming from a consortium of US banks), and a further IMF loan.
126 Timberman, *A Changeless Land*, p. 135.
127 Jackson, "The Philippines," p. 246.
128 Carl H. Lande, "Authoritarian Rule in the Philippines: Some Critical Views," *Pacific Affairs* 55 (1992), 83.
129 Wurfel, *Filipino Politics*, pp. 333–7.
130 Yoshihara, *The Rise of Ersatz*, p. 87.
131 World Bank, *World Tables, 1995*, pp. 532–3.
132 Dohner and Intal, "Debt Crisis and Adjustment," p. 178.
133 Ranis and Mahmood, *The Political Economy of Development Policy Change*, p. 196.
134 Haggard, "The Political Economy of the Philippine Debt," pp. 215–55.
135 Hutchcroft, "Oligarchs and Cronies," pp. 425–6.
136 *Ibid.*, pp. 430–2.
137 *Ibid.*, p. 434.
138 Montes, "The Politics of Liberalization," p. 92.
139 Pacific Economic Cooperation Council, *Milestones in APEC Liberalisation: A Map of Market Opening Measures by APEC*, Singapore: APEC Secretariat, 1995, p. 139.
140 Timberman, *A Changeless Land*, p. 135.
141 World Bank, *World Tables, 1994*, tables 9, 10.
142 Timberman, *A Changeless Land*, p. 322.
143 World Bank, *World Tables, 1994*, table 15.
144 Dohner and Intal, "Debt Crisis and Adjustment," p. 171.

145 Jackson, "The Philippines," p. 248.
146 Wurfel, *Filipino Politics*, pp. 187–8.
147 Naya, "Role of Trade Policies," p. 180.
148 McCarthy *et al.*, "Measuring the Effect of External Shocks," p. 18.
149 World Bank, *World Tables, 1994*, pp. 532–5.
150 Wurfel, *Filipino Politics*, p. 194.
151 *Ibid.*
152 Jackson, "The Philippines," pp. 250–1.
153 Wurfel, *Filipino Politics*, pp. 53–6.
154 World Bank, *World Tables, 1994*, pp. 532–5; Asian Development Bank, *Key Indicators, 1994*, pp. 280–1.
155 *Far Eastern Economic Review* (December 14, 1989), 15.
156 *Far Eastern Economic Review* (July 12, 1990), 33–4.
157 Montes, "The Politics of Liberalization," p. 92.
158 In the mid-1990s, between 4.2 and 6 million Filipinos were working abroad and remitting some $3 billion a year. *Washington Post* (November 3, 1995), A1.
159 *Far Eastern Economic Review* (June 13, 1991), 42.
160 *The Economist* (May 20, 1995), 7.
161 *Los Angeles Times* (June 24, 1991), D1.
162 *Far Eastern Economic Review* (April 21, 1994), 74.
163 Timberman, *A Changeless Land*, p. 333.
164 *The Economist* (March 25, 1989), 35–7.
165 Timberman, *A Changeless Land*, p. 333.
166 Asian Development Bank, *Key Indicators 1994*, p. 261; Keizai Koho Center, *APEC 1995*, Tokyo: Keizai Koho Center, 1995, pp. 6–7, 24–5.
167 *Financial Times* (October 2, 1995), survey.
168 *Far Eastern Economic Review* (July 23, 1992), 44–5.
169 *The Economist* (May 8, 1993), 85–6.
170 *Far Eastern Economic Review* (April 21, 1994), 74.
171 Timberman, *A Changeless Land*, pp. 338–9.
172 Montes, "The Politics of Liberalization," pp. 93, 97–107.
173 Timberman, *A Changeless Land*, pp. 338–9.
174 Pacific Economic Cooperation Council, *Milestones*, pp. 146–7.
175 Pacific Economic Cooperation Council, *Survey of Impediments to Trade and Investment in the APEC Region*, Singapore: APEC Secretariat, 1995, pp. 87–8, 102.
176 Pacific Economic Cooperation Council, *Milestones*, pp. 160–1.
177 *Ibid.*, p. 139.
178 *Far Eastern Economic Review* (June 16, 1994), 48–57.
179 *Ibid.*
180 *Far Eastern Economic Review* (February 15, 1990), 68–70.
181 *Far Eastern Economic Review* (May 23, 1991), 64; *Far Eastern Economic Review* (November 24, 1994), 110; *Far Eastern Economic Review* (January 19, 1995), 54; *The Economist* (January 14, 1995), 35.
182 David G. Timberman, "The Philippines in 1990," *Asian Survey* 31 (1991), 154–5.
183 *Far Eastern Economic Review* (December 8, 1994), 18; *The Economist* (April 15, 1995), 34.
184 Timberman, "The Philippines in 1990," 159–61.
185 Montes, "The Politics of Liberalization," pp. 99–107.
186 *Far Eastern Economic Review* (March 17, 1994), 24; *Far Eastern Economic Review* (April 21, 1994), 74.
187 *Far Eastern Economic Review* (July 21, 1994), 76.

188 The coalition supporting Ramos picked up nine of twelve contested seats in the Senate and over half of those in the House.

189 *The Economist* (July 30, 1994), 32–4.

190 Montes, "The Politics of Liberalization," p. 100.

191 *Ibid.*, p. 97.

192 Hutchcroft, "Oligarchs and Cronies," p. 444.

193 *Ibid.*, p. 437.

6 Thailand

1 W. M. Corden and H. V. Richter, "Trade and the balance of payments," in T. H. Silcock (ed.), *Thailand: Social and Economic Studies in Development*, Durham, N. C.: Duke University Press, 1967, pp. 149–50.

2 For a discussion of labor organization during this period, see Bevars D. Mabry, *The Development of Labor Institutions in Thailand*, Ithaca: Cornell University Southeast Asia Program, Data Paper no. 112, April 1979, pp. 25–7.

3 James C. Ingram, *Economic Change in Thailand, 1850–1970*, Stanford: Stanford University Press, 1971, pp. 37–8.

4 Chai-Anan Samudavanija, "The Military and Politics in Thailand," *Democratic Institutions*, 1 (1992), 21–37.

5 Fred Riggs, *Thailand: The Modernization of a Bureaucratic Policy*, Honolulu: East–West Center Press, 1966, pp. 311–26.

6 David Feeny, *The Political Economy of Productivity: Thai Agricultural Development, 1880–1975*, Vancouver: University of British Columbia Press, 1982.

7 Ingram, *Economic Change*, pp. 203–19.

8 A 1992 amendment to the constitution requires the prime minister to be a member of parliament.

9 Anek Laothamatas, *Business Associations and the New Political Economy of Thailand: From Bureaucratic Polity to Liberal Corporatism*, Boulder: Westview Press, 1992, pp. 4–8.

10 Personal interview with Snoh Unakul, 1987.

11 Formerly the Association of Thai Industries. The Board of Trade long played private sector governance roles in managing Thai exports, including quality control schemes. In the case of the Thai Bankers Association, regular and systematic contact with the Bank of Thailand has varied less with changes in the political leadership.

12 Gustav Ranis and Syed Akhtar Mahmood, *The Political Economy of Development Policy Change*, Cambridge, Mass.: Blackwell, 1992, pp. 175, 192.

13 Kraisak Choonhavan, "The Growth of Domestic Capital and Thai Industrialization," *Journal of Contemporary Asia* 14 (1984), 142.

14 David Elliott, *Thailand: Origins of Military Rule*, London: Zed Press, 1978, pp. 129–33; Scott R. Christensen, "The Politics of Democratization in Thailand: State and Society Since 1932," unpublished paper, Thailand Development Research Institute, Bangkok, 1991, p. 18.

15 Chattip Nartsupha, *Foreign Trade, Foreign Finance and the Development of Thailand, 1956–1965*, Bangkok: Prae Pittaya Ltd., 1970, pp. 99–115; Robert J. Muscat, *The Fifth Tiger: A Study of Thai Development Policy*, Armonk, N.Y.: M. E. Sharpe, 1994, p. 101.

16 I. M. D. Little, Richard N. Cooper, W. Max Corden, and Sarath Rajapatirana, *Boom, Crisis, and Adjustment: The Macroeconomic Experience of Developing Countries*, New York: Oxford University Press, 1993, p. 272.

17 Shinichi Ichimura, "The Pattern and Prospects of Asian Economic Development,"

in Shinichi Ichimura (ed.), *Challenge of Asian Developing Countries: Issues and Analyses*, Tokyo: Asian Productivity Organization, 1988, p. 26. Industrial exports as a whole accounted for 16.5 percent of Thai exports in 1969. Kiyoshi Kojima and Tsuneo Nakauchi, "Economic Conditions in East and Southeast Asia and Development Perspective," in Shinichi Ichimura (ed.), *Challenge of Asian Developing Countries: Issues and Analyses*, Tokyo: Asian Productivity Organization, 1988, p. 114. In 1970, raw materials and agricultural and food products accounted for about 90 percent of Thai exports. Seiji Naya, "Role of Trade Policies: Competition and Cooperation," in Shinichi Ichimura (ed.), *Challenge of Asian Developing Countries: Issues and Analyses*, Tokyo: Asian Productivity Organization, 1988, p. 178.

18 Muscat, *The Fifth Tiger*, p. 61.
19 *Ibid.*, see also T. H. Silcock, "Money and Banking," in T. H. Silcock (ed.), *Thailand: Social and Economic Studies in Development*, Durham, N.C.: Duke University Press, 1967, p. 205.
20 Pasuk Phongpaichit and Sungsidh Piriyarangsan, *Corruption and Democracy in Thailand*, Bangkok: Political Economy Centre, Faculty of Economics, Chulalongkorn University, 1994, p. 13.
21 Akira Suehiro, *Capital Accumulation in Thailand*, Tokyo: Center for East Asian Cultural Studies, 1989, p. 139.
22 Muscat, *The Fifth Tiger*, p. 106.
23 World Bank, *Thailand, Toward a Development Strategy of Full Participation*, Washington, D.C.: The World Bank, 1980, p. 13.
24 Rashid Amjad, "An Overview," in Amjad (ed.), *The Development of Labor Intensive Industry in ASEAN Countries*, Geneva: International Labor Organization, 1981, p. 15.
25 Ichimura, "Pattern and Prospects," p. 16.
26 Naya, "Role of Trade," p. 172.
27 Ranis and Mahmood, *The Political Economy of Development Policy Change*, pp. 167, 189.
28 This paragraph draws on Richard Doner and Danny Unger, "The Politics of Finance in Thai Economic Development," in Stephen Haggard, Chung H. Lee, and Sylvia Maxfield (eds.), *The Politics of Finance in Developing Countries*, Ithaca: Cornell University Press, 1993.
29 Ranis and Mahmood, *The Political Economy of Development Policy Change*, p. 177.
30 *Ibid.*, pp. 177, 199.
31 *Ibid.*, p. 193.
32 *Ibid.*, p. 176.
33 Muscat, *The Fifth Tiger*, p. 101.
34 Amjad, "An Overview," p. 18.
35 Using an export concentration index, Thai exports were considerably more diversified in 1970 than those of Indonesia, Malaysia, or the Philippines, the last of which was also not an energy exporter. In fact, the Thai index in both 1970 and 1982 was closer to that of South Korea than to the other ASEAN Four. Naya, "Role of Trade," p. 176.
36 W. M. Corden, "The Exchange Rate System and the Taxation of Trade," in T. H. Silcock (ed.), *Thailand: Social and Economic Studies in Development*, Durham, N. C.: Duke University Press, 1967, pp. 163–8.
37 A large share of that spending, nearly one-third, was capital expenditure. Little *et al.*, *Boom, Crisis*, pp. 301, 303.
38 Muscat, *The Fifth Tiger*, p. 101.
39 Corden, "The Exchange Rate System," p. 168; Corden and Richter, "Trade," p. 149.
40 Kevin Hewison, *Bankers and Bureaucrats: Capital and the Role of the State in Thailand* (Yale Univesity Southeast Asian Studies), New Haven: Yale University Center for International and Area Studies, 1989, p. 106.

41 World Bank, *World Tables, 1994*, Baltimore: Johns Hopkins University Press, 1994, pp. 358–9.

42 World Bank, *Thailand*, p. 14.

43 Narongchai Akrasanee, Karel Jansen, and Jeerasak Pongpisanupichit, *International Capital Flows and Economic Adjustment in Thailand*, Bangkok: Thailand Development Research Institute, 1993, p. 57.

44 Chaipat Sahasakul, *Lessons from the World Bank's Experience of Structural Adjustment Loans (SALs): A Case Study of Thailand*, Research Monograph no. 8, Bangkok: Thailand Development Research Institute, 1992, pp. 4, 8; Little *et al.*, *Boom, Crisis*, p. 30.

45 Little *et al.*, *Boom, Crisis*, p. 72.

46 World Bank, *World Tables, 1994*, p. 650.

47 Akrasanee *et al.*, *International Capital Flows*, p. 66.

48 Muscat, *The Fifth Tiger*, p. 102.

49 Little *et al.*, *Boom, Crisis*, pp. 35–6; Ranis and Mahmood, *The Political Economy of Development Policy Change*, pp. 175–9.

50 Marcus Noland, *Pacific Basin Developing Countries, Prospects for the Future*, Washington, D.C.: Institute for International Economics, 1990, p. 72.

51 Somsak Tambunlertchai and Chesada Loohawenchit, "Labour Intensive and Small Scale Manufacturing in Thailand," in Rashid Amjad (ed.), *The Development of Labor Intensive Industry in ASEAN Countries*, Geneva: International Labor Organization, 1981, p. 193.

52 Ranis and Mahmood, *The Political Economy of Development Policy Change*, pp. 185–6.

53 Sahasakul, *Lessons from the World Bank's Experience*, p. 4.

54 Mabry, *Development of Labor Institutions*, pp. 52–62.

55 In 1978, the *Far Eastern Economic Review* quoted the estimate by the US Embassy in Thailand that five "Chinese" banking families controlled or "substantially influence[d]" over half of Thailand's private economy. See John L. S. Girling, *Thailand, Society and Politics*, Ithaca: Cornell University Press, 1981, p. 78, n. 39.

56 Little *et al.*, *Boom, Crisis*, pp. 301, 303, 306.

57 Sahasakul, *Lessons from the World Bank's Experience*, pp. 4–5; World Bank, *World Tables, 1994*, pp. 648–51; Little *et al.*, *Boom, Crisis*, p. 78.

58 Kunal Sen, "Thailand: Stabilization with Growth," in Pradeep Agrawal *et al.* (eds.), *Economic Restructuring in East Asia and India: Perspectives on Policy Reform*, New York: St. Martin's Press, 1995, pp. 134–58.

59 Muscat, *The Fifth Tiger*, p. 158.

60 Sahasakul, *Lessons from the World Bank's Experience*, pp. 4–5.

61 Akrasanee *et al.*, *International Capital Flows*, p. 66.

62 World Bank, *World Tables, 1994*, pp. 650–1; Little *et al.*, *Boom, Crisis*, pp. 72, 104.

63 Little *et al.*, *Boom, Crisis*, pp. 86–7; Sahasakul, *Lessons from the World Bank's Experience*, p. 5.

64 Sen, "Thailand," p. 137.

65 Little *et al.*, *Boom, Crisis*, p. 145.

66 Akrasanee *et al.*, *International Capital Flows*, p. 46.

67 Girling, *Thailand*, pp. 225–6.

68 Muscat, *The Fifth Tiger*, pp. 155–7.

69 *Ibid.*, p. 163.

70 Sahasakul, *Lessons from the World Bank's Experience*, p. 28.

71 *Ibid.*, pp. 4–5.

72 Muscat, *The Fifth Tiger*, p. 176.

73 Chris Dixon, "Thailand's Rapid Economic Growth: Causes, Sustainability and Lessons," in Michael J. G. Parnwell (ed.), *Uneven Development in Thailand*, Aldershot, England: Avebury, 1996, p. 33.

74 Little *et al.*, *Boom, Crisis*, pp. 75, 410–11.
75 Muscat, *The Fifth Tiger*, pp. 185–7.
76 World Bank, *Thailand*, p. 14.
77 Little *et al.*, *Boom, Crisis*, pp. 75, 410–11.
78 *Ibid.*, pp. 43, 47, 86.
79 Muscat, *The Fifth Tiger*, p. 188.
80 World Bank, *Thailand*, p. 19.
81 Kiyoshi and Nakauchi, "Economic Conditions," p. 109; Naya, "Role of Trade," p. 174.
82 Naya, "Role of Trade," p. 178.
83 Jean-Christophe Simon, "The Thai Manufacturing Sector: New Patterns of Expansion," in Michael J. G. Parnwell (ed.), *Uneven Development in Thailand*, Aldershot, England: Avebury, 1996, p. 86.
84 Muscat, *The Fifth Tiger*, pp. 163–7.
85 Noland, *Pacific Basin*, p. 72.
86 Ranis and Mahmood, *The Political Economy of Development Policy Change*, p. 193.
87 Pacific Economic Cooperation Council, *Survey of Impediments to Trade and Investment in the APEC Region*, Singapore: APEC Secretariat, 1995, p. 139.
88 Little *et al.*, *Boom, Crisis*, pp. 86–7.
89 Muscat, *The Fifth Tiger*, p. 188.
90 Little *et al.*, *Boom, Crisis*, pp. 86–7.
91 World Bank, *The East Asian Miracle: Economic Growth and Public Policy*, New York: Oxford University Press, 1993, p. 300. Seiji Naya *et al.*'s calculations suggest that over the period of both oil shocks the Thai economy made significant adjustments. This need not imply, however, that Thai officials made significant policy adjustments. William E. James' calculations suggest that policy measures did slightly offset the large negative terms-of-trade effect. Cited in Ichimura, "Pattern and Prospects," pp. 39–43.
92 Little *et al.*, *Boom, Crisis*, p. 97.
93 Pasuk Phongpaichit, "The Politics of Economic Reform in Thailand," in David G. Timberman (ed.), *The Politics of Economic Reform in Southeast Asia, The Experiences of Thailand, Indonesia and the Philippines*, Manila: Asian Institute of Management, 1992, p. 14.
94 Ichimura, "Pattern and Prospects," p. 29; Ranis and Mahmood, *The Political Economy of Development Policy Change*, p. 197.
95 Little *et al.*, *Boom, Crisis*, pp. 301–6.
96 *Ibid.*, p. 75.
97 Laothamatas, *Business Associations*, pp. 123–6.
98 Little *et al.*, *Boom, Crisis*, p. 113; Ranis and Mahmood, *The Political Economy of Development Policy Change*, p. 188.
99 World Bank, *World Tables, 1994*, pp. 650–1.
100 Little *et al.*, *Boom, Crisis*, p. 145.
101 *Ibid.*, p. 104.
102 Naya, "Role of Trade," p. 172.
103 Dixon, "Thailand's Rapid Economic Growth," p. 35.
104 Revenue expansion from 1984 to 1986 was between 3 and 8 percent per year. Sahasakul, *Lessons from the World Bank's Experience*, pp. 5, 28.
105 Little *et al.*, *Boom, Crisis*, p. 72.
106 Muscat, *The Fifth Tiger*, p. 219.
107 Little *et al.*, *Boom, Crisis*, pp. 119, 226.
108 Sahasakul, *Lessons from the World Bank's Experience*, pp. 43–5.

109 *Ibid.*, p. 44.
110 Noland, *Pacific Basin*, p. 72.
111 Pacific Economic Cooperation Council, *Survey of Impediments*, p. 223.
112 Johannes Drasbaek Schmidt, "Paternalism and Planning in Thailand: Facilitating Growth Without Social Benefits," in Michael J. G. Parnwell (ed.), *Uneven Development in Thailand*, Aldershot, England: Avebury, 1996, p. 74.
113 Little *et al.*, *Boom, Crisis*, pp. 301–6.
114 Muscat, *The Fifth Tiger*, pp. 217–18.
115 Little *et al.*, *Boom, Crisis*, pp. 412–13.
116 Muscat, *The Fifth Tiger*, p. 218.
117 Phongpaichit, "The Politics of Economic Reform," p. 14; Dixon, "Thailand's Rapid Economic Growth," pp. 37–8.
118 Phongpaichit, "The Politics of Economic Reform," p. 17.
119 The failing institutions did not include any of the large commercial banks or their affiliated finance companies. Doner and Unger, "The Politics of Finance in Thai Economic Development."
120 Sen, "Thailand," p. 138.
121 Peter A. Petri, *The Lessons of East Asia: Common Foundations of East Asian Success*, Washington, D.C.: World Bank, 1993, p. 9.
122 Masato Hayashida, "The Three Mini Dragons: Economic Development in Thailand, Malaysia, and Indonesia," in *Asia-Pacific Review, 1995*, p. 175.
123 Japan Institute for Social and Economic Affairs, *APEC 1995: A Statistical Compilation*, Tokyo: Keizai Koho Center, 1995, pp. 24, 27.
124 Japan Institute for Social and Economic Affairs, *APEC 1995*, p. 29.
125 Little *et al.*, *Boom, Crisis*, p. 272.
126 Simon, "The Thai Manufacturing Sector," p. 89.
127 Little *et al.*, *Boom, Crisis*, p. 113.
128 Asian Development Bank, *Key Indicators of Developing Asian and Pacific Countries, 1994*, Manila: Oxford University Press, 1994, p. 317.
129 Bank of Thailand, *Quarterly Bulletin* 34 (June 1994), 42, 50.
130 Kunio Yoshihara, "Culture, Institutions, and Economic Growth: A Comparative Study of Korea and Thailand," *Tonan Ajia Kenkyu* [Southeast Asia Studies] 33 (1995), 106.
131 International Monetary Fund, *World Economic Outlook* (May 1995) Washington D.C.: IMF, p. 129; Little *et al.*, *Boom, Crisis*, pp. 410–11.
132 World Bank, *World Tables, 1994*, p. 649.
133 Pacific Economic Cooperation Council, *Milestones*, pp. 99, 161.
134 *The Nation* (July 6, 1991), p. 1.
135 Pacific Economic Cooperation Council, *Survey of Impediments*, p. 223.
136 Teerana Bhongmakapat, "Income Distribution in a Rapidly Growing Economy of Thailand," *Chulalongkorn Journal of Economics* 5 (1993), p. 115; World Bank, *Thailand*, p. 24.
137 Sen, "Thailand," pp. 144, 157–8; Dixon, "Thailand's Rapid Economic Growth," pp. 38–40; Kunio Yoshihara, *The Nation and Economic Growth: The Philippines and Thailand*, New York: Oxford University Press, 1994, p. 106.
138 Sen, "Thailand," p. 142.
139 *Ibid.*, pp. 147–8.
140 Pacific Economic Cooperation Council, *Survey of Impediments*, pp. 223, 19.
141 Schmidt, "Paternalism and Planning," p. 76.
142 Sen, "Thailand," p. 156.
143 Richard Doner first pointed out this development to us.

144 T. H. Silcock, "Summary and Assessment," in T. H. Silcock (ed.), *Thailand: Social and Economic Studies in Development*, Durham, N.C.: Duke University Press, 1967, pp. 294–5.
145 Personal interview with Anand Panyarachul, 1987.

7 Conclusion

1 See, for example, David A. Lake, *Power, Protection, and Free Trade: International Sources of U.S. Commercial Strategy, 1887–1939*, Ithaca: Cornell University Press, 1988.
2 John S. Odell, "Understanding International Trade Policies: An Emerging Synthesis," *World Politics* 43 (1990),147–8.
3 See, for example, Ellen Kennedy, *The Bundesbank, Germany's Central Bank in the International Monetary System*, New York: Council on Foreign Relations Press, 1991, pp. 1–12, 21–5, 30–55.
4 For example, Peter J. Katzenstein, *Small States in World Markets,* Ithaca: Cornell University Press, 1985, pp. 39–79.
5 See Odell's discussion of conditioning hypotheses, "Understanding International Trade Policies," 165–7.
6 This conclusion bears some similarity to conclusions reached by Geoffrey Garrett and Peter Lange concerning economic openness and the organization of labor in Western European states. See "Performance in a Hostile World: Economic Growth in Capitalist Democracies, 1974–1980," *World Politics* 38 (1986), 517–45.
7 See Daniel I. Okimoto, *Between MITI and the Market: Japan's Industrial Policy for High Technology,* Stanford: Stanford University Press, 1989, p. 226.
8 Danny Kin-Kong Lam and Ian Lee, "Guerrilla Capitalism and the Limits of Statist Theory: Comparing the Chinese NICs," in Cal Clark and Steve Chan (eds.), *The Evolving Pacific Basin in the Global Political Economy,* Boulder: Lynne Rienner Publishers, 1992, pp. 107–24.
9 See, for example, Gary Hamilton (ed.), *Business Networks and Economic Development in East and Southeast Asia,* Hong Kong: Centre of Asian Studies, University of Hong Kong, 1991.
10 Louis T. Wells, Jr., "Mobile Exporters: New Foreign Investors in East Asia," in Kenneth A. Froot (ed.), *Foreign Direct Investment*, Chicago: University of Chicago Press, 1993, pp. 173–96.
11 Gary Gereffi, Miguel Korzeniewicz, and Roberto P. Korzeniewicz, "Introduction," in G. Gereffi and M. Korzeniewicz (eds.), *Commodity Chains and Global Capitalism,* Westport, Conn.: Greenwood Press, 1994, pp. 1–14.
12 Lawrence B. Krause, "Introduction," in Lawrence B. Krause and Kim Kihwan (eds.), *Liberalization in the Process of Economic Development,* Berkeley: University of California Press, 1991, p. 2. Barbara Geddes, *Politicians' Dilemma, Building State Capacity in Latin America*, Berkeley: University of California Press, 1994, p. 5. Robert Bates and Anne Krueger emphasize economic stagnation, if not actual crisis, in Robert H. Bates and Anne O. Krueger, "Generalizations Arising from the Country Studies," in Robert H. Bates and Anne O. Krueger (eds.), *Political and Economic Interactions in Economic Policy Reform*, Cambridge, Mass.: Blackwell, 1993, p. 454. Peter A. Gourevitch, *Politics in Hard Times: Comparative Responses to International Economic Crises*, Ithaca: Cornell University Press, 1986, p. 19. Stephan Haggard, *Pathways from the Periphery*, Ithaca: Cornell University Press, 1990, p. 28. Tun-jen Cheng, "Political Regimes and Development Strategies: South Korea and Taiwan," in Gary Gereffi and Donald L. Wyman (eds.), *Manufacturing Miracles*, Princeton: Princeton University Press, 1990, pp. 139–78.

13 It also applies, though less dramatically, to the shifts implemented by Sarit in Thailand beginning in the late 1950s.

14 Charles P. Kindleberger, "The Rise of Free Trade in Western Europe," *Journal of Economic History* 35 (1975), reprinted in Jeffrey A. Frieden and David A. Lake, *International Political Economy: Perspectives on Global Power and Wealth*, 2nd edn., New York: St. Martin's Press, 1991, pp. 72–88.

15 See Stephan Haggard, *Developing Nations and the Politics of Global Integration*, Washington, D.C.: Brookings Institution, 1995.

16 See Robert Putnam, "Diplomacy and Domestic Politics: The Logic of Two-Level Games," *International Organization* 42 (1988), 427–60; Len Schoppa, "Gaiatsu and Economic Bargaining Outcomes," *International Organization* 47 (1993), 353–86.

17 Peter J. Katzenstein, *Between Power and Plenty*, Madison: University of Wisconsin Press, 1978.

18 Interviews with officials in Tokyo.

19 Odell, "Understanding International Trade Policies," 143.

20 Yoshihara offers a more straightforward, functionalist variation on this argument when he concludes that Thai leaders, unlike those in South Korea, opened their country to foreign investment because they were unable to realize rapid economic growth without it – unlike the South Korean case. Kunio Yoshihara, "Culture, Institutions, and Economic Growth: A Comparative Study of Korea and Thailand," *Tonan Ajia Kenkyu* [Southeast Asian Studies] 33 (1995), 387.

21 Marcus Noland, *Pacific Basin Developing Countries, Prospects for the Future*, Washington, D.C.: Institute for International Economics, 1990.

22 Kunio Yoshihara, *The Nation and Economic Growth: The Philippines and Thailand*, New York: Oxford University Press, 1994, pp.106–9.

23 Paul Krugman argues, however, that it is precisely such high levels of investment that account for most of the East Asian "miracles." Paul Krugman, "The Myth of Asia's Miracle," *Foreign Affairs* 73 (1994), 62–78. An Australian government study of OECD countries in 1996 found that tariff cuts served better than domestic economic reforms in explaining relative rates of economic growth after 1970. A 1 percent tariff reduction was associated with productivity increases of over 3 percent and 2 percent growth in GDP. These achievements stemmed from efficiency gains rather than rising investment. *Financial Times* (April 9, 1996), 3.

24 See Odell, "Understanding International Trade Policies," 147.

25 Manuel F. Montes, "The Politics of Liberalization: The Aquino Government's 1990 Tariff Reform Initiative," in David G. Timberman (ed.), *The Politics of Economic Reform in Southeast Asia: The Experiences of Thailand, Indonesia and the Philippines*, Manila: Asian Institute of Management, 1992, p. 92.

26 An interesting recent discussion of some of these issues appears in *Newsletter of the APSA Organized Section in Comparative Politics* 7 (1996), 1–18.

Bibliography

"20% Surcharge on Propylene Imports," *Jakarta Post* (February 15, 1996), 1.

"Indonesia: Chandra Asri – Olefin Tariff Causes Controversy," *Asian Chemical News* (March 2, 1995), electronic newsletter.

"Indonesia: Jakarta Observed – Soeharto's Trade Two-Step Leads to Credibility Twist," *Australian Financial Review* (January 11, 1995), 7.

"Indonesia's Rising Prosperity Feeds a Push for Democracy," *New York Times* (June 21, 1996), A3.

"June 1996 Deregulation," press release of Coordinating Ministry for Economy, Finance and Development Supervision, Government of Indonesia.

"Malaysia: What Price Success?" *Southeast Asia Chronicle* 49 (April 1980), 1–28.

"Periodic Economic Roundup," (unclassified) US Embassy, Jakarta, March 1995 (Source: on-line Lexis International News).

Akrasnee, Narongchai, Karel Jansen, and Jeerasak Pongpisanupichit, *International Capital Flows and Economic Adjustment in Thailand*, Bangkok: Thailand Development Research Institute, 1993.

Ali, S. Husin (ed.), *Ethnicity, Class and Development in Malaysia*, Kuala Lumpur: Persatuan Sains Sosial Malaysia, 1984.

Amjad, Rashid, "An Overview," in Amjad (ed.), *The Development of Labour Intensive Industry in ASEAN Countries*.

(ed.), *The Development of Labour Intensive Industry in ASEAN Countries*, Geneva: ILO, 1981.

Anderson, Benedict, *Imagined Communities: Reflections on the Origin and Spread of Nationalism*, London: Verso, 1991.

ASEAN Centre, *ASEAN–Japan Statistical Pocketbook*, Tokyo: ASEAN Centre, 1993.

Asian Development Bank, *Key Indicators of Developing Asian and Pacific Countries*, Manila: Oxford University Press, various years.

Asian Wall Street Journal Weekly, various issues.

Bangkok Post, various issues.

Bank of Thailand, *Quarterly Bulletin* 34 (June 1994).

"National Government Actual Revenue Classified by Major Sources", mimeo.

Bates, Robert H. and Anne O. Krueger (eds.), *Political and Economic Interactions in Economic Policy Reform*, Cambridge, Mass.: Blackwell, 1993.

"Generalizations Arising from the Country Studies," in Bates and Krueger (eds.), *Political and Economic Interactions*.

"Introduction," in Bates and Krueger (eds.), *Political and Economic Interactions*.

Beaglehole, J. H., "Malay Participation in Commerce and Industry: The Role of RIDA and MARA," *Journal of Commonwealth Political Studies* 7 (November 1969), 216–45.

Bello, Walden, David Kinley, and Elaine Elinson (eds.), *Development Debacle: The World Bank in the Philippines*, San Francisco: Institute for Food and Development Policy, Philippine Solidarity Network, 1982.

Bello, Walden, David O'Connor, and Robin Broad, "Export-Oriented Industrialization: The Short-Lived Illusion," in Bello *et al.* (eds.), *Development Debacle*, pp. 127–64.

Bernard, Mitchell, and John Ravenhill, "Beyond Product Cycles and Flying Geese: Regionalization, Hierarchy, and the Industrialization of East Asia," *World Politics* 47 (1995), 171–209.

Bhongmakapat, Teerana, "Income Distribution in a Rapidly Growing Economy of Thailand," *Chulalongkorn Journal of Economics* 5 (1993), 109–35.

Black, Stanley W., "The Impact of Changes in the World Economy on Stabilization Policies in the 1970s," in Cline and Weintraub (eds.), *Economic Stabilization*, 1981, pp. 43–82.

Blecker, Robert A. (ed.), *U.S. Trade Policy and Global Growth*, Armonk, N.Y.: M. E. Sharpe, 1996.

Borden, William S., *The Pacific Alliance: United States Foreign Economic Policy and Japanese Trade Recovery, 1947–1955*, Madison: University of Wisconsin Press, 1984.

Bowie, Alasdair, "Responding to the International Challenge: Shaping Policy in Indonesia and Malaysia," paper to the 47th Annual Meeting of the Association for Asian Studies, Washington, D.C., April 6–9, 1995.

"The Dynamics of Business–Government Relations in Industrialising Malaysia," in MacIntyre (ed.), *Business and Government in Industrialising Asia*, pp. 167–94.

Crossing the Industrial Divide, New York: Columbia University Press, 1991.

Callaghy, Thomas R., "Vision and Politics in the Transformation of the Global Political Economy: Lessons from the Second and Third Worlds," in Slater *et al.* (eds.), *Global Transformation and the Third World*, pp. 161–258.

Cameron, David R., "Social Democracy, Corporatism, and Labor Quiescence: The Representation of Economic Institutions in Advanced Capitalist Society," in John H. Goldthorpe (ed.), *Order and Conflict in Contemporary Capitalism*, New York: Oxford University Press, 1984, pp. 143–78.

Carlson, Sevinc, *Indonesia's Oil*, Washington, D.C.: Center for Strategic and International Studies, 1976.

Chee, Peng Lim, *Industrial Development: An Introduction to the Malaysian Industrial Master Plan*, Petaling Jaya, Selangor: Pelanduk, 1987.

Cheng, Tun-jen, "Political Regimes and Development Strategies: South Korea and Taiwan," in Gereffi and Wyman (eds.), *Manufacturing Miracles*, pp. 139–78.

Cheng, Tun-jen, and Stephan Haggard, *Newly Industrializing Asia in Transition: Policy Reform and American Response*, Berkeley: Institute of International Studies, University of California, 1987.

Chhibber, Ajay, Division Chief, World Bank, address to a conference on "Uncovering Indonesia," Washington, D.C., March 15, 1995.

Choonhavan, Kraisak, "The Growth of Domestic Capital and Thai Industrialization," *Journal of Contemporary Asia* 14 (1984), 135–46.

Christensen, Scott R., "The Politics of Democratization in Thailand: State and Society Since 1932," unpublished paper, Thailand Development Research Institute, Bangkok, 1991.

Clark, Cal, and Steve Chan (eds.), *The Evolving Pacific Basin in the Global Political Economy*, Boulder: Lynne Rienner Publishers, 1992.

Cline, William R. and Sidney Weintraub (eds.), *Economic Stabilization in Developing Countries*, Washington D.C.: Brookings Institution, 1981.

Corden, W. M., "The Exchange Rate System and the Taxation of Trade," in Silcock (ed.), *Thailand, Social and Economic Studies in Development*, pp. 151–69.

Corden, W. M. and H. V. Richter, "Trade and the Balance of Payments," in Silcock (ed.), *Thailand, Social and Economic Studies in Development*, pp. 128–50.

Crone, Donald K., "State, Social Elites, and Government Capacity in Southeast Asia," *World Politics* 40 (1988), 252–68.

Cumings, Bruce, "The Origins and Development of the Northeast Asian Political Economy: Industrial Sectors, Product Cycles, and Political Consequences," in Deyo (ed.), *The Political Economy of the New Asian Industrialism*, pp. 44–83.

Davidson, Paul, "Reforming the International Payments System," in Blecker (ed.), *U.S. Trade Policy and Global Growth*, pp. 215–36.

Deyo, Frederic C. (ed.), *The Political Economy of the New Asian Industrialism*, Ithaca: Cornell University Press, 1987.

Diamond, Larry, Juan J. Linz, and Seymour Martin Lipset (eds.), *Democracy in Developing Countries*, vol. III, *Asia*, Boulder: Lynne Rienner Publishers, 1988.

Dixon, Chris, "Thailand's Rapid Economic Growth: Causes, Sustainability and Lessons," in Parnwell (ed.), *Uneven Development in Thailand*, pp. 28–48.

Dohner, Robert S. and Ponciano Intal, Jr., "Debt Crisis and Adjustment in the Philippines," in R. S. Dohner and P. Intal, Jr. (eds.), *Developing Country Debt and the World Economy*, Chicago: University of Chicago Press, 1989.

Doner, Richard, and Danny Unger, "The Politics of Finance in Thai Economic Development," in Haggard *et al.* (eds.), *The Politics of Finance in Developing Countries*, pp. 93–122.

Drabble, J. H., "Some Thoughts on the Economic Development of Malaya Under British Administration," *Journal of Southeast Asian Studies* 5 (1974), 199–208.

Drake, P. J., *Financial Development in Malaya and Singapore*, Canberra: Australian National University Press, 1969.

East–West Center, *Annual Report*, Honolulu: East–West Center, various years, 1987–88.

The Economist, various issues.

Elliott, David, *Thailand: Origins of Military Rule*, London: Zed Press, 1978.

Ensign, Margee M., *Doing Good or Doing Well: Japan's Foreign Aid Program*, New York: Columbia University Press, 1992.

Evans, Peter, "The State as Problem and Solution: Predation, Embedded Autonomy, and Structural Change," in Haggard and Kaufman (eds.), *The Politics of Economic Adjustment*, pp. 139–81.

Export-Import Bank of the United States, *Report to the U.S. Congress on Tied Aid and Credit Practices*, Washington, D.C.: Eximbank, 1989.

Far Eastern Economic Review, various issues.

Far Eastern Economic Review, *Asia Yearbook*, various issues.

Feeny, David, *The Political Economy of Productivity: Thai Agricultural Development, 1880–1975*, Vancouver: University of British Columbia Press, 1982.

The Financial Times, various issues.

Fishlow, Albert, *et al.*, *Miracle or Design? Lessons From the East Asian Experience*, Washington, D.C.: Overseas Development Council, 1994.

Frieden, Jeffrey A., *Debt, Development, and Democracy*, Princeton: Princeton University Press, 1991.

Froot, Kenneth A. (ed.), *Foreign Direct Investment*, Chicago: University of Chicago Press, 1993.

Funston, Neil John, *Malay Politics in Malaysia: A Study of UMNO and Party Islam*, Kuala Lumpur: Heinemann Educational Books, 1980.

Gale, Bruce, *Politics and Public Enterprise in Malaysia*, Singapore: Eastern Universities Press, 1981.

Garrett, Geoffrey, and Peter Lange, "Performance in a Hostile World: Economic Growth in Capitalist Democracies, 1947–1980," *World Politics* 38 (1986), 517–45.

Geddes, Barbara, *Politicians' Dilemma: Building State Capacity in Latin America*, Berkeley: University of California Press, 1994.

Gelb, Alan H., *Oil Windfalls, Blessing or Curse?*, New York: Oxford University Press, for the World Bank, 1988.

Gelston, Sally, "Indonesia: Tariff Task Force Reshuffled," *East Asian Executive Reports* 16 (November 15, 1994), pp. 4–6.

Gereffi, Gary, and Miguel Korzeniewicz (eds.), *Commodity Chains and Global Capitalism*, Westport, Conn.: Greenwood Press, 1994.

Gereffi, Gary, Miguel Korzeniewicz, and Roberto P. Korzeniewicz, "Introduction," in Gereffi and Korzeniewicz (eds.), *Commodity Chains and Global Capitalism*, pp. 1–14.

Gereffi, Gary, and Donald L. Wyman (eds.), *Manufacturing Miracles*, Princeton: Princeton University Press, 1990.

Girling, John L. S., *Thailand, Society and Politics*, Ithaca: Cornell University Press, 1981.

Go, Evelyn M. and Jungsoo Lee, "Foreign Capital, Balance of Payments and External Debt in Developing Asia," in Ichimura (ed.), *Challenge of Asian Developing Countries*, pp. 227–84.

Golay, Frank H., *The Philippines: Public Policy and National Economic Development*, Ithaca: Cornell University Press, 1961.

Gourevitch, Peter A., *Politics in Hard Times: Comparative Responses to International Economic Crises*, Ithaca: Cornell University Press, 1986.

Griffith-Jones, Steffany, "Introduction," in Griffith-Jones and Harvey (eds.), *World Prices and Development*, pp. 1–12.

Griffith-Jones, Steffany, and Charles Harvey (eds.), *World Prices and Development*, Brookfield, Vt.: Gower Publishers, 1985.

Gullick, J.M. and Bruce Gale, *Malaysia: Its Political and Economic Development*, Petaling Jaya, Selangor: Pelanduk, 1986.

Haggard, Stephan, *Developing Nations and the Politics of Global Integration*, Washington, D.C.: Brookings Institution, 1995.

Pathways from the Periphery, Ithaca: Cornell University Press, 1991.

"The Political Economy of the Philippine Debt Crisis," in Nelson (ed.), *Economic Crisis and Policy Choice* pp. 215–55.

"The Philippines: Picking up After Marcos," in *The Promise of Privatization*, New York: Council on Foreign Relations, 1988.

Haggard, Stephan, and Robert R. Kaufman (eds.), *The Politics of Economic Adjustment: International Constraints, Distributive Conflicts, and the State*, Princeton: Princeton University Press, 1992.

Haggard, Stephan, Chung H. Lee, and Sylvia Maxfield (eds.), *The Politics of Finance in Developing Countries*, Ithaca: Cornell University Press, 1993.

Halim, Fatimah, "The Transformation of the Malaysian State," *Journal of Contemporary Asia* 20 (1990), 64–88.

Halliday, Jon, and Gavan McCormack, *Japanese Imperialism Today, "Co-Prosperity in Greater East Asia,"* New York: Monthly Review Press, 1973.

Hamilton, Gary (ed.), *Business Networks and Economic Development in East and Southeast Asia*, Hong Kong: Centre of Asian Studies, University of Hong Kong, 1991.

Hasan, Parvez, "Adjustment to External Shocks," in Krause and Kihwan (eds.), *Liberalization in the Process of Economic Development*, pp. 170–210.

Hawes, Gary, "Marcos, His Cronies, and the Philippines' Failure to Develop," in Ruth McVey (ed.), *Southeast Asian Capitalists*, Ithaca: Cornell University Southeast Asia Program, 1992, pp. 145–60.

The Philippine State and the Marcos Regime, Ithaca: Cornell University Press, 1987.

Hayashida, Masato, "The Three Mini Dragons: Economic Development in Thailand, Malaysia, and Indonesia," in *Asia-Pacific Review, 1995*, pp. 165–87.

Hefner, Robert W., "Islam, State, and Civil Society: ICMI and the Struggle for the Indonesian Middle Class," *Indonesia* 56 (1993), 1–35.

Hewison, Kevin, *Bankers and Bureaucrats: Capital and the Role of the State in Thailand (Yale University Southeast Asian Studies)*, New Haven: Yale Center for International and Area Studies, 1989.

Higgott, Richard, and Richard Robinson (eds.), *Southeast Asia: Essays in the Political Economy of Structural Change*, London: Routledge & Kegan Paul, 1985.

Hill, Hal, "The Philippine Economy Under Aquino: New Hopes, Old Problems," *Asian Survey* 28 (1988), 261–85.

Hing, Ai Yun, "Capitalist Development, Class and Race," in Ali (ed.), *Ethnicity, Class and Development in Malaysia*, pp. 296–328.

Hirschman, Albert O., *National Power and the Structure of International Trade*, Berkeley: University of California Press, 1945.

Hong, Evelyn (ed.), *Malaysian Women: Problems and Issues*, Penang: Consumers Association of Penang, 1983.

Hui, Lim Mah, "Contradictions in the Development of Malay Capital: State, Accumulation and Legitimation," *Journal of Contemporary Asia* 15 (1985), 37–63.

Hutchcroft, Paul D., "Preferential Credit Allocation in the Philippines," in Haggard *et al.* (eds.), *The Politics of Finance in Developing Countries*, pp. 165–98.

"Oligarchs and Cronies in the Philippine State," *World Politics* 43 (1991), 414–50.

Ichimura, Shinichi, "The Pattern and Prospects of Asian Economic Development," in Ichimura (ed.), *Challenge of Asian Developing Countries*, pp. 7–64.

(ed.), *Challenge of Asian Developing Countries: Issues and Analyses*, Tokyo: Asian Productivity Organization, 1988.

Ikenberry, G. John, "The State and Strategies of International Adjustment," *World Politics* 39 (1986), 53–77.

Ingram, James C., *Economic Change in Thailand, 1850–1970*, Stanford: Stanford University Press, 1971.

International Bank for Reconstruction and Development, *The Economic Development of Malaya*, Baltimore: Johns Hopkins University Press, for IBRD, 1955.

International Monetary Fund, *World Economic Outlook* (May 1995), Washington, D.C.: IMF.

Iriye, Akira, "Continuities in U.S.–Japanese Relations, 1941–1949," in Yonosuke Nagai and Akira Iriye (eds.), *The Origins of the Cold War in Asia*, Tokyo: University of Tokyo Press, 1977, pp. 378–407.

Iriye, Akira, and Warren I. Cohen (eds.), *The United States and Japan in the Postwar World*, Lexington: University Press of Kentucky, 1989.

Jackson, Karl D., "The Philippines: The Search for a Suitable Democratic Solution, 1946–1986," in Diamond, *et al.* (eds.), *Democracy in Developing Countries*, vol. III, pp. 231–66.

"Bureaucratic Polity: A Theoretical Framework for the Analysis of Power and Communications in Indonesia," in Jackson and Pye (eds.), *Political Power and Communications in Indonesia*, pp. 3–22.

Jackson, Karl D. and Lucian Pye (eds.), *Political Power and Communications in Indonesia*, Berkeley: University of California Press, 1978.

Japan External Trade Organization (JETRO), *Jetro White Paper on International Trade (Summary)*, Tokyo: JETRO, 1992.

Japan Institute for Social and Economic Affairs, *APEC 1995*, Tokyo: Keizai Koho Center, 1995.

APEC 1995: A Statistical Compilation, Tokyo: Keizai Koho Center, 1995.

Japan, Ministry of Foreign Affairs, *Official Development Assistance, 1992*, Tokyo: Ministry of Foreign Affairs, 1992.

Johnson, Chalmers, "Political Institutions and Economic Performance: The Government–Business Relationship in Japan, South Korea, and Taiwan," in Deyo (ed.), *The Political Economy of the New Asian Industrialism*, pp. 136–64.

Conspiracy at Matsukawa, Berkeley: University of California Press, 1972.

Jomo, Kwame Sundaram, *A Question of Class: Capital, the State and Uneven Development in Malaya*, Singapore: Oxford University Press, 1986.

(ed.), *The Sun Also Sets*, Petaling Jaya, Selangor: INSAN, 1983.

Jowitt, Kenneth, "A World Without Leninism," in Slater *et al.* (eds.), *Global Transformation and the Third World*, pp. 9–27.

The New World Disorder, Berkeley: University of California Press, 1992.

Kahler, Miles, "External Influence, Conditionality, and the Politics of Adjustment," in Haggard and Kaufman (eds.), *The Politics of Economic Adjustment*, pp. 89–136.

Katzenstein, Peter J., *Small States in World Markets*, Ithaca: Cornell University Press, 1985.

Between Power and Plenty, Madison: University of Wisconsin Press, 1978.

Keizai Koho Center, *APEC 1995*, Tokyo: Keizai Koho Center, 1995.

Kennedy, Ellen, *The Bundesbank, Germany's Central Bank in the International Monetary System*, New York: Council on Foreign Relations Press, 1991.

Khamchoo, Chaiwat, "A Historical Perspective on Japan–Thai Relations," in *Japan and Thailand: Historical Perspective and Future Directions* (Proceedings of the Fourth Japan–Thai Symposium in Bangkok, June 1987), Tokyo: The Japan Center for International Exchange, 1987.

Kindleberger, Charles P., "The Rise of Free Trade in Western Europe," *Journal of Economic History* 35 (1975), 20–55.

Kojima, Kiyoshi, and Tsuneo Nakauchi, "Economic Conditions in East and Southeast Asia and Development Perspective," in Ichimura (ed.), *Challenge of Asian Developing Countries*, Tokyo: Asian Productivity Organization, 1988, pp. 102–32.

Krasner, Stephen, "Oil is the Exception," *Foreign Policy* 14 (1974), 68–84.

Krause, Lawrence B., "Introduction," in Krause and Kihwan (eds.), *Liberalization in the Process of Economic Development*, pp. 1–26.

Krause, Lawrence B. and Kim Kihwan (eds.), *Liberalization in the Process of Economic Development*, Berkeley: University of California Press, 1991.

Krueger, Anne O., *Political Economy of Policy Reform in Developing Countries*, Cambridge, Mass.: MIT Press, 1993.

Krugman, Paul, "The Myth of Asia's Miracle," *Foreign Affairs* 73 (November/December 1994), 62–78.

Lake, David A., *Power, Protection, and Free Trade: International Sources of United States Commercial Strategy, 1887–1939*, Ithaca: Cornell University Press, 1988.

Lam, Danny Kin-Kong, and Ian Lee, "Guerrilla Capitalism and the Limits of Statist Theory: Comparing the Chinese NICs," in Clark and Chan (eds.), *The Evolving Pacific Basin in the Global Political Economy*, pp. 107–24

Lande, Carl H., "Authoritarian Rule in the Philippines: Some Critical Views," *Pacific Affairs* 55 (1982), 80–93.

Langdon, Frank C., "Japanese Policy Toward Southeast Asia," in Zacher and Milne (eds.), *Conflict and Stability in Southeast Asia*, pp. 327–54.

Laothamatas, Anek, *Business Associations and the New Political Economy of Thailand: From Bureaucratic Polity to Liberal Corporatism*, Boulder: Westview Press, 1992.

Lee, Eddy (ed.), *Export-Led Industrialisation and Development*, Singapore: International Labor Organization, 1981.

Liddle, R. William, "Indonesia in 1986: Contending With Scarcity," *Asian Survey* 27 (1987), 206–18.

"The Politics of Shared Growth: Some Indonesian Cases," *Comparative Politics* 19 (1987), 127–46.

Lim, David, "East Malaysia in Malaysian Development Planning," *Journal of Southeast Asian Studies* 17 (1986), 156–70.

Economic Growth and Development in West Malaysia 1947–1970, Kuala Lumpur: Oxford University Press, 1973.

Lincoln, Edward J., *Japan's Unequal Trade*, Washington D.C.: Brookings Institution, 1990.

Lindsey, Charles W., "In Search of Dynamism: Foreign Investment in the Philippines Under Martial Law," *Pacific Affairs* 56 (1983), 477–94.

Little, I. M. D., Richard N. Cooper, W. Max Corden, and Sarath Rajapatirana, *Boom, Crisis, and Adjustment: The Macroeconomic Experience of Developing Countries*, New York: Oxford University Press, for the World Bank, 1993.

Los Angeles Times, various issues.

Mabry, Bevars D., *The Development of Labor Institutions in Thailand*, Ithaca: Cornell University Southeast Asia Program, Data Paper no. 112, April 1979.

McCarthy, F. Desmond, J. Peter Neary, and Giovanni Zanalda, "Measuring the Effect of External Shocks and the Policy Response to Them: Empirical Methodology Applied to the Philippines," Policy Research Working Paper 1271, World Bank, Washington, D.C., March 1994.

Machiavelli, Niccolo, *Machiavelli, The Chief Works and Others*, translated by Allen Gilbert, vol. I, Durham, N.C.: Duke University Press, 1958.

MacIntyre, Andrew J., "Power, Prosperity and Patrimonialism: Business and Government in Indonesia," in MacIntyre (ed.), *Business and Government in Industrialising Asia*, pp. 244–67.

Business and Politics in Indonesia, Sydney: Allen & Unwin, 1990.

(ed.), *Business and Government in Industrialising Asia*, Ithaca: Cornell University Press, 1994.

Mackie, J. A. C., "Changing Patterns of Chinese Big Business in Southeast Asia," paper presented at the conference on Industrializing Elites in Southeast Asia, Sukhothai, Thailand, December 9–12, 1986.

McVey, Ruth (ed.), *Southeast Asian Capitalists*, Ithaca: Cornell University Southeast Asia Program, 1992.

Malaya, Federation of, *Report of the Industrial Development Working Party*, Kuala Lumpur: Government Printer, 1957.

Malaya, Federation of, Department of Labor, *Annual Report 1959*.

Monthly Report, June 1948.

Malaysia, *Second Malaysia Plan, 1971–1975*, Kuala Lumpur: Government Printer, 1971.

Malaysia, Heavy Industries Corporation of (HICOM), *Annual Report 1985*, Kuala Lumpur: Government Printer 1986.

Malaysian Industrial Development Authority, *Malaysia: Investment in the Manufacturing Sector*, Kuala Lumpur: MIDA, 1991.

Mastanduno, Michael, David A. Lake, and G. John Ikenberry, "Toward a Realist Theory of State Action," *International Studies Quarterly* 33 (1989), 457–74.

Means, Gordon P., *Malaysian Politics*, 2nd edn., London: Hodder & Stoughton, 1976.

Milne, R. S., "Malaysia – Beyond the New Economic Policy," *Asian Survey* 26 (1986), 1364–82.

Milne, R. S. and Diane K. Mauzy, *Politics and Government in Malaysia*, rev. edn., Vancouver: University of British Columbia Press, 1980.

Milner, Helen, *Resisting Protectionism: Global Industries and the Politics of International Trade*, Princeton: Princeton University Press, 1988.

Montes, Manuel F., "The Politics of Liberalization: The Aquino Government's 1990 Tariff Reform Initiative," in Timberman (ed.), *The Politics of Economic Reform in Southeast Asia*, pp. 91–116.

Monthly Energy Review (Energy Information Administration, United States Department of Energy), June 1995, 46–55.

Mukerjee, Dilip, *Lessons From Korea's Industrial Experience*, Kuala Lumpur: Institute of Strategic and International Studies, 1986.

Muscat, Robert J., *The Fifth Tiger: A Study of Thai Development Policy*, Armonk, N.Y.: M. E. Sharpe, 1994.

Thailand and the United States: Development, Security, and Foreign Aid, New York: Columbia University Press, 1991.

Nagai, Yonosuke, and Akira Iriye (eds.), *The Origins of the Cold War in Asia*, Tokyo: University of Tokyo Press, 1977.

Nartsupha, Chattip, *Foreign Trade, Foreign Finance and the Development of Thailand, 1956–1965*, Bangkok: Prae Pittaya, 1970.

Nathan, K. S., "Malaysia in 1989: Communists End Armed Struggle," *Asian Survey* 30 (1990), 210–20.

"Malaysia in 1988: The Politics of Survival," *Asian Survey* 29 (1989), 129–39.

Nathan, K. S. and M. Pathmnathan (eds.), *Trilateralism in Asia: Problems and Prospects in U.S.–Japan–ASEAN Relations*, Kuala Lumpur: Antara Book Company, 1986.

Nau, Henry (ed.), *Domestic Trade Politics and the Uruguay Round*, New York: Columbia University Press, 1989.

Naya, Seiji, "Role of Trade Policies: Competition and Cooperation," in Ichimura (ed.), *Challenge of Asian Developing Countries*, pp.169–202.

Neher, Clark, *Southeast Asia in the New International Era*, Boulder: Westview Press, 1991.

Nelson, Joan M., "Introduction: The Politics of Economic Adjustment in Developing Nations," in Nelson (ed.), *Economic Crisis and Policy Choice*, pp. 3–32.

(ed.), *Economic Crisis and Policy Choice: The Politics of Adjustment in the Third World*, Princeton: Princeton University Press, 1990.

New Straits Times (August 3, 1991), 1.

Newsletter of the APSA Organized Section in Comparative Politics 7 (Summer 1996), 1–18.

Nishikawa, Jun, "ASEAN Countries: Economic Performance and Tasks Ahead," in Ichimura (ed.), *Challenge of Asian Developing Countries*, pp. 357–405.

Noland, Marcus, *Pacific Basin Developing Countries: Prospects for the Future*, Washington, D.C.: Institute for International Economics, 1990.

Odell, John S., "Understanding International Trade Policies: An Emerging Synthesis," *World Politics* 43 (1990), 139–67.

Okimoto, Daniel I., *Between MITI and the Market: Japanese Industrial Policy for High Technology*, Stanford: Stanford University Press, 1989.

Okiuzumi, Kaoru, Kent E. Calder, and Gerrit W. Wong (eds.), *The U.S.–Japan Economic Relationship in East and Southeast Asia: A Policy Framework for Asia-Pacific Economic Cooperation*, Washington, D.C.: Center for Strategic and International Studies, 1992.

Olson, Mancur, *The Rise and Decline of Nations: Economic Growth, Stagflation, and Social Rigidities*, New Haven: Yale University Press, 1982.

Organization for Economic Co-operation and Development (OECD), *Geographic Distribution of Financial Flows*, OECD, Paris, 1982, 1992.

Overholt, William, "The Rise and Fall of Ferdinand Marcos," *Asian Survey* 26 (1986), 1137–63.

Paauw, Douglas S., "Frustrated Labor-Intensive Development: The Case of Indonesia," in Lee (ed.), *Export-Led Industrialisation and Development*, pp. 145–74.

Pacific Economic Cooperation Council, *Milestones in APEC Liberalisation: A Map of Market Opening Measures by APEC*, Singapore: APEC Secretariat, 1995.

Survey of Impediments to Trade and Investment in the APEC Region, Singapore: APEC Secretariat, 1995.

Parnwell, Michael J. G. (ed.), *Uneven Development in Thailand*, Aldershot, England: Avebury, 1996.

Petri, Peter A., *The Lessons of East Asia: Common Foundations of East Asian Success*, Washington, D.C.: World Bank, 1993.

"One Bloc, Two Blocs, or None? Political Economic Forces in Pacific Trade Policy," in Okiuzumi *et al.*, *The U.S.–Japan Economic Relationship in East and Southeast Asia*, pp. 39–70.

Phongpaichit, Pasuk, "The Politics of Economic Reform in Thailand," in Timberman (ed.), *The Politics of Economic Reform in Southeast Asia*, pp. 1–30.

Phongpaichit, Pasuk, and Sungsidh Piriyarangsan, *Corruption and Democracy in Thailand*, Bangkok: The Political Economy Centre, Faculty of Economics, Chulalongkorn University, 1994.

Pura, Raphael, "Doubts Over Heavy Industrialization Strategy," in Jomo (ed.), *The Sun Also Sets*, pp. 377–82.

Puthucheary, Mavis, *The Politics of Administration: The Malaysian Experience*, New York: Oxford University Press, 1978.

Putnam, Robert, "Diplomacy and Domestic Politics: The Logic of Two-Level Games," *International Organization* 42 (1988), 427–60.

Pye, Lucian W., *Asian Power and Politics*, Cambridge, Mass.: The Belknap Press of Harvard University Press, 1985.

Ranis, Gustav, "Contrasts in the Political Economy of Development Policy Change," in Gereffi and Wyman (eds.), *Manufacturing Miracles*, pp. 207–30.

Ranis, Gustav, and Syed Akhtar Mahmood, *The Political Economy of Development Policy Change*, Cambridge, Mass.: Blackwell, 1992.

Rao, Bhanoji, *Malaysia: Development Pattern and Policy, 1947–1971*, Singapore: Singapore University Press, 1980.

Riedinger, Jeffrey, "The Philippines in 1993: Halting Steps Toward Liberalization," *Asian Survey* 34 (1994), 139–46.

Riggs, Fred, *Thailand: The Modernization of a Bureaucratic Polity*, Honolulu: East–West Center Press, 1966.

Riker, William, *The Theory of Political Coalitions*, New Haven: Yale University Press, 1962.

Rogowski, Ronald, *Commerce and Coalitions: How Trade Affects Domestic Political Alignments*, Princeton: Princeton University Press, 1989.

Rosecrance, Richard, *The Rise of the Trading State: Commerce and Conquest in the Modern World*, New York: Basic Books, 1986.

Rosecrance, Richard, and Arthur A. Stein, "Beyond Realism: The Study of Grand Strategy," in Rosecrance and Stein (eds.), *The Domestic Bases of Grand Strategy*, pp. 3–21.

(eds.), *The Domestic Bases of Grand Strategy*, Ithaca: Cornell University Press, 1993.

Sahasakul, Chaipat, *Lessons from the World Bank's Experience of Structural Adjustment Loans (SALs): A Case Study of Thailand*, Research Monograph no. 8, Thailand Development Research Institute, Bangkok, 1992.

Samudavanija, Chai-Anan, "The Military and Politics in Thailand," *Democratic Institutions* 1 (1992), 21–37.

Schmidt, Johannes Drasbaek, "Paternalism and Planning in Thailand: Facilitating

Growth Without Social Benefits," in Parnwell (ed.), *Uneven Development in Thailand,* pp. 63–81.

Schonhardt-Bailey, Cheryl, "Specific Factors, Capital Markets, Portfolio Diversification, and Free Trade: Domestic Determinants of the Repeal of the Corn Laws," *World Politics* 43 (1991), 545–69.

Schoppa, Len, "*Gaiatsu* and Economic Bargaining Outcomes," *International Organization* 47 (1993), 353–86.

Sell, Susan, "Intellectual Property Protection and Antitrust in the Developing World: Crisis, Coercion, and Choice," *International Organization* 49 (1995), 315–49.

Sen, Kunal, "Thailand: Stabilization with Growth," in Pradeep Agrawal *et al.* (eds.), *Economic Restructuring in East Asia and India: Perspectives on Policy Reform,* New York: St. Martin's Press, 1995, pp. 134–58.

Shafer, D. Michael, *Winners and Losers,* Ithaca: Cornell University Press, 1994.

Sherk, Donald R., "Foreign Investment in Southeast Asia," in Zacher and Milne (eds.), *Conflict and Stability in Southeast Asia,* pp. 355–82.

Shibusawa, Masahide, *Japan and the Asian Pacific Region,* New York: St. Martin's Press, 1984.

Shibusawa, Masahide, *et al., Pacific Asia in the 1990s,* New York: Routledge, 1992.

Silcock, T. H., "Money and Banking," in Silcock (ed.), *Thailand, Social and Economic Studies in Development,* pp. 170–205.

"Summary and Assessment," in Silcock (ed.), *Thailand, Social and Economic Studies in Development,* pp. 289–307.

(ed.), *Thailand, Social and Economic Studies in Development,* Durham, N.C.: Duke University Press, 1967.

Simon, Jean-Christophe, "The Thai Manufacturing Sector: New Patterns of Expansion," in Parnwell (ed.), *Uneven Development in Thailand,* pp. 82–108.

Slater, Robert O., Barry M. Schutz, and Steven R. Dorr (eds.), *Global Transformation and the Third World,* Boulder: Lynne Rienner Publishers, 1993.

Smith-Morris, Miles, *The Economist Book of Vital World Statistics,* New York: Times Books, 1990.

Soesastro, M. Hadi, "The Political Economy of Deregulation in Indonesia," *Asian Survey* 29 (1989), 853–69.

Spinanger, Dean, *Industrialization Politics and Regional Economic Development in Malaysia,* Singapore: Oxford University Press, 1986.

Regional Industrialization Policies in a Small Developing Country: A Case Study of West Malaysia, Kiel, Germany: Institute for World Economics, 1980.

The Star [Petaling Jaya, Malaysia] (July 31, 1991), bus. 1.

The Star [Petaling Jaya, Malaysia] (December 14, 1989), 1.

Stauffer, Robert B., "The Philippine Political Economy: (Dependent) State Capitalism in the Corporatist Mode," in Higgott and Robinson (eds.), *Southeast Asia,* pp. 241–65.

Steinberg, David J. (ed.), *In Search of Southeast Asia: A Modern History,* New York: Praeger Publishers, 1971.

Steinberg, David J. *et al.,* "Social Change and the Emergence of Nationalism: Indonesia," in Steinberg (ed.), *In Search of Southeast Asia,* pp. 292–311.

Steinberg, David J. *et al.,* "Framework for Nations: Economic Transformation, 1870–1940," in Steinberg (ed.), *In Search of Southeast Asia,* pp. 219–44.

Stepan, Alfred, *The State and Society,* Princeton: Princeton University Press, 1978.

Stubbs, Richard, *Hearts and Minds in Guerrilla Warfare: The Malayan Emergency 1948–1960,* Oxford: Oxford University Press, 1989.

"Geopolitics and the Political Economy of Southeast Asia," *International Journal* 44 (1989), 517–40.

Sudo, Sueo, "The Road to Becoming a Regional Leader: Japanese Attempts in Southeast Asia, 1975–1980," *Pacific Affairs* 61 (1988), 27–50.

Suehiro, Akira, *Capital Accumulation in Thailand*, Tokyo: Center for East Asian Cultural Studies, 1989.

Sukehiro, Hasegawa, *Japanese Foreign Aid, Policy and Practice*, New York: Praeger Publishers, 1975.

Sundhaussen, Ulf, "Indonesia: Past and Present Encounters with Democracy," in Diamond *et al.* (eds.), *Democracy in Developing Countries*, vol. III, pp. 423–74.

Sundrum, R. M., "Manpower and Educational Development in East and Southeast Asia: A Summary of Conference Proceedings," *Malaysian Economic Review* 16 (1971), 78–90.

Tambunlertchai, Somsak, and Chesada Loohawenchit, "Labour Intensive and Small Scale Manufacturing in Thailand," in Amjad (ed.) *The Development of Labour Intensive Industry in ASEAN Countries*, pp. 175–234.

Tan, Pek Leng, "Women Factory Workers and the Law," in Hong (ed.), *Malaysian Women*, pp. 64–78.

Tanaka, Shoko, *Post-War Japanese Resource Policies and Strategies: The Case of Southeast Asia*, Ithaca: Cornell University East Asia Papers, no. 43, 1986.

Thomas, Vinod, and Yan Wang, *The Lessons of East Asia: Government Policy and Productivity Growth. Is East Asia an Exception?*, Washington, D.C.: World Bank, 1993.

Thorn, Bret, "Co-Prosperity or Co-Recession?," *Manager*, no. 92 (April 1993), 40–9.

Timberman, David G., "The Philippines in 1990: On Shaky Ground," *Asian Survey* 31 (1991), 153–63.

    A Changeless Land: Continuity and Change in the Philippines, New York: M. E. Sharpe, 1991.

    (ed.), *The Politics of Economic Reform in Southeast Asia: The Experiences of Thailand, Indonesia and the Philippines*, Manila: Asian Institute of Management, 1992.

Times Straits, various issues.

Tsuru, Shigeto, *Japan's Capitalism: Creative Defeat and Beyond*, New York: Cambridge University Press, 1993.

UNCTAD, *UNCTAD Commodity Yearbook, 1993*, New York: United Nations, 1993.

    UNCTAD Commodity Yearbook, 1990, New York: United Nations, 1990.

UNDP, *Human Development Report*, New York: Oxford University Press, 1994.

Unger, Danny, "Japan's Capital Exports: Molding East Asia," in Unger and Blackburn (eds.), *Japan's Emerging Global Role*, pp. 155–70.

    "Big Little Japan," in Slater *et al.* (eds.), *Global Transformation and the Third World*, pp. 283–308.

Unger, Danny, and Paul Blackburn (eds.), *Japan's Emerging Global Role*, Boulder: Lynne Rienner Publishers, 1993.

United Nations, *Salient Features and Trends in Foreign Direct Investment*, New York: United Nations Centre on Transnational Corporations, 1983.

    World Economic Survey, 1975, New York: United Nations Department of Economic and Social Affairs, 1976.

    Economic Bulletin for Asia and the Far East 7 (February 1957).

    Economic Bulletin for Asia and the Far East 6 (February 1956).

United States Department of Agriculture, *Sugar, Background for 1995 Farm Legislation*, Agricultural Economic Report no. 711, Washington, D.C.: USDA, 1995.

United States General Accounting Office, "Foreign Assistance: International Resource Flows and Development Assistance to Developing Countries," GAO/NSIAD-91-25FS (Fact Sheet for the Honorable Lee H. Hamilton, Chairman, Joint Economic Committee, US Congress), Washington, D.C., October 1990.

Vandenbosch, Amry, and Richard Butwell, *The Changing Face of Southeast Asia*, Lexington: University of Kentucky Press, 1966.

Vernon, Raymond, *Sovereignty at Bay*, New York: Basic Books, 1971.

Vyas, Vijay S. and William E. James, "Agricultural Development in Asia: Performance, Issues and Policy Options," in Ichimura (ed.), *Challenge of Asian Developing Countries*, pp. 133–68.

Wall Street Journal (September 22, 1975), 24.

Washington Post, various issues.

Watanabe, Akio, "Southeast Asia in U.S.–Japanese Relations," in Iriye and Cohen (eds.), *The United States and Japan in the Postwar World*, pp. 80–95.

Waterbury, John, "The Heart of the Matter? Public Enterprise and the Adjustment Process," in Haggard and Kaufman (eds.), *The Politics of Economic Adjustment* pp. 182–220.

Wells, Louis T., Jr., "Mobile Exporters: New Foreign Investors in East Asia," in Froot (ed.), *Foreign Direct Investment*, pp. 173–96.

Williamson, John, "Washington Consensus," in Williamson (ed.), *The Political Economy of Policy Reform*, pp. 1–28.

   The Progress of Policy Reform in Latin America, Washington, D.C.: Institute for International Economics, 1990.

   (ed.), *The Political Economy of Policy Reform*, Washington, D.C.: Institute for International Economics, 1994.

Williamson, John, and Stephan Haggard, "The Political Conditions for Economic Reform," in Williamson (ed.), *The Political Economy of Policy Reform*, pp. 525–96.

Willner, Ann Ruth, "The Neotraditional Accommodation to Political Independence: The Case of Indonesia," in Lucian Pye (ed.), *Cases in Comparative Politics: Asia*, Boston: Little, Brown, 1970, pp. 242–306.

Wong, Tai Chee, "Industrial Development, the New Economic Policy in Malaysia, and the International Division of Labor," *ASEAN Economic Bulletin* 7 (1990), 106–19.

World Bank, *The East Asian Miracle: Economic Growth and Public Policy*, New York: Oxford University Press, 1993.

   Thailand: Toward a Development Strategy of Full Participation, Washington, D.C.: The World Bank, 1980.

   Economic Development of Malaya, Baltimore: Johns Hopkins University Press, for the World Bank, 1955.

   World Development Report, New York: Oxford University Press, for the World Bank, various years.

   World Tables, Baltimore: Johns Hopkins University Press, for the World Bank, various years.

Wurfel, David, *Filipino Politics: Development and Decay*, Ithaca: Cornell University Press, 1988.

Yarbrough, Beth V. and Robert M. Yarbrough, "International Institutions and the New Economics of Organization," *International Organization* 44 (1990), 235–60.

Yoshihara, Kunio, "Culture, Institutions, and Economic Growth: A Comparative Study of Korea and Thailand," *Tonan Ajia Kenkyu* [Southeast Asia Studies] 33 (1995), 97–144.

   The Nation and Economic Growth: The Philippines and Thailand, New York: Oxford University Press, 1994.

   The Rise of Ersatz Capitalism in South-East Asia, Oxford: Oxford University Press, 1988.

Zacher, Mark W. and R. S. Milne (eds.), *Conflict and Stability in Southeast Asia*, Garden City, N.Y.: Anchor Press, 1974.

Index

236